758

AU.

TITL.

ACCESS:

LYTTON STRACHEY
Literary Essays

Literary Essays

by
LYTTON STRACHEY

1948
Chatto and Windus
LONDON

PUBLISHED BY
Chatto and Windus
LONDON

★

Bibliographical Note

LYTTON STRACHEY's shorter essays have previously appeared in three volumes: *Books and Characters, French and English*, published in 1922 and dedicated to John Maynard Keynes; *Portraits in Miniature and Other Essays*, published in 1931 and dedicated 'with gratitude and admiration' to Max Beerbohm; and *Characters and Commentaries*, published posthumously in 1933.

The exigencies of the moment have made it desirable to reduce the three volumes to two. For this purpose their contents have been reshuffled and divided into two collections of approximately equal length made up respectively of 'Biographical' and 'Literary' Essays. In each of these volumes the essays are arranged in the chronological order, not of their composition, but, roughly, of the subjects with which they deal.

Six of the essays in *Characters and Commentaries* have been omitted from the present volumes: 'Versailles', 'Avons-nous changé tout cela?', 'Bonga-Bonga in Whitehall', 'French Poets through Boston Eyes', 'Militarism and Theology' and 'The Claims of Patriotism'. On the other hand an essay on Charles Greville, which was not included in any of the three former books, will be found among the Biographical Essays.

Particulars are given in the table of contents of the date and place at which each essay originally appeared, and acknowledgments are due to the Editors of the various periodicals concerned.

J. S.

Contents

CONTENTS

SHAKESPEARE'S FINAL PERIOD

THE whole of the modern criticism of Shakespeare has been fundamentally affected by one important fact. The chronological order of the plays, for so long the object of the vaguest speculation, of random guesses, or at best of isolated 'points,' has been now discovered and reduced to a coherent law. It is no longer possible to suppose that *The Tempest* was written before *Romeo and Juliet*; that *Henry VI* was produced in succession to *Henry V*; or that *Antony and Cleopatra* followed close upon the heels of *Julius Caesar*. Such theories were sent to limbo for ever, when a study of those plays of whose date we have external evidence revealed the fact that, as Shakespeare's life advanced, a corresponding development took place in the metrical structure of his verse. The establishment of metrical tests, by which the approximate position and date of any play can be readily ascertained, at once followed; chaos gave way to order; and, for the first time, critics became able to judge, not only of the individual works, but of the whole succession of the works of Shakespeare.

Upon this firm foundation modern writers have been only too eager to build. It was apparent that the Plays, arranged in chronological order, showed something more than a mere development in the technique of verse—a development, that is to say, in the general treatment of characters and subjects, and in the sort of feelings which those characters and subjects were intended to arouse; and from this it was easy to draw conclusions as to the development of the mind of Shakespeare itself. Such conclusions have, in fact, been constantly drawn. But it must be noted that they all rest upon the tacit assumption, that the character of any given drama is, in fact, a true index to the state of mind of the dramatist composing it. The validity of this assumption has never been proved; it has never been shown, for instance, why we should suppose a writer of farces to be habitually merry; or whether we are really justified in concluding, from the fact that Shakespeare wrote nothing but tragedies for six years, that, during that period, more than at any other, he was deeply absorbed in the awful problems of human existence. It is not, however, the purpose of this essay to consider the question of what are the relations between the artist and his art; for it will assume the truth of the generally accepted view, that the character of the one can be inferred from that of the other. What it will attempt to discuss is whether, upon this hypothesis, the most important part of the ordinary doctrine of Shakespeare's mental development is justifiable.

What, then, is the ordinary doctrine? Dr. Furnivall states it as follows:

Shakespeare's course is thus shown to have run from the amorousness and fun of youth, through the strong patriotism of early manhood, to the wrestlings with the dark problems that beset the man of middle age, to the gloom which weighed on Shakespeare (as on so many men) in later life, when, though outwardly successful, the world seemed all against him, and his mind dwelt with sympathy on scenes of faithlessness of friends, treachery of relations and subjects, ingratitude of children, scorn of his kind; till at last, in his Stratford home again, peace came to him, Miranda and Perdita in their lovely freshness and charm greeted him, and he was laid by his quiet Avon side.

And the same writer goes on to quote with approval Professor Dowden's

likening of Shakespeare to a ship, beaten and storm-tossed, but yet entering harbour with sails full-set, to anchor in peace.

Such, in fact, is the general opinion of modern writers upon Shakespeare; after a happy youth and a gloomy middle age he reached at last—it is the universal opinion—a state of quiet serenity in which he died. Professor Dowden's book on 'Shakespeare's Mind and Art' gives the most popular expression to this view, a view which is also held by Mr. Ten

Brink, by Sir I. Gollancz, and, to a great extent, by Dr. Brandes. Professor Dowden, indeed, has gone so far as to label this final period with the appellation of 'On the Heights,' in opposition to the preceding one, which, he says, was passed 'In the Depths.' Sir Sidney Lee, too, seems to find, in the Plays at least, if not in Shakespeare's mind, the orthodox succession of gaiety, of tragedy, and of the serenity of meditative romance.

Now it is clear that the most important part of this version of Shakespeare's mental history is the end of it. That he did eventually attain to a state of calm content, that he did, in fact, die happy—it is this that gives colour and interest to the whole theory. For some reason or another, the end of a man's life seems naturally to afford the light by which the rest of it should be read; last thoughts do appear in some strange way to be really best and truest; and this is particularly the case when they fit in nicely with the rest of the story, and are, perhaps, just what one likes to think oneself. If it be true that Shakespeare, to quote Professor Dowden, 'did at last attain to the serene self-possession which he had sought with such persistent effort'; that, in the words of Dr. Furnivall, 'forgiven and forgiving, full of the highest wisdom and peace, at one with family and friends and foes, in harmony with Avon's flow and Stratford's level meads, Shakespeare closed his life on earth'—we have obtained a piece of knowledge which is both interesting and pleasant. But if it be not true, if, on the contrary, it can be shown that something very different was actually the case, then will it not follow that we must not only reverse our judgment as to this particular point, but also readjust our view of the whole drift and bearing of Shakespeare's 'inner life'?

The group of works which has given rise to this theory of ultimate serenity was probably entirely composed after Shakespeare's final retirement from London, and his establishment at New Place. It consists of three plays—*Cymbeline*, *The Winter's Tale*, and *The Tempest*—and three fragments— the Shakespearean parts of *Pericles*, *Henry VIII*, and *The*

3

Two Noble Kinsmen. All these plays and portions of plays form a distinct group; they resemble each other in a multitude of ways, and they differ in a multitude of ways from nearly all Shakespeare's previous work.

One other complete play, however, and one other fragment, do resemble in some degree these works of the final period; for, immediately preceding them in date, they show clear traces of the beginnings of the new method, and they are themselves curiously different from the plays they immediately succeed—that great series of tragedies which began with *Hamlet* in 1601 and ended in 1608 with *Antony and Cleopatra.* In the latter year, indeed, Shakespeare's entire method underwent an astonishing change. For six years he had been persistently occupied with a kind of writing which he had himself not only invented but brought to the highest point of excellence—the tragedy of character. Every one of his masterpieces has for its theme the action of tragic situation upon character; and, without those stupendous creations in character, his greatest tragedies would obviously have lost the precise thing that has made them what they are. Yet, after *Antony and Cleopatra* Shakespeare deliberately turned his back upon the dramatic methods of all his past career. There seems no reason why he should not have continued, year after year, to produce *Othellos, Hamlets,* and *Macbeths;* instead, he turned over a new leaf, and wrote *Coriolanus.*

Coriolanus is certainly a remarkable, and perhaps an intolerable play: remarkable, because it shows the sudden first appearance of the Shakespeare of the final period; intolerable, because it is impossible to forget how much better it might have been. The subject is thick with situations; the conflicts of patriotism and pride, the effects of sudden disgrace following upon the very height of fortune, the struggles between family affection on the one hand and every interest of revenge and egotism on the other—these would have made a tragic and tremendous setting for some character worthy to rank with Shakespeare's best. But it pleased him to ignore completely all these opportunities; and, in the play he has given us, the

4

situations, mutilated and degraded, serve merely as miserable props for the gorgeous clothing of his rhetoric. For rhetoric, enormously magnificent and extraordinarily elaborate, is the beginning and the middle and the end of *Coriolanus*. The hero is not a human being at all; he is the statue of a demi-god cast in bronze, which roars its perfect periods, to use a phrase of Sir Walter Raleigh's, through a melodious megaphone. The vigour of the presentment is, it is true, amazing; but it is a presentment of decoration, not of life. So far and so quickly had Shakespeare already wandered from the subtleties of *Cleopatra*. The transformation is indeed astonishing; one wonders, as one beholds it, what will happen next.

At about the same time, some of the scenes in *Timon of Athens* were in all probability composed: scenes which resemble *Coriolanus* in their lack of characterisation and abundance of rhetoric, but differ from it in the peculiar grossness of their tone. For sheer virulence of foul-mouthed abuse, some of the speeches in Timon are probably unsurpassed in any literature; an outraged drayman would speak so, if draymen were in the habit of talking poetry. From this whirlwind of furious ejaculation, this splendid storm of nastiness, Shakespeare, we are confidently told, passed in a moment to tranquillity and joy, to blue skies, to young ladies, and to general forgiveness.

From 1604 to 1610 [says Professor Dowden] a show of tragic figures, like the kings who passed before Macbeth, filled the vision of Shakespeare; until at last the desperate image of Timon rose before him; when, as though unable to endure or to conceive a more lamentable ruin of man, he turned for relief to the pastoral loves of Prince Florizel and Perdita; and as soon as the tone of his mind was restored, gave expression to its ultimate mood of grave serenity in *The Tempest*, and so ended.

This is a pretty picture, but is it true? It may, indeed, be admitted at once that Prince Florizel and Perdita are charming creatures, that Prospero is 'grave,' and that Hermione is more or less 'serene'; but why is it that, in our consideration of the later plays, the whole of our attention

5

must always be fixed upon these particular characters? Modern critics, in their eagerness to appraise everything that is beautiful and good at its proper value, seem to have entirely forgotten that there is another side to the medal; and they have omitted to point out that these plays contain a series of portraits of peculiar infamy, whose wickedness finds expression in language of extraordinary force. Coming fresh from their pages to the pages of *Cymbeline*, *The Winter's Tale*, and *The Tempest*, one is astonished and perplexed. How is it possible to fit into their scheme of roses and maidens that 'Italian fiend' the 'yellow Iachimo,' or Cloten, that 'thing too bad for bad report,' or the 'crafty devil,' his mother, or Leontes, or Caliban, or Trinculo? To omit these figures of discord and evil from our consideration, to banish them comfortably to the background of the stage, while Autolycus and Miranda dance before the footlights, is surely a fallacy in proportion; for the presentment of the one group of persons is every whit as distinct and vigorous as that of the other. Nowhere, indeed, is Shakespeare's violence of expression more constantly displayed than in the 'gentle utterances' of his last period; it is here that one finds Paulina, in a torrent of indignation as far from 'grave serenity' as it is from 'pastoral love,' exclaiming to Leontes:

> What studied torments, tyrant, hast for me?
> What wheels? racks? fires? what flaying? boiling
> In leads or oils? what old or newer torture
> Must I receive, whose every word deserves
> To taste of thy most worst? Thy tyranny,
> Together working with thy jealousies,
> Fancies too weak for boys, too green and idle
> For girls of nine, O! think what they have done,
> And then run mad indeed, stark mad; for all
> Thy by-gone fooleries were but spices of it.
> That thou betray'dst Polixenes, 'twas nothing;
> That did but show thee, of a fool, inconstant
> And damnable ingrateful; nor was't much
> Thou would'st have poison'd good Camillo's honour,
> To have him kill a king; poor trespasses,

6

More monstrous standing by; whereof I reckon
The casting forth to crows thy baby daughter
To be or none or little; though a devil
Would have shed water out of fire ere done't.
Nor is't directly laid to thee, the death
Of the young prince, whose honourable thoughts,
Thoughts high for one so tender, cleft the heart
That could conceive a gross and foolish sire
Blemished his gracious dam.

Nowhere are the poet's metaphors more nakedly material; nowhere does he verge more often upon a sort of brutality of phrase, a cruel coarseness. Iachimo tells us how:

> The cloyed will,
> That satiate yet unsatisfied desire, that tub
> Both filled and running, ravening first the lamb,
> Longs after for the garbage.

and talks of:

> an eye
> Base and unlustrous as the smoky light
> That's fed with stinking tallow.

'The south fog rot him!' Cloten burst out to Imogen, cursing her husband in an access of hideous rage.

What traces do such passages as these show of 'serene self-possession,' of 'the highest wisdom and peace,' or of 'meditative romance'? English critics, overcome by the idea of Shakespeare's ultimate tranquillity, have generally denied to him the authorship of the brothel scenes in *Pericles*; but these scenes are entirely of a piece with the grossnesses of *The Winter's Tale* and *Cymbeline*.

> Is there no way for men to be, but women
> Must be half-workers?

says Posthumus when he hears of Imogen's guilt.

> We are all bastards;
> And that most venerable man, which I
> Did call my father, was I know not where
> When I was stamped. Some coiner with his tools

7

Made me a counterfeit; yet my mother seemed
The Dian of that time; so doth my wife
The nonpareil of this—O vengeance, vengeance!
Me of my lawful pleasure she restrained
And prayed me, oft, forbearance; did it with
A pudency so rosy, the sweet view on't
Might well have warmed old Saturn, that I thought her
As chaste as unsunned snow—O, all the devils!—
This yellow Iachimo, in an hour,—was't not?
Or less,—at first: perchance he spoke not; but,
Like a full-acorned boar, a German one,
Cried, oh! and mounted: found no opposition
But what he looked for should oppose, and she
Should from encounter guard.

And Leontes, in a similar situation, expresses himself in
images no less to the point.

There have been,

Or I am much deceived, cuckolds ere now,
And many a man there is, even at this present,
Now, while I speak this, holds his wife by the arm,
That little thinks she has been sluiced in's absence
And his pond fished by his next neighbour, by
Sir Smile, his neighbour: nay, there's comfort in't,
Whiles other men have gates, and those gates opened,
As mine, against their will. Should all despair
That have revolted wives, the tenth of mankind
Would hang themselves. Physic for't there's none;
It is a bawdy planet, that will strike
Where 'tis predominant; and 'tis powerful, think it,
From east, west, north and south: be it concluded,
No barricado for a belly, know't;
It will let in and out the enemy
With bag and baggage: many thousand on's
Have the disease, and feel't not.

It is really a little difficult, in the face of such passages,
to agree with Professor Dowden's dictum: 'In these latest
plays the beautiful pathetic light is always present.'

But how has it happened that the judgment of so many
critics has been so completely led astray? Charm and gravity,

and even serenity, are to be found in many other plays of Shakespeare. Ophelia is charming, Brutus is grave, Cordelia is serene; are we then to suppose that *Hamlet*, and *Julius Caesar*, and *King Lear* give expression to the same mood of high tranquillity which is betrayed by *Cymbeline*, *The Tempest*, and *The Winter's Tale*? 'Certainly not,' reply the orthodox writers, 'for you must distinguish. The plays of the last period are not tragedies; they all end happily'—'in scenes,' says Sir I. Gollancz, 'of forgiveness, reconciliation, and peace.' Virtue, in fact, is not only virtuous, it is triumphant; what would you more?

But to this it may be retorted, that, in the case of one of Shakespeare's plays, even the final vision of virtue and beauty triumphant over ugliness and vice fails to dispel a total effect of horror and of gloom. For, in *Measure for Measure* Isabella is no whit less pure and lovely than any Perdita or Miranda, and her success is as complete; yet who would venture to deny that the atmosphere of *Measure for Measure* was more nearly one of despair than of serenity? What is it, then, that makes the difference? Why should a happy ending seem in one case futile, and in another satisfactory? Why does it sometimes matter to us a great deal, and sometimes not at all, whether virtue is rewarded or not?

The reason, in this case, is not far to seek. *Measure for Measure* is, like nearly every play of Shakespeare's before *Coriolanus*, essentially realistic. The characters are real men and women; and what happens to them upon the stage has all the effect of what happens to real men and women in actual life. Their goodness appears to be real goodness, their wickedness real wickedness; and, if their sufferings are terrible enough, we regret the fact, even though in the end they triumph, just as we regret the real sufferings of our friends. But, in the plays of the final period, all this has changed; we are no longer in the real world, but in a world of enchantment, of mystery, of wonder, a world of shifting visions, a world of hopeless anachronisms, a world in which anything may happen next. The pretences of reality are indeed usually

9

preserved, but only the pretences. Cymbeline is supposed
to be the king of a real Britain, and the real Augustus is supposed to demand tribute of him; but these are the reasons
which his queen, in solemn audience with the Roman ambassador, urges to induce her husband to declare for war:

> Remember, sir, my liege,
> The Kings your ancestors, together with
> The natural bravery of your isle, which stands
> As Neptune's park, ribbed and paled in
> With rocks unscaleable and roaring waters,
> With sands that will not bear your enemies' boats,
> But suck them up to the topmast. A kind of conquest
> Caesar made here; but made not here his brag
> Of 'Came, and saw, and overcame'; with shame—
> The first that ever touched him—he was carried
> From off our coast, twice beaten; and his shipping—
> Poor ignorant baubles!—on our terrible seas,
> Like egg-shells moved upon the surges, crack'd
> As easily 'gainst our rocks; for joy whereof
> The famed Cassibelan, who was once at point—
> O giglot fortune!—to master Caesar's sword,
> Made Lud's town with rejoicing fires bright
> And Britons strut with courage.

It comes with something of a shock to remember that this
medley of poetry, bombast, and myth will eventually reach
the ears of no other person than the Octavius of *Antony and
Cleopatra*; and the contrast is the more remarkable when one
recalls the brilliant scene of negotiation and diplomacy in
the latter play, which passes between Octavius, Maecenas,
and Agrippa on the one side, and Antony and Enobarbus on
the other, and results in the reconciliation of the rivals and
the marriage of Antony and Octavia.

Thus strangely remote is the world of Shakespeare's
latest period; and it is peopled, this universe of his invention,
with beings equally unreal, with creatures either more or less
than human, with fortunate princes and wicked step-mothers,
with goblins and spirits, with lost princesses and insufferable
kings. And of course, in this sort of fairy land, it is an essential

condition that everything shall end well; the prince and princess are bound to marry and live happily ever afterwards, or the whole story is unnecessary and absurd; and the villains and the goblins must naturally repent and be forgiven. But it is clear that such happy endings, such conventional closes to fantastic tales, cannot be taken as evidences of serene tranquillity on the part of their maker; they merely show that he knew, as well as anyone else, how such stories ought to end.

Yet there can be no doubt that it is this combination of charming heroines and happy endings which has blinded the eyes of modern critics to everything else. Iachimo, and Leontes, and even Caliban, are to be left out of account, as if, because in the end they repent or are forgiven, words need not be wasted on such reconciled and harmonious fiends. It is true they are grotesque; it is true that such personages never could have lived; but who, one would like to know, has ever met Miranda, or become acquainted with Prince Florizel of Bohemia? In this land of faery, is it right to neglect the goblins? In this world of dreams, are we justified in ignoring the nightmares? Is it fair to say that Shakespeare was in 'a gentle, lofty spirit, a peaceful, tranquil mood,' when he was creating the Queen in *Cymbeline*, or writing the first two acts of *The Winter's Tale?*

Attention has never been sufficiently drawn to one other characteristic of these plays, though it is touched upon both by Professor Dowden and Dr. Brandes—the singular carelessness with which great parts of them were obviously written. Could anything drag more wretchedly than the *dénouement* of *Cymbeline?* And with what perversity is the great pastoral scene in *The Winter's Tale* interspersed with long-winded intrigues, and disguises, and homilies! For these blemishes are unlike the blemishes which enrich rather than lessen the beauty of the earlier plays; they are not, like them, interesting or delightful in themselves; they are usually merely necessary to explain the action, and they are sometimes purely irrelevant. One is, it cannot be denied, often bored, and occasionally irritated, by Polixenes and Camillo and Sebastian and Gonzalo and Belarius; these personages have not even the life of ghosts; they are hardly more than speaking names, that give patient utterance to involution upon involution. What a contrast to the minor characters of Shakespeare's earlier works!

It is difficult to resist the conclusion that he was getting bored himself. Bored with people, bored with real life, bored with drama, bored, in fact, with everything except poetry and poetical dreams. He is no longer interested, one often feels, in what happens, or who says what, so long as he can find place for a faultless lyric, or a new, unimagined rhythmical effect, or a grand and mystic speech. In this mood he must have written his share in *The Two Noble Kinsmen*, leaving the plot and characters to Fletcher to deal with as he pleased, and reserving to himself only the opportunities for pompous verse. In this mood he must have broken off halfway through the tedious history of *Henry VIII*; and in this mood he must have completed, with all the resources of his rhetoric, the miserable archaic fragment of *Pericles*.

Is it not thus, then, that we should imagine him in the last years of his life? Half enchanted by visions of beauty and loveliness, and half bored to death; on the one side inspired by a soaring fancy to the singing of ethereal songs, and on the other urged by a general disgust to burst occasionally through his torpor into bitter and violent speech? If we are to learn anything of his mind from his last works, it is surely this.

And such is the conclusion which is particularly forced upon us by a consideration of the play which is in many ways most typical of Shakespeare's later work, and the one which critics most consistently point to as containing the very essence of his final benignity—*The Tempest*. There can be no doubt that the peculiar characteristics which distinguish *Cymbeline* and *The Winter's Tale* from the dramas of Shakespeare's prime, are present here in a still greater degree. In *The Tempest*, unreality has reached its apotheosis. Two of the principal characters are frankly not human beings at all; and the whole action passes, through a series of impossible occurrences, in a place which can only by courtesy be said to exist. The Enchanted Island, indeed, peopled, for a timeless moment, by this strange fantastic medley of persons and of things, has been cut adrift for ever from common sense, and floats buoyed up by a sea, not of waters, but of poetry. Never did Shakespeare's magnificence of diction reach more marvellous heights than in some of the speeches of Prospero, or his lyric art a purer beauty than in the songs of Ariel; nor is it only in these ethereal regions that the triumph of his language asserts itself. It finds as splendid a vent in the curses of Caliban:

> All the infection that the sun sucks up
> From bogs, fens, flats, on Prosper fall, and make him
> By inch-meal a disease!

and in the similes of Trinculo:

> Yond' same black cloud, yond' huge one, looks like a foul
> bombard that would shed his liquor.

The *dénouement* itself, brought about by a preposterous piece of machinery, and lost in a whirl of rhetoric, is hardly more than a peg for fine writing.

> O, it is monstrous, monstrous!
> Methought the billows spoke and told of it;
> The winds did sing it to me; and the thunder,
> That deep and dreadful organ-pipe, pronounced
> The name of Prosper; it did bass my trespass.
> Therefore my son i' th' ooze is bedded, and
> I'll seek him deeper than e'er plummet sounded,
> And with him there lie mudded.

And this gorgeous phantasm of a repentance from the mouth of the pale phantom Alonzo is a fitting climax to the whole fantastic play.

A comparison naturally suggests itself, between what was perhaps the last of Shakespeare's completed works, and that early drama which first gave undoubted proof that his imagination had taken wings. The points of resemblance between *The Tempest* and *A Midsummer Night's Dream*, their common atmosphere of romance and magic, the beautiful absurdities of their intrigues, their studied contrasts of the grotesque with the delicate, the ethereal with the earthly, the charm of their lyrics, the *verve* of the vulgar comedy—these, of course, are obvious enough; but it is the points of difference which really make the comparison striking. One thing, at any rate, is certain about the wood near Athens—it is full of life. The persons that haunt it—though most of them are hardly more than children, and some of them are fairies, and all of them are too agreeable to be true—are nevertheless substantial creatures, whose loves and jokes and quarrels receive our thorough sympathy; and the air they breathe—the lords and the ladies, no less than the mechanics and the elves—is instinct with an exquisite good-humour, which makes us as happy as the night is long. To turn from Theseus and Titania and Bottom to the Enchanted Island, is to step out of a country lane into a conservatory. The roses and the dandelions have vanished before preposterous cactuses, and fascinating orchids too delicate for the open air; and, in the artificial atmosphere, the gaiety of youth has been replaced by the disillusionment of middle age. Prospero is the central figure of *The Tempest*; and it has often been wildly asserted that he is a portrait of the author—an embodiment of that spirit of wise benevolence which is supposed to have thrown a halo over Shakespeare's later life. But, on closer inspection, the portrait seems to be as imaginary as the original. To an irreverent eye, the ex-Duke of Milan would perhaps appear as an unpleasantly crusty personage, in whom a twelve years' monopoly of the conversation had developed an inordinate propensity for talking. These may have been the sentiments of Ariel, safe at the Bermoothes; but to state them is to risk at least ten years in the knotty entrails of an oak, and it is sufficient to point out, that if Prospero is wise, he is also self-opinionated and sour, that his gravity is often another name for pedantic severity, and that there is no character in the play to whom, during some part of it, he is not studiously disagreeable. But his Milanese countrymen are not even disagreeable; they are simply dull. 'This is the silliest stuff that e'er I heard,' remarked Hippolyta of Bottom's amateur theatricals; and one is tempted to wonder what she would have said to the dreary puns and interminable conspiracies of Alonzo, and Gonzalo, and Sebastian, and Antonio, and Adrian, and Francisco, and other shipwrecked noblemen. At all events, there can be little doubt that they would not have had the entrée at Athens.

The depth of the gulf between the two plays is, however, best measured by a comparison of Caliban and his masters with Bottom and his companions. The guileless group of English mechanics, whose sports are interrupted by the mischief of Puck, offers a strange contrast to the hideous trio of the 'jester,' the 'drunken butler,' and the 'savage and deformed slave,' whose designs are thwarted by the magic of Ariel. Bottom was the first of Shakespeare's masterpieces in characterisation, Caliban was the last: and what a world of bitterness and horror lies between them! The charming coxcomb it is easy to know and love; but the 'freckled whelp hag-born' moves us mysteriously to pity and to terror, eluding us for ever in fearful allegories, and strange coils of disgusted laughter and phantasmagorical tears. The physical vigour of the presentment is often so remorseless as to shock us. 'I left them,' says Ariel, speaking of Caliban and his crew:

> I' the filthy-mantled pool beyond your cell,
> There dancing up to the chins, that the foul lake
> O'erstunk their feet.

But at other times the great half-human shape seems to swell like the 'Pan' of Victor Hugo, into something unimaginably vast.

> You taught me language, and my profit on't
> Is, I know how to curse.

Is this Caliban addressing Prospero, or Job addressing God? It may be either; but it is not serene, nor benign, nor pastoral, nor 'On the Heights.'

1904.

WORDS AND POETRY[1]

A STORY is told of Degas, who, in the intervals of painting, amused himself by writing sonnets, and on one occasion found that his inspiration had run dry. In his distress, he went to his friend Mallarmé. 'I cannot understand it,' he said; 'my poem won't come out, and yet I am full of excellent ideas.' 'My dear Degas,' was Mallarmé's reply, 'poetry is not written with ideas; it is written with words.'

Mr. George Rylands' book is a commentary on Mallarmé's dictum. Was it a platitude? Was it a paradox? Both and neither, perhaps, like most profound observations; and Mr. Rylands explains to us how this may be—explains with the delicate amplitude of sensitive enthusiasm and the fresh learning of youth.

It is pleasant to follow him, as he explains and explores. The wide rich fields of English literature lie open before us— the paths are flowery—the nosegays many and sweet. We are lured down fascinating avenues of surmises; we ask questions, and all is made clear by some cunningly chosen bunch that is put into our hands, full of unexpected fragrances, or, perhaps, by the moon. We begin to understand why it is that the glory of an April day cannot be fickle and must be uncertain; we realise the difference between hills and mountains; to our surprise we detect a connection between Dr. Johnson and the Shropshire Lad. With such a clever guide, we may well at last grow presumptuous and long to do a little exploring on our own account.

But it is not an easy business. Perhaps of all the creations of man language is the most astonishing. Those small articulated sounds, that seem so simple and so definite, turn out, the more one examines them, to be the receptacles of subtle

[1] [Originally published as an introduction to *Words and Poetry*. By George H. W. Rylands, M.A. The Hogarth Press. 1928.]

mystery and the dispensers of unanticipated power. Each one
of them, as we look, shoots up into

> A palm with winged imagination in it,
> And roots that stretch even beneath the grave.

It is really a case of Frankenstein and his monster. These
things that we have made are as alive as we are, and we have
become their slaves. Words are like coins (a dozen metaphors
show it), and in nothing more so than in this—that the verbal
currency we have so ingeniously contrived has outrun our
calculations, and become an enigma and a matter for endless
controversy. We say something; but we can never be quite
certain what it is that we have said. In a single written sentence a hundred elusive meanings obscurely palpitate. With
Mr. Rylands' help we analyse the rainbow; we dissect and
compare and define; but the ultimate solution escapes us; we
are entranced by an inexplicable beauty—an intangible
loveliness more enduring than ourselves.

The value of a word depends in part upon the obscure
influences of popular expression and in part upon the fiat of
poets and masters of prose. A great artist can invest a common
word with a miraculous significance—can suddenly turn a
halfpenny into a five-pound note. He can do more; he can
bring back a word that has been dead for centuries into the
life and usage of every day. What now passes as a Bradbury
was once—before the poet touched it with his muttered
abracadabra—a rusty bit of metal in a collector's cabinet. The
romantic writers of the early nineteenth century were the
great masters of this particular enchantment; and it is owing
to them that to-day a multitude of words and phrases go
familiarly among us, which, no less familiar to the Elizabethans, were unknown and unintelligible even to the learned
men of the age of Pope and Gray.

But neither can the poets themselves escape the thraldom
of their own strange handiwork. They, too, are the slaves as
well as the masters of words. Even the greatest of them all,
perhaps! There is one name that no English writer on English

literature can hope, or wish, to avoid for more than a very few moments together. Before we are aware of it, we all of us find that we are talking about Shakespeare. And Mr. Rylands is no exception. Naturally, inevitably, he devotes the latter half of his book to a consideration of Shakespeare as a user of words, and to the history—the romance, one might almost say—of his adventures among them.

It is curious that Shakespeare—by far the greatest word-master who ever lived—should have been so rarely treated of from this point of view. We know almost nothing of the facts of his life; we can only conjecture, most hazardously, about his opinions and his emotions; but there, fixed and palpable before us, lie the vast accumulations of his words, like geological strata, with all their wealth of information laid bare to the eye of the patient and curious observer. How very remarkable, for instance, is the development, which Mr. Rylands points out to us—a late and unexpected development —in Shakespeare's use of prose! How extremely interesting is the story of his dealings with words of classical derivation! The early youthful *engouement* for a romance vocabulary, the more mature severity, and the recoil towards Saxon influences, and then the sudden return to a premeditated and violent classicism—the splendid latinistic passion, which, though it grew fainter with time, left such ineffaceable traces on all his later life!

A drama might almost be made of it—and a drama that could hardly have passed unconsciously in Shakespeare's mind. The supreme artist must have known well enough what was happening among those innumerable little creatures who did his bidding with so rare a felicity—his words. Did he, perhaps, for his own amusement, write an account of the whole affair? A series of sonnets. . . . ? If an allegory must be found in those baffling documents, why should not this be the solution of it? One can fancy that the beautiful youth was merely a literary expression for the classical vocabulary, while the dark lady personified the Saxon one. Their relations, naturally enough, were strained, yet intimate. . . . The theory is offered gratis to the next commentator on the Sonnets. There have been many more far-fetched.

Shakespeare, certainly, knew what he was doing; and yet, in the end, he found that those little creatures were too much for him. So it appears; the geological strata put it almost beyond a doubt. The supreme word-master lorded it no less over character and drama; for many years he carried those three capacities together in an incredible combination, pushing them on from glory to glory; until something most unexpected happened: the words asserted themselves, and triumphed, with extraordinary results. In Shakespeare's later works character has grown unindividual and unreal; drama has become conventional or operatic; the words remain more tremendously, more exquisitely, more thrillingly alive than ever—the excuse and the explanation of the rest. The little creatures had absolutely fascinated their master; he had become their slave. At their bidding he turned Coriolanus from a human being into a glorious gramophone; they spoke, and a fantastic confusion, a beautiful impossibility, involved the constructions of *The Winter's Tale* and *Cymbeline*. To please them, he called up out of nothingness, in *The Tempest*, an Island, not of Romance, but of Pure Style. At last, it was simply for style that Shakespeare lived; everything else had vanished. He began as a poet, and as a poet he ended. Human beings, life, fate, reality—he cared for such things no longer. They were figments—mere ideas; and poetry is not written with ideas; it is written with words.

1928.

SHAKESPEARE AT CAMBRIDGE

Perhaps the best way of realising the implications involved in the fact that the war is over is to pay a visit to one of the Universities. In London the enormous human mechanism, in the country the inevitable processes of nature, serve to conceal the depth of the social change. Somehow or other, in war as in peace, London lives and works and amuses itself; and the woods grow green, and the rain and the sun bring in the harvest. But, to the Universities, the difference between war and peace was literally the difference between death and life; when the war ended, they went through a transformation as complete and sudden as that of a Russian spring; all at once, after the icy season of sterility, the sap has begun to flow again, and the exuberance of youth is made manifest. It is delightful —it is almost incredible—to see college courts with caps and gowns in them, and swishing boats tearing after one another on academic streams. Among other symptoms of this rejuvenescence one welcomes with peculiar pleasure the reappearance at Cambridge of the Marlowe Society which, with unhesitating vigour, has been reviving its pre-war traditions by a production of the First Part of *King Henry IV*. The Marlowe Society is an undergraduate body, full of the spirit of youth; and it was primarily as a spontaneous expression both of the high purposes of youth and of youthful delight in beauty that its rendering of *Henry IV* must have struck the more mature among the audience. That young men should have come together, so soon and so eagerly, to enjoy themselves thus—with candour, with painstaking, with geniality—was surely an admirable thing.

Yet it was not merely from the symptomatic point of view that the performance was interesting. The *blasé* critic might naturally have expected that the pleasure of the evening would be found mainly on the other side of the footlights—

that on *his* side it would be chiefly of the reflected kind. The play is not an easy one to act. The Falstaff scenes, with their extraordinary mingling of brilliant wit, sheer fun, and psychological profundity, seem to cry out for acting that is something more than passable—for acting that is really great—and, in addition, for that most difficult product of stage artistry—a perfectly manipulated *ensemble*. On the other hand, the 'historical' scenes, with their long speeches and sonorous verse, seem to lack action, and, except for the figure of Hotspur, to be too deficient in character to be made much of, save by actors of high accomplishment. The event, however, was full of surprises. The first, instantaneous impression was one of immense relief. The King was speaking. The *blasé* critic might well prick up his ears. How very rarely has a King been heard to speak on any stage! Yet that was what this King, unmistakably, was doing. He was neither mouthing, nor gesticulating, nor rolling his eyes, nor singing, nor chopping his words into mincemeat, nor dragging them out in slow torment up and down the diatonic scale; he was simply speaking; and as he spoke one became conscious of a singular satisfaction—of soothing harmonies, of lovely language flowing in fine cadences, of beautiful images unwinding beautifully, of the subtle union of thought and sound. He ceased, and another speaker followed, and yet another; and the charm remained unbroken. This, then, was the first surprise—the delight of hearing the blank verse of Shakespeare spoken unaffectedly and with the intonation of civilised English; the next was the perception of the fact that, given a good delivery of the verse, the interest of drama and character automatically followed. These scenes, one realised, were something more than mere poetical declamation; for poetical declamation grows dull, and the King, and Worcester, and Westmoreland, and the rest, were never dull for a moment. The words, devised with the supreme skill of Shakespeare's early maturity, required the minimum of acting; all that was needed was their straightforward enunciation by living human beings on a stage; Shakespeare did the rest. Without effort, without fuss, one's imagination was seized and occupied: a few undergraduates became a group of intriguing statesmen, whose minds were full of interest, and whose deliberations were full of moment. Curiously enough, the one character which failed to make an impression was the very one which seemed to offer the easiest opportunity for a success. But here the exception proved the rule; for the part of Hotspur was taken by an actor who had evidently learned to 'act.' The result was inevitable. A thick veil of all the elocutionary arts and graces—points, gestures, exaggerations, and false emphases—was thrown over the words of Shakespeare, and in the process Hotspur vanished as effectually as if he had been at His Majesty's. In the Falstaff scenes Shakespeare again triumphed. A Prince Hal who is really young, a Poins who really laughs, a Falstaff who is neither inaudible nor inebriated—with such blessings one can put up with a weak *ensemble*, and only momentarily reflect upon the opportunities for great acting.

It is difficult not to wish that all performances of Shakespeare could resemble that of the Marlowe Society. Is it impossible that they should? Clearly, one great difficulty stands in the way. The actors at Cambridge were obviously amateurs in the fullest sense of the term. They had never learned to act, and therefore their acting had the charm of unself-consciousness—the charm of primitive art and the drawing and poetry of children. But as soon as the amateur becomes the professional—as soon, that is to say, as he makes a serious and continued practice of his art—self-consciousness necessarily arises, and with self-consciousness the way is opened to the preposterous conventions of the modern stage. The young actor begins to 'act,' and all is over. But is this inevitable? Is there no means of arriving at self-consciousness without the fatal accompaniments of a bad tradition? It is plain that what is needed is a new tradition, and the conclusion suggests itself that the best hope for a new tradition lies in the deliberate development of the instinctive style of the amateur. If the young actor could only be taught that he has to unlearn nothing, that he must preserve at all costs his natural enunciation, his economy of gesture, his sobriety of emotional expression, that it is his business, not to 'interpret' Shakespeare's words, but to speak them, that the first rule for acting Shakespeare is to trust him—how incalculable would the improvement be! One can conceive, with a very little direction, a very little imaginative control, the actors of the Marlowe Society evolving a style of Shakespeare acting which would attain to a permanent excellence—which would be classical, like the acting of Molière at the *théâtre français*. But this is still far off. At present, while dreaming of a perfect instrument, one is fortunate to hear, now and then, the breath of Apollo in a reed.

1919.

OTHELLO

With *Hamlet*, Shakespeare had reached one of the turning-points of his career; he had constructed a tragedy of character —an æsthetic form which had been unknown in Europe since the Greeks. But he had certainly not gone to the Greeks for a model. Romantic, metaphysical, complicated, *Hamlet* seems at times to be almost a psychological treatise, and at other times to be almost a novel. The achievement was vast—perhaps too vast—so Ben Jonson may have remarked, between a growl and a laugh at the Mermaid; and Shakespeare may well have felt that such a criticism was not unfounded. At any rate, he would not repeat himself; he would not write another *Hamlet*; on the contrary, his next work, while preserving the essential quality of the former—the interplay of character and tragic circumstance—should differ from it in almost every other respect; it should be simple, both in treatment and scope; it should avoid philosophical implications and spiritual mysteries; it should depend for its effect upon force, intensity, and concentration.

That Shakespeare, this time intentionally, submitted himself to Greek influence may be a fanciful suggestion; but it is not an impossibility. Even if he could not read Greek, his 'small Latin' was probably enough to enable him to go through one of the Latin translations of Sophocles, and to gather from it a perception, if not of the poetical sublimity, at least of the constructive principles, of the original. Be that as it may, there is undoubtedly a curious analogy between the basic scheme of *Othello* and that of the *Œdipus Tyrannus*. It might almost be said that the first is, in essence, the converse of the second. The dramatic idea of the *Œdipus* is that of a man who deliberately discovers a horror—a horror which is a fact and which, when he knows it, is his undoing. The play consists of this crescendo of discovery, leading to the foreseen and inevitable catastrophe. In *Othello*, on the other hand, the hero is gradually deluded into believing a horror—a horror which is a figment; and the culmination of the tragedy comes, not with the knowledge of a fact, but with the realisation of a delusion. The crescendo, this time, is one of *false* discovery; but in both cases the essence of the drama lies in a mental progression on the part of the hero—a progression whose actual nature and necessary conclusion is not understood by him, but is realised and foreseen at every point by the audience.

The comparison may be carried a step further: whether or no Shakespeare was aware of it, for us it is illuminating to observe the likeness and the contrast between, not only the situations, but the characters of the two heroes. Given the scheme of Sophocles's play, it is clear that it becomes a dramatic necessity for Œdipus to possess certain qualities. It is clear that he must be a very intelligent and an extremely self-willed man. It must be his nature to put two and two together, to refuse to be taken in, to insist with all the force of obstinacy and passion upon unravelling the mystery with which he is faced. A detective-autocrat, his ironic tragedy comes when, utterly unaware of what he is doing, he turns his power and his intellect against himself. One other quality he must have, to complete the effect of the story: he must be royal, not only in position but in nature; the soul that is overwhelmed by this strange nemesis must be a great one, if pity and terror are to reach their full height.

But what are the dramatic requirements for Othello's situation? A great soul certainly; a passionate nature; but his intellectual equipment must be exactly the reverse of that of Œdipus—he must be simple-minded, unsuspicious, easily thrown off his mental balance, a creature eminently susceptible to deceit. The tragedy here is not ironical but pathetic; and the pathos will be deepest if the victim whom one watches led step by step to his ruin, is both magnificent and blind.

Such, stated in the most general terms possible, is the nucleus of the tragedy of *Othello*—the axiomatic starting-point from which—given the genius of Shakespeare—the whole of the rest of the play might be deduced. Actually, of course, Shakespeare did not proceed in any such abstract manner. According to his almost invariable habit, he found the suggestion for his play in another work, which he used as the rough material for his own construction. From this point of view, the case of *Othello* is particularly informing, since it is drawn from a single source, and we are thus able to observe, without doubt or difficulty, the process of manipulation which Shakespeare applied to his original. Cinthio's story—the seventh in the third decade of his *Hecatommithi*—is a 'novella' written in the manner of Boccaccio, a perfectly straightforward narrative, which, brief, matter-of-fact, with hardly a touch of colour or comment, might almost be the report of an actual occurrence, based upon the proceedings of a police-court. In its main lines, the story, up to the death of Desdemona, is nearly identical with Shakespeare's: the marriage of the Venetian lady and the Moorish general; the plot of the Ancient to make the Moor believe that his wife was guilty of adultery with the Captain; the Captain's disgrace, and Desdemona's attempt to obtain his forgiveness from the Moor; the incident of the stolen handkerchief; the Moor's determination to avenge himself by the deaths of his wife and the Captain; and the wounding of the Captain in the leg by the Ancient—all this is common to the story and the play. But in Cinthio, Desdemona is murdered by the Ancient at the instigation and in the presence of the Moor; after which they make her death appear a natural one, so that the murder is undetected; then the Moor and the Ancient quarrel; the Ancient persuades the Captain that it was the Moor who wounded him in the leg (which by this time had been amputated), with the result that the Moor is arrested by the Signoria of Venice, is put to the torture, and, on refusing to confess, is banished—to be eventually slain by the kinsfolk of his wife. As for the Ancient, in consequence of the failure of another of his plots, his end comes in death following upon torture.

Certainly, to anyone who bears in mind what Shakespeare

made out of Cinthio's story, its most striking feature is its lack of characterisation. The persons who, with the exception of the Venetian lady, Disdemona, are not even named, are furnished with a few crude and obvious qualities, and then set off into action. The Moor, we are told, was 'molto valoroso,' he was 'prò della persona,' had given proof 'nelle cose della guerra, di gran prudenza e di vivace ingegno,' and had an 'amore singolare' for his wife. She on her side was 'una virtuosa donna di maravigliosa bellezza,' who 'altro bene non haveva al mondo che il Moro.' Of the Captain we simply learn that he was 'carissimo al Moro,' and of the Ancient's wife that she was a 'bella e honesta giovane.' The Ancient alone receives a slightly more elaborate label. He was 'di bellissima presenza, ma della più scelerata natura che mai fosse huomo del mondo,' and 'quantunque egli fosse di vilissimo animo, copriva nondimeno, coll'alte e superbe parole e colla sua presenza, di modo la viltà ch'egli chiudea nel cuore, che si scopriva nella sembianza un'Ettore od un'Achille.' Yet, with all this black and white, it is difficult to make sure where our sympathies are expected to lie, or even if we are intended to have any. For when at last Othello is killed, the author's casual comment is 'com'egli meritava'—a curious piece of moral bleakness, which reminds us once again of the magistrate's court.

Shakespeare's way was different: his persons are elaborate human beings, towards whom our feelings are directed with an extraordinary certainty and intensity. The Moor becomes Othello; and, whether Shakespeare met with the name in some obscure book of stories or whether he invented it, it was certainly a marvellous *trouvaille*. The essential elements of the character—grandeur and simplicity—are immediately evoked: the bearer of such a name, one feels instinctively, could never have been a clever, puny man. At the same time, the suggestions aroused by the idea of a Moor—which Cinthio had made no use of whatever—were seized upon by Shakespeare with the greatest skill to reinforce his dominating intention. An Italian meant primarily to an Englishman of those days a creature of unscrupulous cunning—a Mac-chiavel—and Othello was *not* an Italian; he was *not* a 'super-subtle Venetian'; he was—the point is constantly insisted upon—utterly foreign to all that. Actually, of course, a Moor might have been as unscrupulously cunning as any Italian; but the antithesis, once established, is effective, and the imagination is set going on the required lines. Among a multitude of minor details, all introduced for the same purpose, one in particular deserves remark. Othello—so Shakespeare more than once gives us to understand—was not merely a fighter and an explorer, he was a sailor; and a certain grand simplicity is a sailor's obvious attribute. There is some reason to believe that, after the first production of the play, Shakespeare decided to accentuate this note still further. At one of the supreme moments of Othello's tragedy—when he finally abandons himself to the delusion that destroys him—Shakespeare put into his mouth the astonishing lines about the Propontic and the Euxine. What manner of man is this? We need no telling: it is the mariner, whose mind, in the stress of an emotional crisis, goes naturally to the sea.

The delusion, yes; but it is time to consider the deluder. It is at this point that we find Shakespeare making, not merely expansions, but definite alterations in the material provided by Cinthio. The Ancient, in Cinthio's story, concealed his wickedness under a heroic guise; he wore the semblance of a Hector or an Achilles. Now it is obvious that, in Shakespeare's scheme, this would not do. To have had two heroic figures, a real one and a false one—as protagonists, would have turned the tragedy into something very like a comedy; and, though we can imagine Shakespeare treating such a theme in another mood—the mood of *Troilus and Cressida*, for instance—any such confusion of *genres* was now quite alien to his purpose. No; the cloak of Iago's villainy must be of an altogether different stuff; clearly it must be the very contrary of the heroic—the downrightness, the outspokenness of bluff integrity. This conception needed no great genius to come by—it might have occurred to half a dozen of the Elizabethan

28

dramatists, even without Iago as a model—but Shakespeare's next readjustment is of quite another class. In Cinthio's story, the Ancient's motive for his villainy is—just what one would expect it to be: he was in love with the lady; she paid no heed to him; his love turned to hatred; he imagined, in his fury, that she loved the Captain; and he determined to be revenged upon them both. Now this is the obvious, the regulation plot, which would have been followed by any ordinarily competent writer. And Shakespeare rejected it. Why? In the first place, let us recall once more the nature of the theme, and let us put it this time less schematically: Othello is to be deluded into believing that Desdemona is faithless; he is to kill her; and then he is to discover that his belief was false. This is the situation, the horror of which is to be intensified in every possible way: the tragedy must be enormous, and unrelieved. But there is one eventuality that might, in some degree at any rate, mitigate the atrocity of the story. If Iago had been led to cause this disaster by his love for Desdemona, in that very fact would lie some sort of comfort; the tragedy would have been brought about by a motive not only comprehensible but in a sense sympathetic; the hero's passion and the villain's would be the same. Let it be granted, then, that the completeness of the tragedy would suffer if its origin lay in Iago's love for Desdemona; therefore let that motive be excluded from Iago's mind. The question immediately presents itself—in that case, for what reason are we to suppose that Iago acted as he did? The whole story depends upon his plot, which forms the machinery of the action; yet, if the Desdemona impulsion is eliminated, what motive for his plot can there be? Shakespeare supplied the answer to this question with one of the very greatest strokes of his genius. By an overwhelming effort of creation he summoned up out of the darkness a psychological portent that was exactly fitted to the requirements of the tragic situation with which he was dealing, and endowed it with reality. He determined that Iago should have no motive at all. He conceived of a monster, whose wickedness should lie far deeper than anything that could be explained by a motive—the very essence of whose being should express itself in the machinations of malignity. This creature might well suppose himself to have a motive; he might well explain his purposes both to himself and his confederate; but his explanations should contradict each other; he should put forward first one motive, and then another, and then another still; so that, while he himself would be only half-aware of the falsity of his self-analysis, to the audience it would be clear; the underlying demonic impulsion would be manifest as the play developed, it would be seen to be no common affair of love and jealousy, but a tragedy conditioned by something purposeless, profound, and terrible; and, when the moment of revelation came, the horror that burst upon the hero would be as inexplicably awful as evil itself. This triumphant invention of the motivelessness of Iago has been dwelt upon by innumerable commentators; but none, so far as I know, has pointed out the purpose of it, and the dramatic necessity which gave it birth. . . .

*   *   *   *   *

[*The MS. of this essay was left unfinished.*]

1931.

RABELAIS

IT is difficult to think of any other among the very great writers of the world who is appreciated in such a variety of degrees, and for such a variety of reasons, as Rabelais. There are those who worship him, there are those who admire him at a distance, there are those who frankly cannot put up with him at all. He is read by many as a great humanist and moral teacher; by many more, probably, as a teller of stories, and in particular of improper stories; others are fascinated by his language, and others by the curious problems—literary, bio-graphical, allegorical—which his book suggests. Mr. W. F. Smith, of St. John's College, Cambridge, belongs to another class—and it is a larger one than might have been expected—the class of those who read Rabelais for the sake of making notes.[1] Mr. Smith, indeed, devotes one of his chapters to 'Rabelais as a Humanist,' but it principally consists of a series of jottings upon the French printers of the early sixteenth century, introduced by the remark, 'We cannot lose sight of the fact that the Renaissance could not have had such far-reaching influence but for the invention of printing.' Of Rabelais as a story-teller, Mr. Smith has very little to say; an uninformed reader of his book would hardly guess from it that there was anything amusing about Gargantua and Pantagruel; though he would discover (on the last page but one) a pained reference to the author's 'outspokenness.' 'Outspokenness generally,' Mr. Smith tells us, 'was tolerated and excused more at that time than now'; and he quotes with approval the obser-vation of 'a French writer' who 'has asserted bluntly that, as the early part of Rabelais' life was spent among monks and friars and the later part in the medical world, it is not sur-prising that he fell in with the freedom of speech usual in

[1] *Rabelais in His Writings.* By W. F. Smith, M.A. Cambridge: At the University Press.

those professions.' We are left to suppose that if only Rabelais had read for the Bar, or had gone into the Army, his writings would never have raised a blush in the most Victorian cheek. As for his style, Mr. Smith's chapter upon that subject could, one feels, have originated nowhere but in the University of Cambridge. Only a member of that learned body would set out to discuss one of the most marvellous creations of human art by filling pages with observations on 'the decadence of pure Latinity observable in the writers of the so-called Silver age, as instanced in Juvenal, Persius, Tacitus, and others,' on 'the policy pursued by the Romans of sending out colonies of veterans to garrison their distant conquests,' on 'the system of Roman law, as administered by the Prætors,' on 'the Vulgate which was used in the Roman Church services' (with special reference to 'St. Jerome's edition'), on 'the study of Aristotle, which was introduced through the Arabic philosophers and was taken up by Albertus Magnus'—all leading to the conclusion that Rabelais 'seems to have formed his style, perhaps unconsciously, on the easy-flowing periods of Herodotus, full as they are of conversations, as well as on the cynicism of Lucian, from whom he borrows freely.' Decidedly, Mr. Smith is happier in the less ambitious task of taking notes—in compiling a list of the plants mentioned by Rabelais, or in tracing his medical references to their sources in Galen, Hipparchus, and Pliny. It is unfortunate, however, that so large a number of his observations should have been culled from the pages of that admirable and learned journal, *La Revue des Etudes Rabelaisiennes*. The reader finds it difficult to determine how much of the book is new, and how much is a *réchauffé*; though the originality of some of Mr. Smith's remarks is obvious. In a note, for instance, on one of the fantasies of the disputed Fifth Book—'les chemins qui cheminent'—after quoting a French editor to the effect that a similar idea occurs in Pascal's *Pensées*—'les rivières sont des chemins qui marchent'—Mr. Smith adds that 'the suggestion has been carried out in practice recently in Paris and elsewhere by means of slopes, etc., moved by machinery to take the place of staircases, etc.' This comment, with the charming glimpse it gives of the groves of Academe, is really after Rabelais' own heart.

Upon the question of the authenticity of the Fifth Book—the greatest of all the Rabelais cruxes—Mr. Smith, of course, has something to say, and inclines, on the whole, to a belief in its genuineness. But he does not refer to two of the most serious arguments in favour of the contrary opinion. Neither the style nor the general tone of the book appears to be that of the author of the rest of the work. Upon the point of style, the English reader can only bow to the judgment of French critics; but it may be noticed that those who are only acquainted with Rabelais through the translation of Urquhart and Motteux can hardly escape a false impression of the literary quality of the original. The splendid genius of Urquhart seized upon that side of Rabelais' writing which was congenial to itself, emphasised it, amplified it, and endowed it with a new immortality. But it was not to be expected that even Urquhart's magic could have transmuted more than a *part* of the glorious gold of the Master. What he gives us is the superabundance of Rabelais, his gigantic linguistic facility, his orgiastic love of words. Urquhart, in fact, actually increases from his own stores the verbal wealth of the original; he cannot resist enlarging as he translates, and prolonging, in a kind of competitive ardour, even the enormous lengths of the famous Lists and Litanies. The result is something magnificent, but something that is not quite Rabelais, for the final miracle of Rabelais' writing is that, in spite of its extraordinary fecundity, it yet preserves an exquisite measure, a supreme restraint. There is a beautiful quality of elegance, of cleanness, of economy, of what the French call 'netteté,' in his sentences, which justifies the paradox that he is one of the most concise of writers. His prose, in short, with all its idiosyncrasies, is characteristically French. Now it is precisely this quality of 'netteté' which is absent in the Fifth Book. Even an English reader must be struck by the change from the delicious concluding pages of the Fourth

33   3

Book, where the writing dances along, flashing, with such an easy lightness, such a swift, consummate grace, to the opening of the Fifth, with its heavy, trailing, formless sentences. The hand of the Master has vanished.

In its general tone the Fifth Book seems to be no less unmistakably unrabelaisian. The great Curé of Meudon may perhaps be described as a satirist; but he was certainly the best-natured satirist who ever lived. No doubt, too, he was a reformer—almost a revolutionary; but of all reformers and revolutionaries he was the most genial, the most urbane. In opinions he was doubtless of the school of Voltaire; but his temperament was the rich, full-blooded, Old Tory temperament of Sir Walter Scott. The good-humoured generosity of his hero, Pantagruel, at times almost verges upon a weak complacency. He seems to tolerate not only the scurvy jests of Panurge but the more serious delinquencies of Bridoison, the imbecile old judge. In the Fifth Book all this changes. The *Isle Sonnante* chapters are full of bitterness; in his comments on the 'Papegaut,' Panurge, besides being heretical, is brutal into the bargain. More remarkable still is the virulence of feeling in the famous description of the *Chats Fourrés* and of Grippeminaud upon the bench. Here the satire is fierce, unrelenting, terrible; there is not a trace of laughter about it; it is a direct and savage attack. The unknown writer rises for a moment to greatness, and seems, after all, in his very different manner, not unworthy of his company. It is perhaps the strangest feature of this strange work that it should have been completed so enigmatically, so incongruously, and with such success. Rabelais, so extraordinary in his nature, was no less extraordinary in his posthumous fate. Of this, the mysterious Fifth Book was the earliest manifestation; the latest is Mr. Smith's volume; but no doubt it will not be the last.

1918.

SIR THOMAS BROWNE

THE life of Sir Thomas Browne does not afford much scope
for the biographer. Everyone knows that Browne was a
physician who lived at Norwich in the seventeenth century;
and, so far as regards what one must call, for want of a better
term, his 'life,' that is a sufficient summary of all there is to
know. It is obvious that, with such scanty and unexciting
materials, no biographer can say very much about what Sir
Thomas Browne did; it is quite easy, however, to expatiate
about what he wrote. He dug deeply into so many subjects,
he touched lightly upon so many more, that his works offer innumerable openings for those half-conversational digressions
and excursions of which perhaps the pleasantest kind of
criticism is composed.

Mr. Gosse, in his volume on Sir Thomas Browne in the
'English Men of Letters' Series, has evidently taken this view
of his subject. He has not attempted to treat it with any great
profundity or elaboration; he has simply gone 'about it and
about.' The result is a book so full of entertainment, of discrimination, of quiet humour, and of literary tact, that no
reader could have the heart to bring up against it the obvious
—though surely irrelevant—truth, that the general impression which it leaves upon the mind is in the nature of a composite presentment, in which the features of Sir Thomas have
become somehow indissolubly blended with those of his biographer. It would be rash indeed to attempt to improve upon
Mr. Gosse's example; after his luminous and suggestive
chapters on Browne's life at Norwich, on the *Vulgar Errors*,
and on the self-revelations in the *Religio Medici*, there seems
to be no room for further comment. One can only admire in
silence, and hand on the volume to one's neighbour.

There is, however, one side of Browne's work upon which
it may be worth while to dwell at somewhat greater length.

Mr. Gosse, who has so much to say on such a variety of topics, has unfortunately limited to a very small number of pages his considerations upon what is, after all, the most important thing about the author of *Urn Burial* and *The Garden of Cyrus*—his style. Mr. Gosse himself confesses that it is chiefly as a master of literary form that Browne deserves to be remembered. Why then does he tell us so little about his literary form, and so much about his family, and his religion, and his scientific opinions, and his porridge, and who fished up the *murex*?

Nor is it only owing to its inadequacy that Mr. Gosse's treatment of Browne as an artist in language is the least satisfactory part of his book: for it is difficult not to think that upon this crucial point Mr. Gosse has for once been deserted by his sympathy and his acumen. In spite of what appears to be a genuine delight in Browne's most splendid and characteristic passages, Mr. Gosse cannot help protesting somewhat acrimoniously against that very method of writing whose effects he is so ready to admire. In practice, he approves; in theory, he condemns. He ranks the *Hydriotaphia* among the gems of English literature; and the prose style of which it is the consummate expression he denounces as fundamentally wrong. The contradiction is obvious; but there can be little doubt that, though Browne has, as it were, extorted a personal homage, Mr. Gosse's real sympathies lie on the other side. His remarks upon Browne's effect upon eighteenth-century prose show clearly enough the true bent of his opinions; and they show, too, how completely misleading a preconceived theory may be.

The study of Sir Thomas Browne, Mr. Gosse says, 'encouraged Johnson, and with him a whole school of rhetorical writers in the eighteenth century, to avoid circumlocution by the invention of superfluous words, learned but pedantic, in which darkness was concentrated without being dispelled.' Such is Mr. Gosse's account of the influence of Browne and Johnson upon the later eighteenth-century writers of prose. But to dismiss Johnson's influence as something altogether deplorable, is surely to misunderstand the whole drift of the great revolution which he brought about in English letters. The characteristics of the pre-Johnsonian prose style—the style which Dryden first established and Swift brought to perfection—are obvious enough. Its advantages are those of clarity and force; but its faults, which, of course, are unimportant in the work of a great master, become glaring in that of the second-rate practitioner. The prose of Locke, for instance, or of Bishop Butler, suffers, in spite of its clarity and vigour, from grave defects. It is very flat and very loose; it has no formal beauty, no elegance, no balance, no trace of the deliberation of art. Johnson, there can be no doubt, determined to remedy these evils by giving a new mould to the texture of English prose; and he went back for a model to Sir Thomas Browne. Now, as Mr. Gosse himself observes, Browne stands out in a remarkable way from among the great mass of his contemporaries and predecessors, by virtue of his highly developed artistic consciousness. He was, says Mr. Gosse, 'never carried away. His effects are closely studied, they are the result of forethought and anxious contrivance'; and no one can doubt the truth or the significance of this dictum who compares, let us say, the last paragraphs of *The Garden of Cyrus* with any page in *The Anatomy of Melancholy*. The peculiarities of Browne's style—the studied pomp of its latinisms, its wealth of allusion, its tendency towards sonorous antithesis—culminated in his last, though not his best, work, the *Christian Morals*, which almost reads like an elaborate and magnificent parody of the Book of Proverbs. With the *Christian Morals* to guide him, Dr. Johnson set about the transformation of the prose of his time. He decorated, he pruned, he balanced; he hung garlands, he draped robes; and he ended by converting the Doric order of Swift into the Corinthian order of Gibbon. Is it quite just to describe this process as one by which 'a whole school of rhetorical writers' was encouraged 'to avoid circumlocution' by the invention 'of superfluous words,' when it was this very process that gave us the peculiar savour of polished ease which characterises nearly all the important prose of the last half of the eighteenth century—that of Johnson himself, of Hume, of Reynolds, of Horace Walpole—which can be traced even in Burke, and which fills the pages of Gibbon? It is, indeed, a curious reflection, but one which is amply justified by the facts, that the *Decline and Fall* could not have been precisely what it is, had Sir Thomas Browne never written the *Christian Morals.*

That Johnson and his disciples had no inkling of the inner spirit of the writer to whose outward form they owed so much, has been pointed out by Mr. Gosse, who adds that Browne's 'genuine merits were rediscovered and asserted by Coleridge and Lamb.' But we have already observed that Mr. Gosse's own assertion of these merits lies a little open to question. His view seems to be, in fact, the precise antithesis of Dr. Johnson's; he swallows the spirit of Browne's writing, and strains at the form. Browne, he says, was 'seduced by a certain obscure romance in the terminology of late Latin writers,' he used 'adjectives of classical extraction, which are neither necessary nor natural,' he forgot that it is better for a writer 'to consult women and people who have not studied, than those who are too learnedly oppressed by a knowledge of Latin and Greek.' He should not have said 'oneiro-criticism,' when he meant the interpretation of dreams, nor 'omneity' instead of 'oneness'; and he had 'no excuse for writing about the "pensile" gardens of Babylon, when all that is required is expressed by "hanging." ' Attacks of this kind—attacks upon the elaboration and classicism of Browne's style—are difficult to reply to, because they must seem, to anyone who holds a contrary opinion, to betray such a total lack of sympathy with the subject as to make argument all but impossible. To the true Browne enthusiast, indeed, there is something almost shocking about the state of mind which would exchange 'pensile' for 'hanging,' and 'asperous' for 'rough,' and would do away with 'digladiation' and 'quodlibetically' altogether. The truth is, that there is a great gulf fixed between those who naturally dislike the ornate, and those who naturally love it. There is no remedy; and to attempt to ignore this fact only emphasises it the more. Anyone who is jarred by the expression 'prodigal blazes' had better immediately shut up Sir Thomas Browne. The critic who admits the jar, but continues to appreciate, must present, to the true enthusiast, a spectacle of curious self-contradiction.

If once the ornate style be allowed as a legitimate form of art, no attack such as Mr. Gosse makes on Browne's latinisms can possibly be valid. For it is surely an error to judge and to condemn the latinisms without reference to the whole style of which they form a necessary part. Mr. Gosse, it is true, inclines to treat them as if they were a mere excrescence which could be cut off without difficulty, and might never have existed if Browne's views upon the English language had been a little different. Browne, he says, 'had come to the conclusion that classic words were the only legitimate ones, the only ones which interpreted with elegance the thoughts of a sensitive and cultivated man, and that the rest were barbarous.' We are to suppose, then, that if he had happened to hold the opinion that Saxon words were the only legitimate ones, the *Hydriotaphia* would have been as free from words of classical derivation as the sermons of Latimer. A very little reflection and inquiry will suffice to show how completely mistaken this view really is. In the first place, the theory that Browne considered all unclassical words 'barbarous' and unfit to interpret his thoughts, is clearly untenable, owing to the obvious fact that his writings are full of instances of the deliberate use of such words. So much is this the case, that Pater declares that a dissertation upon style might be written to illustrate Browne's use of the words 'thin' and 'dark.' A striking phrase from the *Christian Morals* will suffice to show the deliberation with which Browne sometimes employed the latter word:—'the areopagy and dark tribunal of our hearts.' If Browne had thought the Saxon epithet 'barbarous,' why should he have gone out of his way to use it, when 'mysterious' or 'secret' would have expressed his meaning? The truth is clear enough. Browne saw that 'dark' was the one word which would give, better than any other, the precise impression of mystery and secrecy which he intended to produce; and so he used it. He did not choose his words according to rule, but according to the effect which he wished them to have. Thus, when he wished to suggest an extreme contrast between simplicity and pomp, we find him using Saxon words in direct antithesis to classical ones. In the last sentence of *Urn Burial*, we are told that the true believer, when he is to be buried, is 'as content with six foot as the Moles of Adrianus.' How could Browne have produced the remarkable sense of contrast which this short phrase conveys, if his vocabulary had been limited, in accordance with a linguistic theory, to words of a single stock?

There is, of course, no doubt that Browne's vocabulary is extraordinarily classical. Why is this? The reason is not far to seek. In his most characteristic moments he was almost entirely occupied with thoughts and emotions which can, owing to their very nature, only be expressed in Latinistic language. The state of mind which he wished to produce in his readers was nearly always a complicated one: they were to be impressed and elevated by a multiplicity of suggestions and a sense of mystery and awe. 'Let thy thoughts,' he says himself, 'be of things which have not entered into the hearts of beasts: think of things long past, and long to come: acquaint thyself with the choragium of the stars, and consider the vast expanse beyond them. Let intellectual tubes give thee a glance of things which visive organs reach not. Have a glimpse of incomprehensibles; and thoughts of things, which thoughts but tenderly touch.' Browne had, in fact, as Dr. Johnson puts it, 'uncommon sentiments'; and how was he to express them unless by a language of pomp, of allusion, and of elaborate rhythm? Not only is the Saxon form of speech devoid of splendour and suggestiveness; its simplicity is still further emphasised by a spondaic rhythm which seems to produce (by some mysterious rhythmic law) an atmosphere of ordinary life, where, though the pathetic may be present, there is no place for the complex or the remote. To understand how unsuitable such conditions would be for the highly subtle and rarefied art of Sir Thomas

Browne, it is only necessary to compare one of his periods with a typical passage of Saxon prose.

Then they brought a faggot, kindled with fire, and laid the same down at Doctor Ridley's feet. To whom Master Latimer spake in this manner: 'Be of good comfort, Master Ridley, and play the man. We shall this day light such a candle, by God's grace, in England, as I trust shall never be put out.'

Nothing could be better adapted to the meaning and sentiment of this passage than the limpid, even flow of its rhythm. But who could conceive of such a rhythm being ever applicable to the meaning and sentiment of these sentences from the *Hydriotaphia*?

To extend our memories by monuments, whose death we daily pray for, and whose duration we cannot hope without injury to our expectations in the advent of the last day, were a contradiction to our beliefs. We, whose generations are ordained in this setting part of time, are providentially taken off from such imaginations; and, being necessitated to eye the remaining particle of futurity, are naturally constituted unto thoughts of the next world, and cannot excusably decline the consideration of that duration, which maketh pyramids pillars of snow, and all that's past a moment.

Here the long, rolling, almost turgid clauses, with their enormous Latin substantives, seem to carry the reader forward through an immense succession of ages, until at last, with a sudden change of the rhythm, the whole of recorded time crumbles and vanishes before his eyes. The entire effect depends upon the employment of a rhythmical complexity and subtlety which is utterly alien to Saxon prose. It would be foolish to claim a superiority for either of the two styles; it would be still more foolish to suppose that the effects of one might be produced by means of the other.

Wealth of rhythmical elaboration was not the only benefit which a highly Latinised vocabulary conferred on Browne. Without it, he would never have been able to achieve those splendid strokes of stylistic *bravura*, which were evidently so dear to his nature, and occur so constantly in his finest passages. The precise quality cannot be easily described, but is impossible to mistake; and the pleasure which it produces seems to be curiously analogous to that given by a piece of magnificent brushwork in a Rubens or a Velazquez. Browne's 'brushwork' is certainly unequalled in English literature, except by the very greatest masters of sophisticated art, such as Pope and Shakespeare; it is the inspiration of sheer technique. Such expressions as: 'to subsist in bones and be but pyramidally extant'—'sad and sepulchral pitchers which have no joyful voices'—'predicament of chimæras'—'the irregularities of vain glory, and wild enormities of ancient magnanimity'— are examples of this consummate mastery of language, examples which, with a multitude of others, singly deserve whole hours of delicious gustation, whole days of absorbed and exquisite worship. It is pleasant to start out for a long walk with such a splendid phrase upon one's lips as: 'According to the ordainer of order and mystical mathematicks of the City of Heaven,' to go for miles and miles with the marvellous syllables still rich upon the inward ear, and to return home with them in triumph. It is then that one begins to understand how mistaken it was of Sir Thomas Browne not to have written in simple, short, straightforward Saxon English.

One other function performed by Browne's latinisms must be mentioned, because it is closely connected with the most essential and peculiar of the qualities which distinguish his method of writing. Certain classical words, partly owing to their allusiveness, partly owing to their sound, possess a remarkable flavour which is totally absent from those of Saxon derivation. Such a word, for instance, as 'pyramidally,' gives one at once an immediate sense of something mysterious, something extraordinary, and, at the same time, something almost grotesque. And this subtle blending of mystery and queerness characterises not only Browne's choice of words, but his choice of feelings and of thoughts. The grotesque side of his art, indeed, was apparently all that was visible to the critics of a few generations back, who admired him simply and solely for what they called his 'quaintness'; while Mr. Gosse has flown to the opposite extreme, and will not allow Browne any sense of humour at all. The confusion no doubt arises merely from a difference in the point of view. Mr. Gosse, regarding Browne's most important and general effects, rightly fails to detect anything funny in them. The Early Victorians, however, missed the broad outlines, and were altogether taken up with the obvious grotesqueness of the details. When they found Browne asserting that 'Cato seemed to dote upon Cabbage,' or embroidering an entire paragraph upon the subject of 'Pyrrhus his Toe,' they could not help smiling; and surely they were quite right. Browne, like an impressionist painter, produced his pictures by means of a multitude of details which, if one looks at them in themselves, are discordant, and extraordinary, and even absurd.

There can be little doubt that this strongly marked taste for curious details was one of the symptoms of the scientific bent of his mind. For Browne was scientific just up to the point where the examination of detail ends, and its co-ordination begins. He knew little or nothing of general laws; but his interest in isolated phenomena was intense. And the more singular the phenomena, the more he was attracted. He was always ready to begin some strange inquiry. He cannot help wondering: 'Whether great-ear'd persons have short necks, long feet, and loose bellies?' 'Marcus Antoninus Philosophus,' he notes in his commonplace book, 'wanted not the advice of the best physicians; yet how warrantable his practice was, to take his repast in the night, and scarce anything but treacle in the day, may admit of great doubt.' To inquire thus is, perhaps, to inquire too curiously; yet such inquiries are the stuff of which great scientific theories are made. Browne, however, used his love of details for another purpose: he co-ordinated them, not into a scientific theory, but into a work of art. His method was one which, to be successful, demanded a self-confidence, an imagination, and a technical power, possessed by only the very greatest artists. Everyone knows Pascal's overwhelming sentence:—'Le silence éternel de ces espaces infinis m'effraie.' It is overwhelming, obviously and immediately; it, so to speak, knocks one down. Browne's ultimate object was to create some such tremendous effect as that, by no knock-down blow, but by a multitude of delicate, subtle, and suggestive touches, by an elaborate evocation of memories and half-hidden things, by a mysterious combination of pompous images and odd unexpected trifles drawn together from the ends of the earth and the four quarters of heaven. His success gives him a place beside Webster and Blake, on one of the very highest peaks of Parnassus. And, if not the highest of all, Browne's peak is—or so at least it seems from the plains below—more difficult of access than some which are no less exalted. The road skirts the precipice the whole way. If one fails in the style of Pascal, one is merely flat; if one fails in the style of Browne, one is ridiculous. He who plays with the void, who dallies with eternity, who leaps from star to star, is in danger at every moment of being swept into utter limbo, and tossed forever in the Paradise of Fools.

Browne produced his greatest work late in life; for there is nothing in the *Religio Medici* which reaches the same level of excellence as the last paragraphs of *The Garden of Cyrus* and the last chapter of *Urn Burial*. A long and calm experience of life seems, indeed, to be the background from which his most amazing sentences start out into being. His strangest fantasies are rich with the spoils of the real world. His art matured with himself; and who but the most expert of artists could have produced this perfect sentence in *The Garden of Cyrus*, so well known, and yet so impossible not to quote?

Nor will the sweetest delight of gardens afford much comfort in sleep; wherein the dullness of that sense shakes hands with delectable odours; and though in the bed of Cleopatra, can hardly with any delight raise up the ghost of a rose.

This is Browne in his most exquisite mood. For his most characteristic, one must go to the concluding pages of *Urn Burial*, where, from the astonishing sentence beginning—

'Meanwhile Epicurus lies deep in Dante's hell'—to the end of the book, the very quintessence of his work is to be found. The subject—mortality in its most generalised aspect—has brought out Browne's highest powers; and all the resources of his art—elaboration of rhythm, brilliance of phrase, wealth and variety of suggestion, pomp and splendour of imagination —are accumulated in every paragraph. To crown all, he has scattered through these few pages a multitude of proper names, most of them gorgeous in sound, and each of them carrying its own strange freight of reminiscences and allusions from the unknown depths of the past. As one reads, an extraordinary procession of persons seems to pass before one's eyes —Moses, Archimedes, Achilles, Job, Hector and Charles the Fifth, Cardan and Alaric, Gordianus, and Pilate, and Homer, and Cambyses, and the Canaanitish woman. Among them, one visionary figure flits with a mysterious pre-eminence, flickering over every page, like a familiar and ghostly flame. It is Methuselah; and, in Browne's scheme, the remote, almost infinite, and almost ridiculous patriarch is—who can doubt?—the only possible centre and symbol of all the rest. But it would be vain to dwell further upon this wonderful and famous chapter, except to note the extraordinary sublimity and serenity of its general tone. Browne never states in so many words what his own feelings towards the universe actually are. He speaks of everything but that; and yet, with triumphant art, he manages to convey into our minds an indelible impression of the vast and comprehensive grandeur of his soul.

It is interesting—or at least amusing—to consider what are the most appropriate places in which different authors should be read. Pope is doubtless at his best in the midst of a formal garden, Herrick in an orchard, and Shelley in a boat at sea. Sir Thomas Browne demands, perhaps, a more exotic atmosphere. One could read him floating down the Euphrates, or past the shores of Arabia; and it would be pleasant to open the *Vulgar Errors* in Constantinople, or to get by heart a chapter of the *Christian Morals* between the paws of a Sphinx. In

England, the most fitting background for his strange ornament must surely be some habitation consecrated to learning,
some University which still smells of antiquity and has learnt
the habit of repose. The present writer, at any rate, can bear
witness to the splendid echo of Browne's syllables amid
learned and ancient walls; for he has known, he believes, few
happier moments than those in which he has rolled the periods
of the *Hydriotaphia* out to the darkness and the nightingales
through the studious cloisters of Trinity.

But, after all, who can doubt that it is at Oxford that
Browne himself would choose to linger? May we not guess
that he breathed in there, in his boyhood, some part of that
mysterious and charming spirit which pervades his words?
For one traces something of him, often enough, in the old
gardens, and down the hidden streets; one has heard his footstep beside the quiet waters of Magdalen; and his smile still
hovers amid that strange company of faces which guard, with
such a large passivity, the circumference of the Sheldonian.

1906.

THE OLD COMEDY

THE rises and falls in the stock market of literature deserve more study than they have received. The greater and more obvious fluctuations have, no doubt, come in for a certain amount of attention—the boom in Ovid at the end of the sixteenth century, for instance, or the slump in Pope at the beginning of the nineteenth. But the minor variations are in their way almost as interesting, and they have been little discussed. What were the subtle causes which led, quite lately, to the rise in Donne, after he had lain for two hundred years a drug on the market? He is still rising, and shareholders who picked him up for next to nothing—an old song, one might say—fifteen years ago, are now congratulating themselves. There are many other such curious cases—the inflation, followed by a rapid collapse, in R. L. Stevenson, is one of them. Another case, which shows some sign of proving interesting, is that of the Comedy of the Restoration. I think, from what I know of the state of the market generally, that I might recommend this stock to purchasers who are willing to wait a little. It is true that it cannot be described as a gilt-edged security; in fact, this particular stock will, I fear, always be a trifle risky; and its reputation with the public has been so bad for so long that no immediate recovery is likely. But, of course, investors must not expect everything. Shakespeare is perfectly safe, but there is a glut in Shakespeare—you cannot get rid of him. Wordsworth, too, is a good sound investment, but he only yields $2\frac{1}{2}$ per cent. It is to those who do not object to an occasional flutter that I recommend the Comedy of the Restoration, which is at present quoted at a very low figure—indeed, it is hardly quoted at all.

Mr. John Palmer's book, *The Comedy of Manners* (Bell & Son), is one of the indications of an approaching change of feeling towards those gay old writers who are perhaps still

47

chiefly familiar to the ordinary reader through the grievous
wigging meted out to them by Macaulay more than seventy
years since. Mr. Palmer's outspoken and interesting attempt
to vindicate the impeached dramatists, and incidentally to
administer a wigging to Macaulay in his turn, shows, I think,
the way in which the critical wind is beginning to blow.
Whether this book does more than this—whether it is likely
to add much force to the breeze already blowing—seems less
certain, partly because of its very anxiety to do so. Mr.
Palmer's attitude is a little too much that of the partisan to be
thoroughly convincing. He is too anxious to argue upon every
point, and perhaps a shade too clever in his arguments. The
truth is that no amount of special pleading, however dexterous,
will do away with the plain fact that the dramatists of the
Restoration were, in the ordinary sense of the word, indecent.
It is simpler to state this at once, for by this means not only
will a good deal of misunderstanding be avoided, but the
dramatists themselves will be given their true place in the
history of literature—in that long line of writers who, from
Aristophanes to Anatole France, have taken as the theme for
their variations of humour and fancy one of the very few
universal elements in the nature of man. Macaulay understood
that this was so, and saw that if he were to make good his
attack upon Wycherley and Congreve he must bring home to
them some more heinous fault than that lack of decency
which is common to such a vast number of illustrious writers
and which, in fact, forms the very essence of the work of some
of the most illustrious of all. He accordingly attempted to
show that the Restoration dramatists were indecent in a
particularly reprehensible way—that they used, so to speak, a
particular brand of indecency which made their works both
morally detestable and artistically bad. And this is the real
question at issue—not whether Wycherley and his successors
were or were not indecent, but whether they were or were
not indecent with the particular *nuance* that Macaulay im-
putes to them. His arguments appear to me unconvincing,
and they certainly have not convinced Mr. Palmer; what is

more important, both Hazlitt and Lamb take the contrary view. Thackeray and Meredith, however, side with Macaulay. When doctors disagree in this way it seems fair to suppose that the underlying difference is less one of principle than one of personal taste. In such delicate and difficult matters individual variations of temperament and of upbringing—to say nothing of the changes in the moral conventions of different epochs, upon which Mr. Palmer lays so much stress—are really the preponderating elements in any judgment. If your stomach is a queasy one, there are many things in this world which will be distasteful to you—among them the Comedies of the Restoration. But that is no reason why the robust gentleman yonder should not wash down his tripe and onions, if the fancy so takes him, with mulled claret and divert his mind with the rollicking scenes of the *Relapse* or the *Plain Dealer*.

If Mr. Palmer had taken this line of defence, rather than the more unyielding one of theoretic disputation, his book would, I think, have gained from the point of view of literary criticism. As it is, the main interest of it seems to lie in its æsthetic doctrines rather than in its appreciations of actual works of art. This is unfortunate, because a sympathetic exposition of what is truly valuable and interesting in this half-forgotten body of literature would have been of real service to the reading public. For instance, there is one very obvious merit in these old plays which, if it had been properly emphasised by critics, would have done much to help the reader to forget their unsavoury reputation, and look into them for their own sakes. It is one of the curious facts about our literature that such a small proportion of it reflects the dominant characteristics of our race. Its greatest achievements are poetical; and we are a nation of shopkeepers. Nor is our poetry of that sober and solid kind which it might have been expected to be; it is for the most part remarkable either for high fantasy, as in Shelley and the Elizabethan lyrists, or for intellectual subtlety, as in Donne and Browning, or for pure artistry, as in Milton and Keats; the very qualities which the ordinary Englishman notoriously lacks. In prose, no doubt,

4

we have Fielding and Scott; but we have also Sir Thomas
Browne, Sterne, Lamb, and George Meredith. Either the
accepted estimate of our national character is altogether
wrong, or the average English reader must be pictured as an
unfortunate wanderer among alien and uncongenial spirits.
Yet, if he would only turn to the Comedy of the Restoration,
he would find there all that his heart most yearns for; and he
would find it especially in the pages of that writer whose name
is familiar to him at present simply as a byword for disgusting
indecorum—Wycherley. Mr. Palmer glances for a moment
at Wycherley's relation to Molière, only to dismiss the
subject as of small importance. In a sense it is certainly
unimportant, for Wycherley's indebtedness to his great
French contemporary was purely formal; but, from the point
of view of the light which it throws upon Wycherley's art,
nothing could be more instructive than a comparison of the
two writers. It is not the resemblance, it is the contrast, that
is so extraordinarily striking. One only grasps to the full the
native vigour of Wycherley's genius when one realises that
he has taken the main situation of Molière's *Misanthrope* and
has had the audacity to use it as the basis for his own *Plain
Dealer*. Surely only an Englishman could have done that—
could have remained so utterly impervious to all those qualities
in the French play which have made it a thing of unique and
undying beauty—the refinement of its atmosphere, the concentration of its purpose, the intimate delicacy of its character-
drawing—could have brushed all this aside like so much
gossamer, and have proceeded to create on its ruins his own
coarse, vivid, solid, rough-and-tumble comedy. He makes his
Alceste a hectoring sea captain, who first comes on to the
stage with a couple of jack tars carrying his luggage. Imagine
an able-bodied seaman in Célimène's drawing-room! Everywhere it is the same: instead of the poignant reserve of
Molière's masterpiece, Wycherley gives us the breadth and
bustle of common life—transports us to Westminster Hall
among lawyers and aldermen, drags in litigious widows and
country bumpkins, or whisks us off to 'the Cock in Bow

Street,' pouring out upon us all the time his jokes and his vituperations in alternate bucketfuls. The effect is Hogarthian; and the atmosphere is unmistakable—it is that which can only be produced by the combination of solid British beef, thick British beer, stout British bodies, and let us add (for even Mr. Palmer, to his regret, is almost obliged to confess it) stolid British moralising. The loose jests have precisely the same quality; and this, no doubt, is why Wycherley's reputation in this respect is so peculiarly bad; he was English even there. As a true-born Briton he had to do his job thoroughly; and so his licentiousness, like English furniture and English cutlery, is the genuine article, turned out regardless of expense.

It would be pleasant to trace out this English vein in further detail, as it runs through the Comedy of Wycherley's successors, and especially as it appears in the works of Sir John Vanbrugh, a writer to whom I think justice has never been done, and who only receives at the hands of Mr. Palmer some rather grudging commendation. What Vanbrugh gives us is not the hot, confused and crowded atmosphere of an English inn, but the jovial, high-hearted gaiety of English outdoor life; in his best scenes one has the sense of being carried off at a gallop after the hounds on a fine morning—so brisk and fresh-humoured are they, so full of the exhilarating spirit of happy improvisation. Vanbrugh was something which has always been more common in England than elsewhere—an amateur of genius. He seems to have been naturally inspired with the capacity for doing with absolute *aplomb* whatever he laid his hand to, from the writing of comedies to the building of castles. Luckily, too, he was able to keep his different talents in separate compartments, for while his architecture (as the famous epitaph declares) was the embodiment of massive grandeur, his drama is all light and air. In the *Relapse* we find him at his best, evoking and combining that jolly company of English humours—Sir Tunbelly Clumsy, Miss Hoyden, Tom Fashion, Parson Bull, and the rest—with the spritely ease of consummate theatrical craftsmanship. 'Cod's my life!' exclaims Sir Tun-belly, the portentous country squire, when he finds that he has a lord for a visitor. 'I ask your lordship's pardon ten thousand times. [*To a Servant*] Here, run in a-doors quickly. Get a Scotch-coal fire in the great parlour; set all the Turkey-work chairs in their places; get the great brass candlesticks out, and be sure stick the sockets full of laurel, run! My lord, I ask your lordship's pardon. And do you hear, run away to nurse, bid her let Miss Hoyden loose again, and if it was not shifting day, let her put on a clean tucker, quick!' Is not this instinct with an admirable vitality? Then there is Miss Hoyden herself with her 'I don't care how often I'm married, not I,' and her 'I never disobey my father in anything but eating of green gooseberries.' And then, among them all, there is the superb figure of Lord Foppington, who, with his delicious absurdities, his preposterous airs and graces, his blood-curdling oaths and lackadaisical pronunciation, yet manages to be incessantly witty, to dominate whatever company he may be in, and, in fact, in some strange way, to be great. Vanbrugh, with true English humour, has resisted the temptation of making an utter fool of his fool, and has shown us, even in that strutting clothes-block, the eminence of the human spirit.

And Congreve? It would be lacking in respect to that great name to let it pass unmentioned in any review, however slight, of the Comedy of the Restoration. But the fag-end of an article is no place for a discussion of so high and potent a genius. I would only say that with him, too, as it seems to me, too little stress has been laid upon the broad, the realistic, the solid qualities of his art. Critics are dazzled by the brilliance of his wit and his marvellous verbal felicity. But, if they looked more closely, they would see, I fancy, that even the ineffable figure of Mistress Millamant is planted firmly upon good English earth.

1913.

CONGREVE, COLLIER, MACAULAY, AND MR. SUMMERS

As the Victorian Age grows dim on the horizon, various neglected luminaries re-emerge—among others the comic dramatists of the Restoration. The work of Sheridan begins to be taken at its true value—as a clever but emasculated *rifacimento*; the supreme master of prose comedy in English is seen to be Congreve. At least, let us hope so. To those who are still in doubt, or in ignorance, the new complete edition of Congreve's works, published by the Nonesuch Press, and edited by Mr. Montague Summers, should bring conviction or conversion. Congreve now appears for the first time as he should have appeared long ago—as a classic. The get-up of these four quarto volumes—though it cannot be said to equal the perfect amenity of the Baskerville edition of 1761—is admirable; and the critical prefaces, notes, and commentaries are a monument of erudition and exactitude. Mr. Summers prints the plays, probably rightly, from the original editions, and not from the last edition published during the author's lifetime, which has formed the basis of all subsequent texts. He thus restores to life several excellent jokes, deleted by Congreve owing to the attacks of Jeremy Collier, though he does so at the cost of relegating various small improvements and polishings to the list of variants; but no doubt—if one must choose—polishings are less valuable than jokes. Another decided gain is the reversion to the original arrangement of the scenes, which had been unnecessarily Frenchified by Congreve himself, and had subsequently undergone a process of serious degradation—still unfortunately visible in the current 'Mermaid' edition. Mr. Summers's interesting introduction is full of learning, argument, and feeling—in fact, perhaps too full. There is an idiosyncratic exuberance about it, which sorts ill with the exquisite impersonality of Congreve. To speak of 'the disastrous Revolution of 1688,' for instance, and to describe the Lollards as 'Wyclif's gang,' is odd; and oddity should not appear in Congreve's editor. One small point may be mentioned, as an illustration of the dangers which attend an excess of zeal: ' 'Tis true we found you and Mr. Fainall in the blue garret,' says Mincing, the lady's maid, to Mrs. Marwood; 'by the same token, you swore us to secrecy upon Messalina's Poems.' Mr. Summers has the following note: ' "Messalina's Poems." Considerable research has failed to trace this book. It is alluded to before as "a book of Verses and Poems," and I would suggest that it was a collection of obscene lyrics and songs clandestinely printed.' Alas, for Mr. Summers's 'considerable research'! A word with Millamant would have brought light in a moment. For the explanation is as simple as it is delightful: Mincing had got the title of the 'Book of Verses and Poems' just a little wrong; instead of 'Messalina's,' she should have said 'Miscellaneous.'

The difficulty of distinguishing between what is Miscellaneous and what is Messalina's is not confined to Mincing. The dividing line has never been absolutely drawn, and learned Magistrates are worried with the question to this hour. But at the end of the seventeenth century discussions upon ethics and æsthetics were even more confused and confusing than they are at the present day. For one thing, there were more red herrings on the track. The divine and mysterious requirements of dogmatic theology had to be attended to—so had the almost equally divine and mysterious pronouncements of Aristotle. Jeremy Collier, however, was troubled with no doubts. He saw Messalina everywhere; and, in his *Short View of the Profaneness and Immorality of the English Stage*, published in 1698, he singled out the dramatists of the time for a violent castigation. To a modern reader, Collier's book is nothing but a curiosity, its only merit being, oddly enough, an æsthetic one—it is written in good plain English. The arguments throughout are grotesque, and it is clear that Collier had never stopped for two minutes to consider the general questions at issue. He supports his contentions by appeals to Tertullian, Minutius Felix, St. Chrysostom, and 'the Bishop of Arras'; the ancient drama, he gravely maintains, was less scurrilous than the modern—did not Sophocles show the deepest respect for oracles? As for his conception of what constitutes stage immorality, it is most extraordinary. Any opinion held by any character in a play is assumed to be the author's. Congreve is seriously pronounced to be obscene and blasphemous because he makes his gentlemen say 'Pox on't,' and his ladies 'Jesu!' while Dryden is savagely hectored for 'abusing the clergy' because in one of his plays an Egyptian Princess rails at the priests of Apis. Obviously, this absurd volume lay open to more than one crushing rejoinder. Several rejoinders were made; but their ineptitude is symptomatic of the age; and the most inept of all was Congreve's. With a strange perversity the wittiest man alive made a complete fool of himself by rushing into the one position that was untenable. He maintained that his plays were not indecent, but that, on the contrary, they were written to subserve the highest ends of virtue. He, too, actually appealed to the Early Fathers. It is impossible to decide which of the two antagonists is the more ridiculous— Collier when he fiercely anathematises Congreve for calling a coachman Jehu, or Congreve when he blandly assumes that there is nothing improper in Lady Plyant and Mr. Scandal.

Unluckily, the true nature of this preposterous controversy has become obscured by Macaulay. In an essay, written in that style which, with its metallic exactness and its fatal efficiency, was certainly one of the most remarkable products of the Industrial Revolution, Macaulay has impressed upon the mind of the ordinary reader his own version of the affair. Wishing to make a dramatic story of it, with a satisfactory moral, he has presented Collier as a hero—not, to be sure, without his little short-comings, but still a hero—who, in the twinkling of an eye, purged not only the English theatre, but English literature itself, of the deplorable and reprehensible grossness which had been disgracing the country for the last forty years. A few inconvenient facts are forgotten—the fact, for instance, that the Restoration Comedies continued to be acted unceasingly throughout the eighteenth century. But, no doubt, it is to the moral revolution effected by the *Short View* that we owe the exquisite propriety of the farces of Fielding and the chaste refinements of *Gulliver's Travels* and the *Dunciad*.

One of the wildest of Macaulay's aberrations is his picture of Collier as a great humorist. As Mr. Summers observes, an utter—a devastating—a positively unnerving lack of humour is the most conspicuous feature of the *Short View*. Yet Macaulay has the effrontery to mention Pascal in connection with this egregious jackass. He was gambling heavily on none of his readers having the curiosity to open the book.

Whether Mr. Summers's account of the dispute will supersede Macaulay's seems to be a little doubtful. He is, perhaps, too much of a partisan. His unwillingness to admit the weakness of Congreve's arguments diminishes the force of his denunciation of Collier's. In truth, the question is not so simple. No doubt, as Mr. Summers says, art and life are different things; but wherein precisely lies the difference? Later, Mr. Summers justifies the comedies of the Restoration on the ground that they were a truthful representation of life as it was lived in the high society of the time. 'A close parallel,' he adds, 'may be found in the decadence of Venice.' Surely he might have pushed the comparison a little further—as far as the present day. One can easily think of a Mr. Tattle in Bloomsbury, and a Lady Froth in Mayfair. Nevertheless, it is plainly paradoxical to find in *The Double Dealer* or *The Way of the World* a faithful presentment of any state of society; it is not in that fashion that real life is lived. What, then, is the explanation of this close resemblance combined with this obvious unlikeness? How is it that we are well acquainted with Mrs. Frail, without for a moment supposing that either she or ourselves are figuring in a Congreve comedy? Perhaps the truth is that pure Comedy, unlike Tragedy and Drama and most forms of fiction, depends for its existence on the construction of a conventional world in which, while human nature and human actions are revealed, their consequences are suspended. The characters in Comedy are real; but they exist *in vacuo*. They are there neither to instruct us nor to exalt us, but simply to amuse us; and therefore the effects which would in reality follow from their conduct must not appear. If they did, the comedy would cease to exist: the jealous husband would become a tragic personage; the heavy father a Galsworthy character; the rake would be revealed as a pest, and the old bore as . . . an old bore. By the magic of Comedy, what is scabrous, what is melancholy, what is vicious, and what is tiresome in the actual life of society is converted into charming laughter and glittering delight.

This being so, it is as futile for the comic writer to pretend that he is, in reality, a moralist in disguise, as it is for the moralist to blame the comic writer for ignoring morality. The true weight of the moral objection lies in a very different consideration. It is perfectly possible that the presentation of such spectacles as Comedy presents may prove, in certain circumstances, undermining to the virtue of the spectators. But it is obvious that here no general rule can be laid down; everything depends upon contingencies. The time, the place, the shifting significations of words, the myriad dispositions of the audience or the reader—all these things are variables which can never be reduced to a single formula. Queen Caroline's meat was Queen Victoria's poison; and perhaps Lord Macaulay's poison was Mr. Aldous Huxley's pap. Every case must be considered on its own merits; but, after all, in any case, such considerations have no bearing upon the intrinsic excellence of works of art. Fireworks do not cease to be exhilarating and beautiful because it is dangerous for inexperienced governesses to play with them. The comedies of Congreve must be ranked among the most wonderful and glorious creations of the human mind, although it is quite conceivable that, in certain circumstances, and at a given moment, a whole bench of Bishops might be demoralised by their perusal.

1923.

RACINE

When Ingres painted his vast 'Apotheosis of Homer,' he represented, grouped round the central throne, all the great poets of the ancient and modern worlds, with a single exception—Shakespeare. After some persuasion, he relented so far as to introduce into his picture a *part* of that offensive personage; and English visitors at the Louvre can now see, to their disgust or their amusement, the truncated image of rather less than half of the author of *King Lear* just appearing at the extreme edge of the enormous canvas. French taste, let us hope, has changed since the days of Ingres; Shakespeare would doubtless now be advanced—though perhaps chiefly from a sense of duty—to the very steps of the central throne. But if an English painter were to choose a similar subject, how would he treat the master who stands acknowledged as the most characteristic representative of the literature of France? Would Racine find a place in the picture at all? Or, if he did, would more of him be visible than the last curl of his full-bottomed wig, whisking away into the outer darkness?

There is something inexplicable about the intensity of national tastes and the violence of national differences. If, as in the good old days, I could boldly believe a Frenchman to be an inferior creature, while he, as simply, wrote me down a savage, there would be an easy end of the matter. But alas! *nous avons changé tout cela.* Now we are each of us obliged to recognise that the other has a full share of intelligence, ability, and taste; that the accident of our having been born on different sides of the Channel is no ground for supposing either that I am a brute or that he is a ninny. But, in that case, how does it happen that while on one side of that 'span of waters' Racine is despised and Shakespeare is worshipped, on the other, Shakespeare is tolerated and Racine is adored? The perplexing question was recently emphasised and illustrated

58

in a singular way. Mr. John Bailey, in a volume of essays en-
titled 'The Claims of French Poetry,' discussed the qualities
of Racine at some length, placed him, not without contumely,
among the second rank of writers, and drew the conclusion
that, though indeed the merits of French poetry are many and
great, it is not among the pages of Racine that they are to
be found. Within a few months of the appearance of Mr.
Bailey's book, the distinguished French writer and brilliant
critic, M. Lemaître, published a series of lectures on Racine,
in which the highest note of unqualified panegyric sounded
uninterruptedly from beginning to end. The contrast is
remarkable, and the conflicting criticisms seem to represent
on the whole, the views of the cultivated classes in the two
countries. And it is worthy of note that neither of these critics
pays any heed, either explicitly or by implication, to the
opinions of the other. They are totally at variance, but they
argue along lines so different and so remote that they never
come into collision. Mr. Bailey, with the utmost sang-froid,
sweeps on one side the whole of the literary tradition of
France. It is as if a French critic were to assert that Shakespeare, the Elizabethans, and the romantic poets of the
nineteenth century were all negligible, and that England's
really valuable contribution to the poetry of the world was
to be found among the writings of Dryden and Pope. M.
Lemaître, on the other hand, seems sublimely unconscious
that any such views as Mr. Bailey's could possibly exist.
Nothing shows more clearly Racine's supreme dominion
over his countrymen than the fact that M. Lemaître never
questions it for a moment, and tacitly assumes on every page
of his book that his only duty is to illustrate and amplify a
greatness already recognised by all. Indeed, after reading M.
Lemaître's book, one begins to understand more clearly why
it is that English critics find it difficult to appreciate to the full
the literature of France. It is no paradox to say that that
country is as insular as our own. When we find so eminent a
critic as M. Lemaître observing that Racine 'a vraiment
"achevé" et porté à son point suprême de perfection *la tragédie*,

cette étonnante forme d'art, et qui est bien de chez nous:
car on la trouve peu chez les Anglais,' is it surprising that we
should hastily jump to the conclusion that the canons and the
principles of a criticism of this kind will not repay, and perhaps
do not deserve, any careful consideration? Certainly they are
not calculated to spare the susceptibilities of Englishmen.
And, after all, this is only natural; a French critic addresses a
French audience; like a Rabbi in a synagogue, he has no
need to argue and no wish to convert. Perhaps, too, whether
he willed or no, he could do very little to the purpose; for the
difficulties which beset an Englishman in his endeavours to
appreciate a writer such as Racine are precisely of the kind
which a Frenchman is least able either to dispel or even to
understand. The object of this essay is, first, to face these difficulties, with the aid of Mr. Bailey's paper, which sums up in
an able and interesting way the average English view of the
matter; and, in the second place, to communicate to the English
reader a sense of the true significance and the immense value
of Racine's work. Whether the attempt succeed or fail, some
important general questions of literary doctrine will have been
discussed; and, in addition, at least an effort will have been
made to vindicate a great reputation. For, to a lover of
Racine, the fact that English critics of Mr. Bailey's calibre
can write of him as they do, brings a feeling not only of
entire disagreement, but of almost personal distress. Strange
as it may seem to those who have been accustomed to think
of that great artist merely as a type of the frigid pomposity
of an antiquated age, his music, to ears that are attuned to
hear it, comes fraught with a poignancy of loveliness whose
peculiar quality is shared by no other poetry in the world.
To have grown familiar with the voice of Racine, to have
realised once and for all its intensity, its beauty, and its depth,
is to have learnt a new happiness, to have discovered something exquisite and splendid, to have enlarged the glorious
boundaries of art. For such benefits as these who would not
be grateful? Who would not seek to make them known to
others, that they too may enjoy, and render thanks?

M. Lemaître, starting out, like a native of the mountains, from a point which can only be reached by English explorers after a long journey and a severe climb, devotes by far the greater part of his book to a series of brilliant psychological studies of Racine's characters. He leaves on one side almost altogether the questions connected both with Racine's dramatic construction, and with his style; and these are the very questions by which English readers are most perplexed, and which they are most anxious to discuss. His style in particular—using the word in its widest sense—forms the subject of the principal part of Mr. Bailey's essay; it is upon this count that the real force of Mr. Bailey's impeachment depends; and, indeed, it is obvious that no poet can be admired or understood by those who quarrel with the whole fabric of his writing and condemn the very principles of his art. Before, however, discussing this, the true crux of the question, it may be well to consider briefly another matter which deserves attention, because the English reader is apt to find in it a stumbling-block at the very outset of his inquiry. Coming to Racine with Shakespeare and the rest of the Elizabethans warm in his memory, it is only to be expected that he should be struck with a chilling sense of emptiness and unreality. After the colour, the moving multiplicity, the imaginative luxury of our early tragedies, which seem to have been moulded out of the very stuff of life and to have been built up with the varied and generous structure of Nature herself, the Frenchman's dramas, with their rigid uniformity of setting, their endless duologues, their immense harangues, their spectral confidants, their strict exclusion of all visible action, give one at first the same sort of impression as a pretentious pseudo-classical summer-house appearing suddenly at the end of a vista, after one has been rambling through an open forest. 'La scène est à Buthrote, ville d'Epire, dans une salle du palais de Pyrrhus' —could anything be more discouraging than such an announcement? Here is nothing for the imagination to feed on, nothing to raise expectation, no wondrous vision of 'blasted heaths,' or the 'seaboard of Bohemia'; here is only a

hypothetical drawing-room conjured out of the void for five
acts, simply in order that the persons of the drama may have a
place to meet in and make their speeches. The 'three unities'
and the rest of the 'rules' are a burden which the English
reader finds himself quite unaccustomed to carry; he grows
impatient of them; and, if he is a critic, he points out the
futility and the unreasonableness of those antiquated conventions. Even Mr. Bailey, who, curiously enough, believes
that Racine 'stumbled, as it were, half by accident into great
advantages' by using them, speaks of the 'discredit' into which
'the once famous unities' have now fallen, and declares that
'the unities of time and place are of no importance in themselves.' So far as critics are concerned this may be true; but
critics are apt to forget that plays can exist somewhere else
than in books, and a very small acquaintance with contemporary drama is enough to show that, upon the stage at any
rate, the unities, so far from having fallen into discredit, are
now in effect triumphant. For what is the principle which
underlies and justifies the unities of time and place? Surely it
is not, as Mr. Bailey would have us believe, that of the 'unity
of action or interest,' for it is clear that every good drama,
whatever its plan of construction, must possess a single dominating interest, and that it may happen—as in *Antony and
Cleopatra*, for instance—that the very essence of this interest
lies in the accumulation of an immense variety of local
activities and the representation of long epochs of time. The
true justification for the unities of time and place is to be
found in the conception of drama as the history of a spiritual
crisis—the vision, thrown up, as it were, by a bull's-eye
lantern, of the final catastrophic phases of a long series of
events. Very different were the views of the Elizabethan
tragedians, who aimed at representing not only the catastrophe,
but the whole development of circumstances of which it was
the effect; they traced, with elaborate and abounding detail,
the rise, the growth, the decline, and the ruin of great causes
and great persons; and the result was a series of masterpieces
unparalleled in the literature of the world. But, for good or

evil, these methods have become obsolete, and to-day our drama seems to be developing along totally different lines. It is playing the part, more and more consistently, of the bull's-eye lantern; it is concerned with the crisis, and nothing but the crisis; and, in proportion as its field is narrowed and its vision intensified, the unities of time and place come more and more completely into play. Thus, from the point of view of form, it is true to say that it has been the drama of Racine rather than that of Shakespeare that has survived. Plays of the type of *Macbeth* have been superseded by plays of the type of *Britannicus*. *Britannicus*, no less than *Macbeth*, is the tragedy of a criminal; but it shows us, instead of the gradual history of the temptation and the fall, followed by the fatal march of consequences, nothing but the precise psychological moment in which the first irrevocable step is taken, and the criminal is made. The method of *Macbeth* has been, as it were, absorbed by that of the modern novel; the method of *Britannicus* still rules the stage. But Racine carried out his ideals more rigorously and more boldly than any of his successors. He fixed the whole of his attention upon the spiritual crisis; to him that alone was of importance; and the conventional classicism so disheartening to the English reader—the 'unities,' the harangues, the confidences, the absence of local colour, and the concealment of the action—was no more than the machinery for enhancing the effect of the inner tragedy, and for doing away with every side issue and every chance of distraction. His dramas must be read as one looks at an airy, delicate statue, supported by artificial props, whose only importance lies in the fact that without them the statue itself would break in pieces and fall to the ground. Approached in this light, even the 'salle du palais de Pyrrhus' begins to have a meaning. We come to realise that, if it is nothing else, it is at least the meeting-ground of great passions, the invisible framework for one of those noble conflicts which 'make one little room an everywhere.' It will show us no views, no spectacles, it will give us no sense of atmosphere or of imaginative romance; but it will allow us to be present at the climax of a tragedy, to follow the closing struggle of high destinies, and to witness the final agony of human hearts.

It is remarkable that Mr. Bailey, while seeming to approve of the classicism of Racine's dramatic form, nevertheless finds fault with him for his lack of a quality with which, by its very nature, the classical form is incompatible. Racine's vision, he complains, does not 'take in the whole of life'; we do not find in his plays 'the whole pell-mell of human existence'; and this is true, because the particular effects which Racine wished to produce necessarily involved this limitation of the range of his interests. His object was to depict the tragic interaction of a small group of persons at the culminating height of its intensity; and it is as irrational to complain of his failure to introduce into his compositions 'the whole pell-mell of human existence' as it would be to find fault with a Mozart quartet for not containing the orchestration of Wagner. But it is a little difficult to make certain of the precise nature of Mr. Bailey's criticism. When he speaks of Racine's vision not including 'the whole of life,' when he declares that Racine cannot be reckoned as one of the 'world-poets,' he seems to be taking somewhat different ground and discussing a more general question. All truly great poets, he asserts, have 'a wide view of humanity,' 'a large view of life'—a profound sense, in short, of the relations between man and the universe; and, since Racine is without this quality, his claim to true poetic greatness must be denied. But, even upon the supposition that this view of Racine's philosophical outlook is the true one—and, in its most important sense, I believe that it is not—does Mr. Bailey's conclusion really follow? Is it possible to test a poet's greatness by the largeness of his 'view of life'? How wide, one would like to know, was Milton's 'view of humanity'? And though Wordsworth's sense of the position of man in the universe was far more profound than Dante's, who will venture to assert that he was the greater poet? The truth is that we have struck here upon a principle which lies at the root, not only of Mr. Bailey's criticism of Racine, but of an

entire critical method—the method which attempts to
define the essential elements of poetry in general, and then
proceeds to ask of any particular poem whether it possesses
these elements, and to judge it accordingly. How often this
method has been employed, and how often it has proved
disastrously fallacious! For, after all, art is not a superior kind
of chemistry, amenable to the rules of scientific induction.
Its component parts cannot be classified and tested, and there
is a spark within it which defies foreknowledge. When
Matthew Arnold declared that the value of a new poem might
be gauged by comparing it with the greatest passages in the
acknowledged masterpieces of literature, he was falling into
this very error; for who could tell that the poem in question
was not itself a masterpiece, living by the light of an unknown
beauty, and a law unto itself? It is the business of the poet
to break rules and to baffle expectation; and all the masterpieces in the world cannot make a precedent. Thus Mr.
Bailey's attempts to discover, by quotations from Shakespeare,
Sophocles, and Goethe, the qualities without which no poet
can be great, and his condemnation of Racine because he is
without them, is a fallacy in criticism. There is only one way
to judge a poet, as Wordsworth, with that paradoxical
sobriety so characteristic of him, has pointed out—and that
is, by loving him. But Mr. Bailey, with regard to Racine at
any rate, has not followed the advice of Wordsworth. Let
us look a little more closely into the nature of his attack.

'L'épithète rare,' said the De Goncourts, 'voilà la marque
de l'écrivain.' Mr. Bailey quotes the sentence with approval,
observing that if, with Sainte-Beuve, we extend the phrase to
'le mot rare,' we have at once one of those invaluable touch-
stones with which we may test the merit of poetry. And
doubtless most English readers would be inclined to agree
with Mr. Bailey, for it so happens that our own literature is
one in which rarity of style, pushed often to the verge of
extravagance, reigns supreme. Owing mainly, no doubt, to
the double origin of our language, with its strange and violent
contrasts between the highly-coloured crudity of the Saxon

words and the ambiguous splendour of the Latin vocabulary; owing partly, perhaps, to a national taste for the intensely imaginative, and partly, too, to the vast and penetrating influence of those grand masters of bizarrerie—the Hebrew Prophets—our poetry, our prose, and our whole conception of the art of writing have fallen under the dominion of the emphatic, the extraordinary, and the bold. No one in his senses would regret this, for it has given our literature all its most characteristic glories, and, of course, in Shakespeare, with whom expression is stretched to the bursting point, the national style finds at once its consummate example and its final justification. But the result is that we have grown so unused to other kinds of poetical beauty, that we have now come to believe, with Mr. Bailey, that poetry apart from 'le mot rare' is an impossibility. The beauties of restraint, of clarity, of refinement, and of precision we pass by unheeding; we can see nothing there but coldness and uniformity; and we go back with eagerness to the fling and the bravado that we love so well. It is as if we had become so accustomed to looking at boxers, wrestlers, and gladiators that the sight of an exquisite minuet produced no effect on us; the ordered dance strikes us as a monotony, for we are blind to the subtle delicacies of the dancers, which are fraught with such significance to the practised eye. But let us be patient, and let us look again.

> Ariane ma sœur, de quel amour blessée,
> Vous mourûtes aux bords où vous fûtes laissée.

Here, certainly, are no 'mots rares'; here is nothing to catch the mind or dazzle the understanding; here is only the most ordinary vocabulary, plainly set forth. But is there not an enchantment? Is there not a vision? Is there not a flow of lovely sound whose beauty grows upon the ear, and dwells exquisitely within the memory? Racine's triumph is precisely this—that he brings about, by what are apparently the simplest means, effects which other poets must strain every nerve to produce. The narrowness of his vocabulary is in fact nothing but a proof of his amazing art. In the following passage, for instance, what a sense of dignity and melancholy and power is conveyed by the commonest words!

> Enfin j'ouvre les yeux, et je me fais justice:
> C'est faire à vos beautés un triste sacrifice
> Que de vous présenter, madame, avec ma foi,
> Tout l'âge et le malheur que je traîne avec moi.
> Jusqu'ici la fortune et la victoire mêmes
> Cachaient mes cheveux blancs sous trente diadèmes.
> Mais ce temps-là n'est plus: je régnais; et je fuis:
> Mes ans se sont accrus; mes honneurs sont détruits.

Is that wonderful 'trente' an 'épithète rare'? Never, surely, before or since, was a simple numeral put to such a use—to conjure up so triumphantly such mysterious grandeurs! But these are subtleties which pass unnoticed by those who have been accustomed to the violent appeals of the great romantic poets. As Sainte-Beuve says, in a fine comparison between Racine and Shakespeare, to come to the one after the other is like passing to a portrait by Ingres from a decoration by Rubens. At first, 'comme on a l'œil rempli de l'éclatante vérité pittoresque du grand maître flamand, on ne voit dans l'artiste français qu'un ton assez uniforme, une teinte diffuse de pâle et douce lumière. Mais qu'on approche de plus près et qu'on observe avec soin: mille nuances fines vont éclore sous le regard; mille intentions savantes vont sortir de ce tissu profond et serré; on ne peut plus en détacher ses yeux.'

Similarly when Mr. Bailey, turning from the vocabulary to more general questions of style, declares that there is no 'element of fine surprise' in Racine, no trace of the 'daring metaphors and similes of Pindar and the Greek choruses'—the reply is that he would find what he wants if he only knew where to look for it. 'Who will forget,' he says, 'the comparison of the Atreidæ to the eagles wheeling over their empty nest, of war to the money-changer whose gold dust is that of human bodies, of Helen to the lion's whelps? . . . Everyone knows these. Who will match them among the formal elegances of Racine?' And it is true that when Racine wished to create a great effect he did not adopt the romantic method;

he did not chase his ideas through the four quarters of the universe to catch them at last upon the verge of the inane; and anyone who hopes to come upon 'fine surprises' of this kind in his pages will be disappointed. His daring is of a different kind; it is not the daring of adventure but of intensity; his fine surprises are seized out of the very heart of his subject, and seized in a single stroke. Thus many of his astonishing phrases burn with an inward concentration of energy, which, difficult at first to realise to the full, comes in the end to impress itself ineffaceably upon the mind.

C'était pendant l'horreur d'une profonde nuit.

The sentence is like a cavern whose mouth a careless traveller might pass by, but which opens out, to the true explorer, into vista after vista of strange recesses rich with inexhaustible gold. But, sometimes, the phrase, compact as dynamite, explodes upon one with an immediate and terrific force—

C'est Vénus toute entière à sa proie attachée!

A few 'formal elegances' of this kind are surely worth having.

But what is it that makes the English reader fail to recognise the beauty and the power of such passages as these? Besides Racine's lack of extravagance and bravura, besides his dislike of exaggerated emphasis and far-fetched or fantastic imagery, there is another characteristic of his style to which we are perhaps even more antipathetic—its suppression of detail. The great majority of poets—and especially of English poets—produce their most potent effects by the accumulation of details—details which in themselves fascinate us either by their beauty or their curiosity or their supreme appropriateness. But with details Racine will have nothing to do; he builds up his poetry out of words which are not only absolutely simple but extremely general, so that our minds, failing to find in it the peculiar delights to which we have been accustomed, fall into the error of rejecting it altogether as devoid of significance. And the error is a grave one, for in truth nothing is more marvellous than the magic with which

68

Racine can conjure up out of a few expressions of the vaguest import a sense of complete and intimate reality. When Shakespeare wishes to describe a silent night he does so with a single stroke of detail—'not a mouse stirring'! And Virgil adds touch upon touch of exquisite minutiæ:

> Cum tacet omnis ager, pecudes, pictaeque volucres,
> Quaeque lacus late liquidos, quaeque aspera dumis
> Rura tenent, etc.

Racine's way is different, but is it less masterly?

> Mais tout dort, et l'armée, et les vents, et Neptune.

What a flat and feeble set of expressions! is the Englishman's first thought—with the conventional 'Neptune,' and the vague 'armée,' and the commonplace 'vents.' And he forgets to notice the total impression which these words produce— the atmosphere of darkness and emptiness and vastness and ominous hush.

It is particularly in regard to Racine's treatment of nature that this generalised style creates misunderstandings. 'Is he so much as aware,' exclaims Mr. Bailey, 'that the sun rises and sets in a glory of colour, that the wind plays deliciously on human cheeks, that the human ear will never have enough of the music of the sea? He might have written every page of his work without so much as looking out of the window of his study.' The accusation gains support from the fact that Racine rarely describes the processes of nature by means of pictorial detail; that, we know, was not his plan. But he is constantly, with his subtle art, suggesting them. In this line, for instance, he calls up, without a word of definite description, the vision of a sudden and brilliant sunrise:

> Déjà le jour plus grand nous frappe et nous éclaire.

And how varied and beautiful are his impressions of the sea! He can give us the desolation of a calm:

> La rame inutile
> Fatigua vainement une mer immobile;

or the agitated movements of a great fleet of galleys:

Voyez tout l'Hellespont blanchissant sous nos rames;

or he can fill his verses with the disorder and the fury of a storm:

Quoi! pour noyer les Grecs et leurs mille vaisseaux,
Mer, tu n'ouvriras pas des abymes nouveaux!
Quoi! lorsque les chassant du port qui les recèle,
L'Aulide aura vomi leur flotte criminelle,
Les vents, les mêmes vents, si longtemps accusés,
Ne te couvriront pas de ses vaisseaux brisés!

And then, in a single line, he can evoke the radiant spectacle of a triumphant flotilla riding the dancing waves:

Prêts à vous recevoir mes vaisseaux vous attendent;
Et du pied de l'autel vous y pouvez monter,
Souveraine des mers qui vous doivent porter.

The art of subtle suggestion could hardly go further than in this line, where the alliterating v's, the mute e's, and the placing of the long syllables combine so wonderfully to produce the required effect.

But it is not only suggestions of nature that readers like Mr. Bailey are unable to find in Racine—they miss in him no less suggestions of the mysterious and the infinite. No doubt this is partly due to our English habit of associating these qualities with expressions which are complex and unfamiliar. When we come across the mysterious accent of fatality and remote terror in a single perfectly simple phrase—

La fille de Minos et de Pasiphaé

we are apt not to hear that it is there. But there is another reason—the craving, which has seized upon our poetry and our criticism ever since the triumph of Wordsworth and Coleridge at the beginning of the last century, for metaphysical stimulants. It would be easy to prolong the discussion of this matter far beyond the boundaries of 'sublunary debate,' but it is sufficient to point out that Mr. Bailey's criticism of Racine affords an excellent example of the fatal effects of this obsession. His pages are full of references to 'infinity' and 'the unseen' and 'eternity' and 'a mystery brooding over a mystery' and 'the key to the secret of life'; and it is only natural that he should find in these watchwords one of those tests of poetic greatness of which he is so fond. The fallaciousness of such views as these becomes obvious when we remember the plain fact that there is not a trace of this kind of mystery or of these 'feelings after the key to the secret of life,' in *Paradise Lost*, and that *Paradise Lost* is one of the greatest poems in the world. But Milton is sacrosanct in England; no theory, however mistaken, can shake that stupendous name, and the damage which may be wrought by a vicious system of criticism only becomes evident in its treatment of writers like Racine, whom it can attack with impunity and apparent success. There is no 'mystery' in Racine —that is to say, there are no metaphysical speculations in him, no suggestions of the transcendental, no hints as to the ultimate nature of reality and the constitution of the world; and so away with him, a creature of mere rhetoric and ingenuities, to the outer limbo! But if, instead of asking what a writer is without, we try to discover simply what he is, will not our results be more worthy of our trouble? And in fact, if we once put out of our heads our longings for the mystery of metaphysical suggestion, the more we examine Racine, the more clearly we shall discern in him another kind of mystery, whose presence may eventually console us for the loss of the first— the mystery of the mind of man. This indeed is the framework of his poetry, and to speak of it adequately would demand a wider scope than that of an essay; for how much might be written of that strange and moving background, dark with the profundity of passion and glowing with the beauty of the sublime, wherefrom the great personages of his tragedies— Hermione and Mithridate, Roxane and Agrippine, Athalie and Phèdre—seem to emerge for a moment towards us, whereon they breathe and suffer, and among whose depths they vanish for ever from our sight! Look where we will, we shall find among his pages the traces of an inward mystery and the obscure infinities of the heart.

Nous avons su toujours nous aimer et nous taire.

The line is a summary of the romance and the anguish of two lives. That is all affection; and this all desire—

J'aimais jusqu'à ses pleurs que je faisais couler.

Or let us listen to the voice of Phèdre, when she learns that Hippolyte and Aricie love one another:

Les a-t-on vus souvent se parler, se chercher?
Dans le fond des forêts alloient-ils se cacher?
Hélas! ils se voyaient avec pleine licence;
Le ciel de leurs soupirs approuvait l'innocence;
Ils suivaient sans remords leur penchant amoureux;
Tous les jours se levaient clairs et sereins pour eux.

This last line—written, let us remember, by a frigidly ingenious rhetorician, who had never looked out of his study-window—does it not seem to mingle, in a trance of absolute simplicity, the peerless beauty of a Claude with the misery and ruin of a great soul?

It is, perhaps, as a psychologist that Racine has achieved his most remarkable triumphs; and the fact that so subtle and penetrating a critic as M. Lemaître has chosen to devote the greater part of a volume to the discussion of his characters shows clearly enough that Racine's portrayal of human nature has lost nothing of its freshness and vitality with the passage of time. On the contrary, his admirers are now tending more and more to lay stress upon the brilliance of his portraits, the combined vigour and intimacy of his painting, his amazing knowledge, and his unerring fidelity to truth. M. Lemaître, in fact, goes so far as to describe Racine as a supreme realist, while other writers have found in him the essence of the modern spirit. These are vague phrases, no doubt, but they imply a very definite point of view; and it is curious to compare with it our English conception of Racine as a stiff and pompous kind of dancing-master, utterly out of date and infinitely cold. And there is a similar disagreement over his style. Mr. Bailey is never tired of asserting that Racine's style is rhetorical, artificial, and monotonous; while M. Lemaître speaks of it as 'nu et familier,' and Sainte-Beuve says 'il rase la prose, mais avec des ailes.' The explanation of these contradictions is to be found in the fact that the two critics are considering different parts of the poet's work. When Racine is most himself, when he is seizing upon a state of mind and depicting it with all its twistings and vibrations, he writes with a directness which is indeed naked, and his sentences, refined to the utmost point of significance, flash out like swords, stroke upon stroke, swift, certain, irresistible. This is how Agrippine, in the fury of her tottering ambition, bursts out to Burrhus, the tutor of her son:

> Prétendez-vous longtemps me cacher l'empereur?
> Ne le verrai-je plus qu'à titre d'importune?
> Ai-je donc élevé si haut votre fortune
> Pour mettre une barrière entre mon fils et moi?
> Ne l'osez-vous laisser un moment sur sa foi?
> Entre Sénèque et vous disputez-vous la gloire
> A qui m'effacera plus tôt de sa mémoire?
> Vous l'ai-je confié pour en faire un ingrat,
> Pour être, sous son nom, les maîtres de l'état?
> Certes, plus je médite, et moins je me figure
> Que vous m'osiez compter pour votre créature;
> Vous, dont j'ai pu laisser vieillir l'ambition
> Dans les honneurs obscurs de quelque légion;
> Et moi, qui sur le trône ai suivi mes ancêtres,
> Moi, fille, femme, sœur, et mère de vos maîtres!

When we come upon a passage like this we know, so to speak, that the hunt is up and the whole field tearing after the quarry. But Racine, on other occasions, has another way of writing. He can be roundabout, artificial, and vague; he can involve a simple statement in a mist of high-sounding words and elaborate inversions.

> Jamais l'aimable sœur des cruels Pallantides
> Trempa-t-elle aux complots de ses frères perfides.

That is Racine's way of saying that Aricie did not join in her brothers' conspiracy. He will describe an incriminating letter as 'De sa trahison ce gage trop sincère.' It is obvious that this kind of expression has within it the germs of the 'noble' style of the eighteenth-century tragedians, one of whom, finding himself obliged to mention a dog, got out of the difficulty by referring to—'De la fidélité le respectable appui.' This is the side of Racine's writing that puzzles and disgusts Mr. Bailey. But there is a meaning in it, after all. Every art is based upon a selection, and the art of Racine selected the things of the spirit for the material of its work. The things of sense—physical objects and details, and all the necessary but insignificant facts that go to make up the machinery of existence —these must be kept out of the picture at all hazards. To have called a spade a spade would have ruined the whole effect; spades must never be mentioned, or, at the worst, they must be dimly referred to as agricultural implements, so that the entire attention may be fixed upon the central and dominating features of the composition—the spiritual states of the characters—which, laid bare with uncompromising force and supreme precision, may thus indelibly imprint themselves upon the mind. To condemn Racine on the score of his ambiguities and his pomposities is to complain of the hastily dashed-in column and curtain in the background of a portrait, and not to mention the face. Sometimes indeed his art seems to rise superior to its own conditions, endowing even the dross and refuse of what it works in with a wonderful significance. Thus when the Sultana, Roxane, discovers her lover's treachery, her mind flies immediately to thoughts of revenge and death, and she exclaims—

Ah! je respire enfin, et ma joie est extrême
Que le traître une fois se soit trahi lui-même.
Libre des soins cruels où j'allais m'engager,
Ma tranquille fureur n'a plus qu'à se venger.
Qu'il meure. Vengeons-nous. Courez. Qu'on le saisisse!
Que la main des muets s'arme pour son supplice;
Qu'ils viennent préparer ces nœuds infortunés
Par qui de ses pareils les jours sont terminés.

To have called a bowstring a bowstring was out of the question; and Racine, with triumphant art, has managed to introduce the periphrasis in such a way that it exactly expresses the state of mind of the Sultana. She begins with revenge and rage, until she reaches the extremity of virulent resolution; and then her mind begins to waver, and she finally orders the execution of the man she loves, in a contorted agony of speech.

But, as a rule, Racine's characters speak out most clearly when they are most moved, so that their words, at the height of passion, have an intensity of directness unknown in actual life. In such moments, the phrases that leap to their lips quiver and glow with the compressed significance of character and situation; the 'Qui te l'a dit?' of Hermione, the 'Sortez' of Roxane, the 'Je vais à Rome' of Mithridate, the 'Dieu des Juifs, tu l'emportes!' of Athalie—who can forget these things, these wondrous microcosms of tragedy? Very different is the Shakespearean method. There, as passion rises, expression becomes more and more poetical and vague. Image flows into image, thought into thought, until at last the state of mind is revealed, inform and molten, driving darkly through a vast storm of words. Such revelations, no doubt, come closer to reality than the poignant epigrams of Racine. In life, men's minds are not sharpened, they are diffused, by emotion; and the utterance which best represents them is fluctuating and agglomerated rather than compact and defined. But Racine's aim was less to reflect the actual current of the human spirit than to seize upon its inmost being and to give expression to that. One might be tempted to say that his art represents the sublimed essence of reality, save that, after all, reality has no degrees. Who can affirm that the wild ambiguities of our hearts and the gross impediments of our physical existence are less real than the most pointed of our feelings and 'thoughts beyond the reaches of our souls'?

It would be nearer the truth to rank Racine among the idealists. The world of his creation is not a copy of our own; it is a heightened and rarefied extension of it; moving, in triumph and in beauty, through 'an ampler ether, a diviner air.' It is a world where the hesitations and the pettinesses and squalors of this earth have been fired out; a world where ugliness is a forgotten name, and lust itself has grown ethereal; where anguish has become a grace and death a glory, and love the beginning and the end of all. It is, too, the world of a poet, so that we reach it, not through melody nor through vision, but through the poet's sweet articulation—through verse. Upon English ears the rhymed couplets of Racine sound strangely; and how many besides Mr. Bailey have dubbed his alexandrines 'monotonous'! But to his lovers, to those who have found their way into the secret places of his art, his lines are impregnated with a peculiar beauty, and the last perfection of style. Over them, the most insignificant of his verses can throw a deep enchantment, like the faintest wavings of a magician's wand. 'A-t-on vu de ma part le roi de Comagène?' How is it that words of such slight import should hold such thrilling music? Oh! they are Racine's words. And, as to his rhymes, they seem perhaps, to the true worshipper, the final crown of his art. Mr. Bailey tells us that the couplet is only fit for satire. Has he forgotten *Lamia*? And he asks, 'How is it that we read Pope's *Satires* and Dryden's, and Johnson's with enthusiasm still, while we never touch *Irene*, and rarely the *Conquest of Granada*?' Perhaps the answer is that if we cannot get rid of our *a priori* theories, even the fiery art of Dryden's drama may remain dead to us, and that, if we touched *Irene* even once, we should find it was in blank verse. But Dryden himself has spoken memorably upon rhyme. Discussing the imputed unnaturalness of the rhymed 'repartee' he says: 'Suppose we acknowledge it: how comes this confederacy to be more displeasing to you than in a dance which is well contrived? You see there the united design of many persons to make up one figure; . . . the confederacy is plain amongst them, for chance could never produce anything so beautiful; and yet there is nothing in it that shocks your sight . . . 'Tis an art which appears; but it appears only like the shadowings of painture, which, being to cause the rounding of it, cannot be absent; but while that is considered, they are lost: so while we attend to the other beauties of the matter, the care and labour of the rhyme is carried from us, or at least drowned in its own sweetness, as bees are sometimes buried in their honey.' In this exquisite passage Dryden seems to have come near, though not quite to have hit, the central argument for rhyme—its power of creating a beautiful atmosphere, in which what is expressed may be caught away from the associations of common life and harmoniously enshrined. For Racine, with his prepossessions of sublimity and perfection, some such barrier between his universe and reality was involved in the very nature of his art. His rhyme is like the still clear water of a lake, through which we can see, mysteriously separated from us and changed and beautified, the forms of his imagination, 'quivering within the wave's intenser day.' And truly not seldom are they 'so sweet, the sense faints picturing them'!

> Oui, prince, je languis, je brûle pour Thésée …
> Il avait votre port, vos yeux, votre langage,
> Cette noble pudeur colorait son visage,
> Lorsque de notre Crète il traversa les flots,
> Digne sujet des vœux des filles de Minos.
> Que faisiez-vous alors? Pourquoi, sans Hippolyte,
> Des héros de la Grèce assembla-t-il l'élite?
> Pourquoi, trop jeune encor, ne pûtes-vous alors
> Entrer dans le vaisseau qui le mit sur nos bords?
> Par vous aurait péri le monstre de la Crète,
> Malgré tous les détours de sa vaste retraite:
> Pour en développer l'embarras incertain
> Ma sœur du fil fatal eût armé votre main.
> Mais non: dans ce dessein je l'aurais devancée;
> L'amour m'en eût d'abord inspiré la pensée;
> C'est moi, prince, c'est moi dont l'utile secours
> Vous eût du labyrinthe enseigné les détours.
> Que de soins m'eût coûtés cette tête charmante!

It is difficult to 'place' Racine among the poets. He has affinities with many; but likenesses to few. To balance him rigorously against any other—to ask whether he is better or worse than Shelley or than Virgil—is to attempt impossibilities; but there is one fact which is too often forgotten in comparing his work with that of other poets—with Virgil's for instance—Racine wrote for the stage. Virgil's poetry is intended to be read, Racine's to be declaimed; and it is only in the theatre that one can experience to the full the potency of his art. In a sense we can know him in our library, just as we can hear the music of Mozart with silent eyes. But, when the strings begin, when the whole volume of that divine harmony engulfs us, how differently then we understand and feel! And so, at the theatre, before one of those high tragedies, whose interpretation has taxed to the utmost ten generations of the greatest actresses of France, we realise, with the shock of a new emotion, what we had but half-felt before. To hear the words of Phèdre spoken by the mouth of Bernhardt, to watch, in the culminating horror of crime and of remorse, of jealousy, of rage, of desire, and of despair, all the dark forces of destiny crowd down upon that great spirit, when the heavens and the earth reject her, and Hell opens, and the terrific urn of Minos thunders and crashes to the ground— that indeed is to come close to immortality, to plunge shuddering through infinite abysses, and to look, if only for a moment, upon eternal light.

1908.

POPE[1]

AMONG the considerations that might make us rejoice or regret that we did not live in the eighteenth century, there is one that to my mind outbalances all the rest—if we had, we might have known Pope. At any rate, we have escaped that. We may lament that flowered waistcoats are forbidden us, that we shall never ride in a sedan-chair, and that we shall never see good Queen Anne taking tea at Hampton Court: but we can at least congratulate ourselves that we run no danger of waking up one morning to find ourselves exposed, both now and for ever, to the ridicule of the polite world— that we are hanging by the neck, and kicking our legs, on the elegant gibbet that has been put up for us by the little monster of Twit'nam. And, on the other hand, as it is, we are in the happy position of being able, quite imperturbably, to enjoy the fun. There is nothing so shamelessly selfish as posterity. To us, after two centuries, the agonies suffered by the victims of Pope's naughtiness are a matter of indifference; the fate of Pope's own soul leaves us cold. We sit at our ease, reading those *Satires* and *Epistles*, in which the verses, when they were written, resembled nothing so much as spoonfuls of boiling oil, ladled out by a fiendish monkey at an upstairs window upon such of the passers-by whom the wretch had a grudge against—and we are delighted. We would not have it otherwise: whatever is, is right.

In this there is nothing surprising; but what does seem strange is that Pope's contemporaries should have borne with him as they did. His attacks were by no means limited to Grub Street. He fell upon great lords and great ladies, duchesses and statesmen, noble patrons and beautiful women of fashion, with an equal ferocity; and such persons, in those days, were very well able to defend themselves. In France,

[1] The Leslie Stephen Lecture for 1925.

the fate suffered by Voltaire, at that very time, and on far less provocation, is enough to convince us that such a portent as Pope would never have been tolerated on the other side of the Channel. The monkey would have been whipped into silence and good manners in double quick time. But in England it was different. Here, though 'the Great,' as they were called, were all-powerful, they preferred not to use their power against a libellous rhymer, who was physically incapable of protecting himself, and who, as a Roman Catholic, lay particularly open to legal pressure. The warfare between Pope and Lady Mary Wortley Montagu illustrates the state of affairs. The origin of their quarrel is uncertain. According to the lady, it was caused by her bursting into fits of laughter upon a declaration of passion from the poet. Another and perhaps more probable story traces the origin of the discord to a pair of sheets, borrowed by Lady Mary from old Mrs. Pope, the poet's mother, and returned by her ladyship, after a fortnight, unwashed. But whatever may have been the hidden cause of the quarrel, its results were obvious enough. Pope, in one of his *Imitations of Horace*, made a reference to 'Sappho,' whom all the world knew to be Lady Mary, in a couplet of extraordinary scurrility. Always a master of the art of compression, he asserted, in a single line of ten syllables, that his enemy, besides being a slanderous virago, was a debauched woman afflicted with a disgraceful malady. If, after this, Lady Mary had sent her friends or her footmen to inflict a personal chastisement upon the poet, or if she had used her influence with the government to have him brought to his senses, nobody could have been very much surprised. But she did nothing of the sort. Instead, she consulted with Lord Hervey, whom Pope had also attacked, and the two together decided to pay back their tormentor in his own coin. Accordingly they decocted and published a lampoon, in which they did their best to emulate both the style and the substance of the poet. 'None,' they declared,

> thy crabbed numbers can endure,
> Hard as thy heart, and as thy birth obscure.

It shows, they said,

> the Uniformity of Fate
> That one so odious should be born to hate.

And if

> Unwhipt, unblanketed, unkick'd, unslain,
> That wretched little carcase you retain,
> The reason is, not that the world wants eyes,
> But thou'rt so mean, they see and they despise.

After sixty lines of furious abuse, they wound up with a shrug, of the shoulders, which was far from convincing.

> You strike unwounding, we unhurt can laugh,

they asseverated. But for the unhurt this was certainly very odd laughter. It was also quite ineffective. Pope's first reply was a prose pamphlet, in which there is at least one amusing passage—'It is true, my Lord, I am short, not well shaped, generally ill-dressed, if not sometimes dirty. Your Lordship and Ladyship are still in bloom, your figures such as rival the Apollo of Belvedere and the Venus of Medicis, and your faces so finished that neither sickness nor passion can deprive them of colour.' But, of course, he reserved his most poisonous shafts for his poetry. Henceforth, his readers might be sure that in any especially unsavoury couplet the name of Sappho would be found immortally embedded; while, as for Lord Hervey, he met his final doom in the Character of Sporus— the most virulent piece of invective in the English language.

Lady Mary and Lord Hervey, clever as they were, had been so senseless as to try to fight Pope on his own ground, and, naturally enough, their failure was dismal. But why had they committed this act of folly? Their own explanation was the exact reverse of the truth. Far from despising the poet, they profoundly admired him. Hypnotised by his greatness, they were unable to prevent themselves from paying him the supreme compliment of an inept and suicidal imitation. And in this they were typical of the society in which they lived. That society was perhaps the most civilised that our history has known. Never, at any rate, before or since, has literature been so respected in England. Prior wrote well, and he became an ambassador. Addison wrote well, and he was made a Secretary of State. The Duke of Wharton gave Young £2,000 for having written a poem on the Universal Passion. Alderman Barber's great ambition was to be mentioned favourably by Pope. He let it be understood that he would be willing to part with £4,000 if the poet would gratify him; a single couplet was all he asked for; but the Alderman begged in vain. On the other hand, Pope accepted £1,000 from the old Duchess of Marlborough in return for the suppression of an attack upon the late Duke. Pope cancelled the lines; but soon afterwards printed an envenomed character of the Duchess. And even the terrific Sarah herself—such was the overwhelming prestige of the potentate of letters—was powerless in face of this affront.

For the first time in our history, a writer, who was a writer and nothing more—Shakespeare was an actor and a theatrical manager—had achieved financial independence. Pope effected this by his translation of Homer, which brought him £9,000—a sum equivalent to about £30,000 to-day. The immense success of this work was a sign of the times. Homer's reputation was enormous: was he not the father of poetry? The literary snobbery of the age was profoundly impressed by that. Yes, it was snobbery, no doubt; but surely it was a noble snobbery which put Homer so *very* high in the table of precedence—probably immediately after the Archbishop of Canterbury. Yet, there were difficulties. It was not only hard to read Homer, it was positively dangerous. Too close an acquaintance might reveal that the mythical figure sweeping along so grandly in front of the Archbishop of York was something of a blackguard—an alarming barbarian, with shocking tastes, small knowledge of the rules, and altogether far from correct. Pope solved these difficulties in a masterly manner. He supplied exactly what was wanted. He gave the eighteenth century a Homer after its own heart—a Homer who was the father—not quite of poetry, indeed, but of something much more satisfactory—of what the eighteenth century believed poetry to be; and, very properly, it gave him a fortune in return.

The eighteenth century has acquired a reputation for scepticism; but this is a mistake. In truth there has never been a less sceptical age. Its beliefs were rigid, intense, and imperturbable. In literature, as in every other department of life, an unquestioning orthodoxy reigned. It was this extraordinary self-sufficiency that gave the age its force; but the same quality caused the completeness of its downfall. When the reaction came, the absolute certainty of the past epoch seemed to invest it with the maximum degree of odium and absurdity. The romantics were men who had lost their faith; and they rose against the old dispensation with all the zeal of rebels and heretics. Inevitably, their fury fell with peculiar vehemence upon Pope. The great idol was overturned amid shouts of execration and scornful laughter. The writer who, for three generations, had divided with Milton the supreme honour of English poetry, was pronounced to be shallow, pompous, monotonous, meretricious, and not a poet at all.

Now that we have perhaps emerged from romanticism, it is time to consider the master of the eighteenth century with a more impartial eye. This is not altogether an easy task. Though we may be no longer in the least romantic, are we not still—I hesitate to suggest it—are we not still slightly Victorian? Do we not continue to cast glances of furtive admiration towards the pontiffs of that remarkable era, whose figures, on the edge of our horizon, are still visible, so lofty, and so large? We can discount the special pleadings of Wordsworth; but the voice of Matthew Arnold, for instance, still sounds with something like authority upon our ears. Pope, said Matthew Arnold, is not a classic of our poetry, he is a classic of our prose. He was without an 'adequate poetic criticism of life'; his criticism of life lacked 'high-seriousness'; it had neither largeness, freedom, insight, nor benignity. Matthew Arnold was a poet, but his conception of poetry reminds us that he was also an inspector of schools. That the essence of poetry is 'high seriousness' is one of those noble platitudes which commend themselves immediately as both obvious and comfortable. But, in reality, obviousness and comfort have very little to do with poetry. It is not the nature of poetry to be what anyone expects; on the contrary, it is its nature to be surprising, to be disturbing, to be impossible. Poetry and high seriousness! Of course, to Dr. Arnold's son, they seemed to be inevitably linked together; and certainly had the world been created by Dr. Arnold they actually would have been. But—perhaps fortunately—it was not. If we look at the facts, where do we find poetry? In the wild fantasies of Aristophanes, in the sordid lusts of Baudelaire, in the gentle trivialities of La Fontaine.

> Dreadful was the din
> Of hissing through the hall, thick swarming now
> With complicated monsters, head and tail,
> Scorpion, and asp, and amphisbaena dire,
> Cerastes horn'd, hydrus, and ellops drear,
> And dipsas—

That is not high seriousness; it is a catalogue of curious names; and it is poetry. There is poetry to be found lurking in the metaphysical system of Epicurus, and in the body of a flea. And so need we be surprised if it invests a game of cards, or a gentleman sneezing at Hampton Court?—

> Just where the breath of life his nostrils drew,
> A charge of snuff the wily virgin threw;
> The gnomes direct, to every atom just,
> The pungent grains of titillating dust.
> Sudden, with starting tears each eye o'erflows,
> And the high dome re-echoes to his nose.

Pope, we are told, was not only without 'high seriousness'; he lacked no less an 'adequate poetic criticism of life.' What does this mean? The phrase is ambiguous; it signifies at once too much and too little. If we are to understand—as the context seems to imply—that, in Matthew Arnold's opinion, no poetic criticism of life can be adequate unless it possesses largeness, freedom, and benignity, we must certainly agree that Pope's poetic criticism of life was far from adequate; for his way of writing was neither large nor free, and there was nothing benignant about him. But the words will bear another interpretation; and in this sense it may turn out that Pope's poetic criticism of life was adequate to an extraordinary degree.

Let us examine for a moment the technical instrument which Pope used—I mean the heroic couplet.

When he was a young man, the poet Walsh gave Pope a piece of advice. 'We have had great poets,' he said, 'but never one great poet that was correct. I recommend you to make your leading aim—correctness.' Pope took the advice, and became the most correct of poets. This was his chief title to glory in the eighteenth century; it was equally the stick that he was most frequently and rapturously beaten with, in the nineteenth. Macaulay, in his essay on Byron, devotes several pages of his best forensic style to an exposure and denunciation of the absurd futility of the 'correctness' of the school of Pope. There is in reality, he declared, only one kind of correctness in literature—that which 'has its foundation in truth and in the principles of human nature.' But Pope's so-called correctness was something very different. It consisted simply in a strict obedience to a perfectly arbitrary set of prosodic rules. His couplet was a purely artificial structure—the product of mere convention; and, so far from there being any possible poetic merit in the kind of correctness which it involved, this 'correctness' was in fact only 'another name for dullness and absurdity.' A short time ago, the distinguished poet, M. Paul Valéry, demolished Macaulay's argument— no doubt quite unconsciously—in an essay full of brilliant subtlety and charming wit. He showed conclusively the essentially poetic value of purely arbitrary conventions. But, for our purposes, so drastic a conclusion is unnecessary. For Macaulay was mistaken, not only in his theory, but in his facts. The truth is that the English classical couplet—unlike the French—had nothing conventional about it. On the

contrary, it was the inevitable, the logical, the natural outcome of the development of English verse.

The fundamental element in the structure of poetry is
rhythmical repetition. In England, the favourite unit of this
repetition very early became the ten-syllabled iambic line.
Now it is clear that the treatment of this line may be developed
in two entirely different directions. The first of these developments is blank verse. Milton's definition of blank verse is
well known, and it cannot be bettered: it consists, he says,
'in apt numbers, fit quantity of syllables, and the sense
variously drawn out from one verse into another.' Its essence,
in other words, is the combination formed by rhythmical
variety playing over an underlying norm; and it is easy to
trace the evolution of this wonderful measure from the
primitive rigidity of Surrey to the incredible virtuosity of
Shakespeare's later plays, where blank verse reaches its
furthest point of development—where rhythmical variety is
found in unparalleled profusion, while the underlying
regularity is just, still, miraculously preserved. After Shakespeare, the combination broke down; the element of variety
became so excessive that the underlying norm disappeared,
with the result that the blank verse of the latest Elizabethans
is virtually indistinguishable from prose.

But suppose the ten-syllabled iambic were treated in precisely the contrary manner. Suppose, instead of developing
the element of variety to its maximum, the whole rhythmical
emphasis were put upon the element of regularity. What
would be the result? This was the problem that presented
itself to the poets of the seventeenth century, when it appeared
to them that the possibilities of blank verse were played out.
(In reality they were not played out, as Milton proved; but
Milton was an isolated and unique phenomenon.) Clearly, the
most effective method of emphasising regularity is the use of
rhyme; and the most regular form of rhyme is the couplet.
Already, in the splendid couplets of Marlowe and in the
violent couplets of Donne, we can find a foretaste of what the
future had in store for the measure. Shakespeare, indeed, as if

to show that there were no limits either to his comprehension or to his capacity, threw off a few lines which might have been written by Pope, and stuck them into the middle of *Othello*.[1] But it was not until the collapse of blank verse, about 1630, that the essential characteristics which lay concealed in the couplet began to be exploited. It was Waller who first fully apprehended the implications of regularity; and it is to this fact that his immense reputation during the succeeding hundred years was due. Waller disengaged the heroic couplet from the beautiful vagueness of Elizabethanism. He perceived what logically followed from a rhyme. He saw that regularity implied balance, that balance implied antithesis; he saw that balance also implied simplicity, that simplicity implied clarity and that clarity implied exactitude. The result was a poetical instrument contrary in every particular to blank verse—a form which, instead of being varied, unsymmetrical, fluid, complex, profound and indefinite, was regular, balanced, antithetical, simple, clear, and exact. But, though Waller was its creator, the heroic couplet remained, with him, in an embryonic state. Its evolution was slow; even Dryden did not quite bring it to perfection. That great genius, with all his strength and all his brilliance, lacked one quality without which no mastery of the couplet could be complete— the elegance of perfect finish. This was possessed by Pope. The most correct of poets—Pope was indeed that; it is his true title to glory. But the phrase does not mean that he obeyed more slavishly than anybody else a set of arbitrary rules. No, it means something entirely different: it means that the system of versification of which the principle is regularity reached in Pope's hands the final plenitude of its nature —its ultimate significance—its supreme consummation.

---

[1] 'She that in wisdom never was so frail
To change the cod's head for the salmon's tail;
She that could think, and ne'er disclose her mind;
See suitors following, and not look behind;
She was a wight, if ever such wight were,
To suckle fools and chronicle small beer.'

That Pope's verse is artificial there can be no doubt. But then there is only one kind of verse that is not artificial, and that is, bad verse. Yet it is true that there is a sense in which Pope's couplet is more artificial than, let us say, the later blank verse of Shakespeare—it has less resemblance to nature. It is regular and neat; but nature is 'divers et ondoyant'; and so is blank verse. Nature and blank verse are complicated; and Pope's couplet is simplicity itself. But what a profound art underlies that simplicity! Pope's great achievement in English literature was the triumph of simplification. In one of his earliest works, the *Pastorals*, there is simplicity and nothing else; Pope had understood that if he could once attain to a perfect simplicity, all the rest would follow in good time—

> O deign to visit our forsaken seats,
> The mossy fountains, and the green retreats!
> Where'er you walk, cool gales shall fan the glade;
> Trees, where you sit, shall crowd into a shade;
> Where'er you tread, the blushing flow'rs shall rise,
> And all things flourish where you turn your eyes.

The lines flow on with the most transparent limpidity—

> But see, the shepherds shun the noon-day heat,
> The lowing herds to murm'ring brooks retreat,
> To closer shades the panting flocks remove;
> Ye Gods! and is there no relief for love?

Everything is obvious. The diction is a mass of *clichés*; the epithets are the most commonplace possible; the herds low, the brooks murmur, the flocks pant and remove, the retreats are green, and the flowers blush. The rhythm is that of a rocking-horse; and the sentiment is mere sugar. But what a relief! What a relief to have escaped for once from *le mot propre*, from subtle elaboration of diction and metre, from complicated states of mind, and all the profound obscurities of Shakespeare and Mr. T. S. Eliot! How delightful to have no trouble at all—to understand so very, very easily every single thing that is said!

This is Pope at his most youthful. As he matured, his verse matured with him. Eventually, his couplets, while retaining to the full their early ease, polish, and lucidity, became charged with an extraordinary weight. He was able to be massive, as no other wielder of the measure has ever been—

> Lo! thy dread empire, Chaos! is restored;
> Light dies before thy uncreating word;
> Thy hand, great Anarch! lets the curtain fall,
> And universal Darkness buries All.

Here the slow solemnity of the effect is produced by a most learned accumulation of accents and quantities; in some of the lines all the syllables save two are either long or stressed. At other times, he uses a precisely opposite method; in line after line he maintains, almost completely, the regular alternation of accented and unaccented syllables; and so conveys a wonderful impression of solidity and force—

> Proceed, great days! till learning fly the shore,
> Till Birch shall blush with noble blood no more,
> Till Thames see Eton's sons for ever play,
> Till Westminster's whole year be holiday,
> Till Isis' Elders reel, their pupils' sport,
> And Alma Mater lie dissolved in Port!

Perhaps the most characteristic of all the elements in the couplet is antithesis. Ordinary regularity demands that the sense should end with every line—that was a prime necessity; but a more scrupulous symmetry would require something more—a division of the line itself into two halves, whose meanings should correspond. And yet a further refinement was possible: each half might be again divided, and the corresponding divisions in the two halves might be so arranged as to balance each other. The force of neatness could no further go; and thus the most completely evolved type of the heroic line is one composed of four main words arranged in pairs, so as to form a double antithesis.

> Willing to wound, and yet afraid to strike

is an example of such a line, and Pope's poems are full of them. With astonishing ingenuity he builds up these exquisite structures, in which the parts are so cunningly placed that they seem to interlock spontaneously, and, while they are all formed on a similar model, are yet so subtly adjusted that they produce a fresh pleasure as each one appears. But that is not all. Pope was pre-eminently a satirist. He was naturally drawn to the contemplation of human beings, their conduct in society, their characters, their motives, their destinies; and the feelings which these contemplations habitually aroused in him were those of scorn and hatred. Civilisation illumined by animosity—such was his theme; such was the passionate and complicated material from which he wove his patterns of balanced precision and polished clarity. Antithesis penetrates below the structure; it permeates the whole conception of his work. Fundamental opposites clash, and are reconciled. The profundities of persons, the futilities of existence, the rage and spite of genius—these things are mixed together, and presented to our eyes in the shape of a Chinese box. The essence of all art is the accomplishment of the impossible. This cannot be done, we say; and it *is* done. What has happened? A magician has waved his wand. It is impossible that Pope should convey to us his withering sense of the wretchedness and emptiness of the fate of old women in society, in five lines, each containing four words, arranged in pairs, so as to form a double antithesis. But the magician waves his wand, and there it is—

> See how the world its veterans rewards!
> A youth of frolics, an old age of cards;
> Fair to no purpose, artful to no end,
> Young without lovers, old without a friend,
> A fop their passion, and their prize a sot;
> Alive ridiculous, and dead forgot!

And now, perhaps, we have discovered what may truly be said to have been Pope's 'poetic criticism of life.' His poetic criticism of life was, simply and solely, the heroic couplet.

Pope was pre-eminently a satirist; and so it is only natural that his enemies should take him to task for not being something else. He had no benignity; he had no feeling for sensuous beauty; he took no interest in nature; he was pompous —did he not wear a wig? Possibly; but if one is to judge poets by what they are without, where is one to end? One might point out that Wordsworth had no sense of humour, that Shelley did not understand human beings, that Keats could not read Greek, and that Matthew Arnold did not wear a wig. And, if one looks more closely, one perceives that there were a good many things that Pope could do very well—when he wanted to. Sensuous beauty, for instance—

> Die of a rose in aromatic pain.

If that is not sensuously beautiful, what is? Then, we are told, he did not 'compose with his eye on the object.' But once Pope looked at a spider, and this was what he composed—

> The spider's touch, how exquisitely fine!
> Feels at each thread, and lives along the line.

Could Wordsworth have done better? It is true that he did not often expatiate upon the scenery; but, when he chose, he could call up a vision of nature which is unforgettable—

> Lo! where Mæotis sleeps, and hardly flows
> The freezing Tanais thro' a waste of snows.

We see, and we shiver. It cannot be denied that Pope wore a wig; it must even be confessed that there are traces, in his earlier work especially, of that inexpressive ornament in the rococo style, which was the bane of his age; but the true Pope was not there. The true Pope threw his wig into the corner of the room, and used all the plainest words in the dictionary. He used them carefully, no doubt, very carefully, but he used them—one-syllabled, Saxon words, by no means pretty— they cover his pages; and some of his pages are among the coarsest in English literature. There are passages in the *Dunciad* which might agitate Mr. James Joyce. Far from being a scrupulous worshipper of the noble style, Pope was a realist—in thought and in expression. He could describe a sordid interior as well as any French novelist—

> In the worst inn's worst room, with mat half-hung,
> The floors of plaster, and the walls of dung,
> On once a flock-bed, but repair'd with straw,
> With tape-tied curtains, never meant to draw,
> The George and Garter dangling from that bed
> Where tawdry yellow strove with dirty red,
> Great Villiers lies. . . .

But these are only the outworks of the citadel. The heart of the man was not put into descriptions of physical things; it was put into descriptions of people whom he disliked. It is in those elaborate Characters, in which, through a score of lines or so, the verse rises in wave upon wave of malice, to fall at last with a crash on the devoted head of the victim—in the sombre magnificence of the denunciation of the great dead Duke, in the murderous insolence of the attack on the great living Duchess, in the hooting mockery of Bufo, in the devastating analysis of Addison—it is here that Pope's art comes to its climax. With what a relish, with what a thrill, we behold once more the impossible feat—the couplet, that bed of Procrustes, fitted exactly and eternally with the sinuous egoism of Addison's spirit, or the putrescent nothingness of Lord Hervey's. In the Character of Sporus, says the great critic and lexicographer, in memory of whom I have had the honour of addressing you to-day, Pope 'seems to be actually screaming with malignant fury.' It is true.

> Let Sporus tremble!—What? that thing of silk,
> Sporus, that mere white curd of ass's milk?
> Satire or sense, alas! can Sporus feel?
> Who breaks a butterfly upon a wheel?
> —Yet let me flap this bug with gilded wings,
> This painted child of dirt, that stinks and stings;
> Whose buzz the witty and the fair annoys,
> Yet wit ne'er tastes, and beauty ne'er enjoys:
> So well-bred spaniels civilly delight
> In mumbling of the game they dare not bite.

Eternal smiles his emptiness betray,
As shallow streams run dimpling all the way.
Whether in florid impotence he speaks,
And, as the prompter breathes, the puppet squeaks,
Or at the ear of Eve, familiar toad,
Half froth, half venom, spits himself abroad
In puns, or politics, or tales, or lies,
Or spite, or smut, or rhymes, or blasphemies.
His wit all see-saw, between that and this,
Now high, now low, now master up, now miss,
And he himself one vile antithesis.
Amphibious thing! that acting either part,
The trifling head, or the corrupted heart,
Fop at the toilet, flatterer at the board,
Now trips a lady, and now struts a lord.
Eve's tempter thus the Rábbins have expressed,
A cherub's face, a reptile all the rest;
Beauty that shocks you, parts that none can trust,
Wit that can creep, and pride that licks the dust.'

It is true: Pope *seems* to be actually screaming; but let us
not mistake. It is only an appearance; actually, Pope is not
screaming at all; for these are strange impossible screams,
unknown to the world of fact—screams endowed with
immortality. What has happened then? Pope has waved
his wand. He has turned his screams into poetry, with the
enchantment of the heroic couplet.

1925.

93

THE LIVES OF THE POETS[1]

No one needs an excuse for re-opening the *Lives of the Poets*; the book is too delightful. It is not, of course, as delightful as Boswell; but who re-opens Boswell? Boswell is in another category; because, as every one knows, when he has once been opened he can never be shut. But, on its different level, the *Lives* will always hold a firm and comfortable place in our affections. After Boswell, it is the book which brings us nearer than any other to the mind of Dr. Johnson. That is its primary import. We do not go to it for information or for instruction, or that our tastes may be improved, or that our sympathies may be widened; we go to it to see what Dr. Johnson thought. Doubtless, during the process, we are informed and instructed and improved in various ways; but these benefits are incidental, like the invigoration which comes from a mountain walk. It is not for the sake of the exercise that we set out; but for the sake of the view. The view from the mountain which is Samuel Johnson is so familiar, and has been so constantly analysed and admired, that further description would be superfluous. It is sufficient for us to recognise that he is a mountain, and to pay all the reverence that is due. In one of Emerson's poems a mountain and a squirrel begin to discuss each other's merits; and the squirrel comes to the triumphant conclusion that he is very much the better of the two, since he can crack a nut, while the mountain can do no such thing. The parallel is close enough between this impudence and the attitude—implied, if not expressed—of too much modern criticism towards the sort of qualities—the easy, indolent power, the searching sense of actuality, the combined command of sanity and paradox, the immovable independence of thought—which went to the

[1] *Lives of the English Poets.* By Samuel Johnson, LL.D. Edited by George Birkbeck Hill, D.C.L. Oxford: at the Clarendon Press, 1905.

making of the *Lives of the Poets*. There is only, perhaps, one
flaw in the analogy: that, in this particular instance, the
mountain was able to crack nuts a great deal better than any
squirrel that ever lived.

That the *Lives* continue to be read, admired, and edited,
is in itself a high proof of the eminence of Johnson's intellect;
because, as serious criticism, they can hardly appear to the
modern reader to be very far removed from the futile. Johnson's æsthetic judgments are almost invariably subtle, or solid,
or bold; they have always some good quality to recommend
them—except one: they are never right. That is an unfortunate deficiency; but no one can doubt that Johnson has made
up for it, and that his wit has saved all. He has managed to be
wrong so cleverly, that nobody minds. When Gray, for instance, points the moral to his poem on Walpole's cat with a
reminder to the fair that all that glisters is not gold, Johnson
remarks that this is 'of no relation to the purpose; if *what
glistered* had been *gold*, the cat would not have gone into the
water; and, if she had, would not less have been drowned.'
Could anything be more ingenious, or more neatly put, or
more obviously true? But then, to use Johnson's own phrase,
could anything be of less 'relation to the purpose'? It is his
wit—and we are speaking, of course, of wit in its widest sense
—that has sanctified Johnson's perversities and errors, that has
embalmed them for ever, and that has put his book, with all
its mass of antiquated doctrine, beyond the reach of time.

For it is not only in particular details that Johnson's
criticism fails to convince us; his entire point of view is
patently out of date. Our judgments differ from his, not only
because our tastes are different, but because our whole method
of judging has changed. Thus, to the historian of letters, the
Lives have a special interest, for they afford a standing example of a great dead tradition—a tradition whose characteristics throw more than one curious light upon the literary
feelings and ways which have become habitual to ourselves.
Perhaps the most striking difference between the critical
methods of the eighteenth century and those of the present

95

day, is the difference in sympathy. The most cursory glance at Johnson's book is enough to show that he judged authors as if they were criminals in the dock, answerable for every infraction of the rules and regulations laid down by the laws of art, which it was his business to administer without fear or favour. Johnson never inquired what poets were trying to do; he merely aimed at discovering whether what they had done complied with the canons of poetry. Such a system of criticism was clearly unexceptionable, upon one condition—that the critic was quite certain what the canons of poetry were; but the moment that it became obvious that the only way of arriving at a conclusion upon the subject was by consulting the poets themselves, the whole situation completely changed. The judge had to bow to the prisoner's ruling. In other words, the critic discovered that his first duty was, not to criticise, but to understand the object of his criticism. That is the essential distinction between the school of Johnson and the school of Sainte-Beuve. No one can doubt the greater width and profundity of the modern method; but it is not without its drawbacks. An excessive sympathy with one's author brings its own set of errors: the critic is so happy to explain everything, to show how this was the product of the age, how that was the product of environment, and how the other was the inevitable result of inborn qualities and tastes—that he sometimes forgets to mention whether the work in question has any value. It is then that one cannot help regretting the Johnsonian black cap.

But other defects, besides lack of sympathy, mar the *Lives of the Poets.* One cannot help feeling that no matter how anxious Johnson might have been to enter into the spirit of some of the greatest of the masters with whom he was concerned, he never could have succeeded. Whatever critical method he might have adopted, he still would have been unable to appreciate certain literary qualities, which, to our minds at any rate, appear to be the most important of all. His opinion of *Lycidas* is well known: he found that poem 'easy, vulgar, and therefore disgusting.' Of the songs in *Comus* he remarks: 'they are harsh in their diction, and not very musical in their numbers.' He could see nothing in the splendour and elevation of Gray, but 'glittering accumulations of ungraceful ornaments.' The passionate intensity of Donne escaped him altogether; he could only wonder how so ingenious a writer could be so absurd. Such preposterous judgments can only be accounted for by inherent deficiencies of taste; Johnson had no ear, and he had no imagination. These are, indeed, grievous disabilities in a critic. What could have induced such a man, the impatient reader is sometimes tempted to ask, to set himself up as a judge of poetry?

The answer to the question is to be found in the remarkable change which has come over our entire conception of poetry, since the time when Johnson wrote. It has often been stated that the essential characteristic of that great Romantic Movement which began at the end of the eighteenth century was the re-introduction of Nature into the domain of poetry. Incidentally, it is curious to observe that nearly every literary revolution has been hailed by its supporters as a return to Nature. No less than the school of Coleridge and Wordsworth, the school of Denham, of Dryden, and of Pope, proclaimed itself as the champion of Nature; and there can be little doubt that Donne himself—the father of all the conceits and elaborations of the seventeenth century—wrote under the impulse of a Naturalistic reaction against the conventional classicism of the Renaissance. Precisely the same contradictions took place in France. Nature was the watchword of Malherbe and of Boileau; and it was equally the watchword of Victor Hugo. To judge by the successive proclamations of poets, the development of literature offers a singular paradox. The further it goes back, the more sophisticated it becomes; and it grows more and more natural as it grows distant from the State of Nature. However this may be, it is at least certain that the Romantic revival peculiarly deserves to be called Naturalistic, because it succeeded in bringing into vogue the operations of the external world—'the Vegetable Universe,' as Blake called it—as subject-matter for poetry. But it would have done very little, if it had done nothing more than this. Thomson, in the full meridian of the eighteenth century, wrote poems upon the subject of Nature; but it would be foolish to suppose that Wordsworth and Coleridge merely carried on a fashion which Thomson had begun. Nature, with them, was something more than a peg for descriptive and didactic verse; it was the manifestation of the vast and mysterious forces of the world. The publication of *The Ancient Mariner* is a landmark in the history of letters, not because of its descriptions of natural objects, but because it swept into the poet's vision a whole new universe of infinite and eternal things; it was the discovery of the Unknown. We are still under the spell of *The Ancient Mariner*; and poetry to us means, primarily, something which suggests, by means of words, mysteries and infinitudes. Thus, music and imagination seem to us the most essential qualities of poetry, because they are the most potent means by which such suggestions may be invoked. But the eighteenth century knew none of these things. To Lord Chesterfield and to Pope, to Prior and to Horace Walpole, there was nothing at all strange about the world; it was charming, it was disgusting, it was ridiculous, and it was just what one might have expected. In such a world, why should poetry, more than anything else, be mysterious? No! Let it be sensible; that was enough.

The new edition of the *Lives*, which Dr. Birkbeck Hill prepared for publication before his death, and which has been issued by the Clarendon Press, with a brief Memoir of the editor, would probably have astonished Dr. Johnson. But, though the elaborate erudition of the notes and appendices might have surprised him, it would not have put him to shame. One can imagine his growling scorn of the scientific conscientiousness of the present day. And indeed, the three tomes of Dr. Hill's edition, with all their solid wealth of information, their voluminous scholarship, their accumulation of vast research, are a little ponderous and a little ugly; the hand is soon wearied with the weight, and the eye is soon distracted by the varying types, and the compressed columns of the notes, and the paragraphic numerals in the margins. This is the price that must be paid for increased efficiency. The wise reader will divide his attention between the new business-like edition and one of the charming old ones, in four comfortable volumes, where the text is supreme upon the page, and the paragraphs follow one another at leisurely intervals. The type may be a little faded, and the paper a little yellow; but what of that? It is all quiet and easy; and, as one reads, the brilliant sentences seem to come to one, out of the Past, with the friendliness of a conversation.

1906.

TWO FRENCHMEN

THE greatest misfortune that can happen to a witty man is to be born out of France. The French tongue is the appointed vehicle of brilliant thought; an Englishman, if he would be polished, pregnant, and concise, must command, like Bacon or like Burke, not only a wit but an inspiration; and it is perhaps as difficult for him to translate a French epigram as to compose an English one. A Frenchman, however, can always sparkle easily, even if he be stupid, and, if he be profound, the aphorism is his instinctive instrument of expression. The aphorism, indeed, dominates the literature of France, as the imagination dominates the literature of England. Even French tragedies are epigrammatic, and in French prose the epigrammatic style is the link which unites minds of such diverse genius as La Rochefoucauld and Vauvenargues, La Bruyère and Saint-Simon, Pascal and Voltaire. In coupling together La Bruyère and Vauvenargues for translation into English,[1] Miss Lee has clearly been influenced by the fact that both these masters of aphorism were at the same time writers of 'Characters,' or short portrait sketches, a form whose genesis is Theophrastus, and best known to English readers in the *Microcosmographie* of Earle. But this seems hardly sufficient reason for a combination which is interesting by virtue neither of resemblance nor of contrast, and Miss Lee, if she could not do with less than two authors, would have made, if she had substituted La Rochefoucauld for La Bruyère, a very much better book. For between Vauvenargues and La Rochefoucauld the contrast is complete. Many of Vauvenargues' maxims were written in direct opposition to those of La Rochefoucauld; he left a detailed criticism of the

---

[1] *La Bruyère and Vauvenargues: Selections from the Characters, Reflections, and Maxims.* Translated, with Introductory Notes and Memoirs, by Elizabeth Lee. Constable & Co. 1903.

great *Maximes et Réflexions* among his posthumous papers; and, indeed, the casts of mind of the two men were in every respect curiously and radically antipathetic.

La Rochefoucauld, there can be no doubt, was the cleverest duke who ever lived. His brilliant, embittered little book is like a narrow strip of perfectly polished parquet whereon a bored and aristocratic dancer exquisitely moves. Too proud not to be a master of his art, too magnificent to care whether he was or no, he shows, in every line he wrote, that supreme detachment which gives him a place either above or below humanity. When he speaks of love, he is as icy as when he speaks of death; when he speaks of death, it is as if he were already dead. 'Vanity of vanities, all is vanity' is his perpetual text (but in a sense different from the Preacher's) ; and in the safe isolation of this *parti pris*, hedged round by his pride, nourished by his scorn, illuminated by his wit, La Rochefoucauld felt clearly enough how well he could dispense with everything besides—even, perhaps, with the truth itself.

The passionate heart of Vauvenargues revolted against a portrait of humanity restricted and distorted to the extent of being (for all the sobriety of the presentment) really nothing more than a highly ingenious caricature. His mind, so sympathetic as to be often sentimental, so averse from paradox as to be sometimes platitudinous, opposed to La Rochefoucauld's paradoxical cynicism a profound belief in the simple goodness which resides in the emotions of men. 'Le corps a ses grâces,' he says, 'l'esprit a ses talents; le cœur n'aurait-il que des vices, et l'homme capable de raison serait-il incapable de vertu?' And to La Rochefoucauld's 'Nous ne ressentons nos biens et nos maux qu'à proportion de notre amour-propre,' he replies with a question which cuts the ground from under the feet of his antagonist: 'Est-il contre la raison ou la justice de s'aimer soi-même? Et pourquoi voulons-nous que l'amour-propre soit toujours un vice?'

Vauvenargues, however, needs no foil to make him worthy of study, though perhaps it is difficult to obtain a true view of him through a small selection from his writings. Nor has Miss

Lee made up, in her Introduction, for what she cannot give us of Vauvenargues himself. To say that his work betrays no sign of the age in which it was written, shows an entire misconception either of the age or of his work. The truth is, that Vauvenargues was typically eighteenth century; his literary treatment of philosophy, his philosophical treatment of literature, his love of emotion, his sarcasms upon the Church, are almost absurdly characteristic of the period of Voltaire. On every other page of his writings there is a reference to that 'Nature' so dear to philosophers from the days of Locke to the days of Rousseau, and so hard for us children of evolution to understand. There is the constant implication that 'natural' sentiments must be good; there are the usual contradictory assertions that Racine is too 'natural' to write badly, and Shakespeare too 'natural' to write well; there is even the conventional 'American' who converses philosophically with a Portuguese traveller upon the respective merits of civilisation and the 'state of Nature.' Such was the intellectual atmosphere which Vauvenargues necessarily breathed. But it was not only in his writings that he was typical of his time; it was in his mind as well. His letters, the letters of Voltaire, and the stray notices of others who knew him, show clearly enough that he possessed that combination of passionate emotions and love of truth which characterises the great Frenchmen of the eighteenth century. That they were sometimes sentimental, these great Frenchmen, and sometimes doctrinaire, cannot be denied; but is this all that can be said (it is too often all that *is* said) of Diderot, of d'Alembert, of Turgot, and of Condorcet? Their defects were the defects of their qualities, and how splendid these qualities were is precisely what the study of Vauvenargues most plainly shows. It shows Voltaire, it shows the 'Philosophes,' in their true light. 'Aimable créature, beau génie!' exclaims the former of Vauvenargues; to how many others of those true Humanists, those worthy heirs of the Renaissance, those noble and charming spirits, might the same words have been addressed!

'Vauvenargues,' we find in Miss Lee's Introduction,

'understood the art of writing, as an art, scarcely at all.' He understood it better than Miss Lee, whose English is never good, and who writes, on p. 135, 'Who would believe that others exist who pride themselves in not thinking *like* anyone else thinks?' The actual translation, too, is often unfortunately careless; several times the sense of the original has been quite mistaken; entire phrases have been sometimes omitted without apparent reason; and no effort has been made, by avoiding, for instance, the needless repetition of the same word in the same sentence, to obtain either the ease or the distinction of the original. The style of Vauvenargues is so simple, following, like all eighteenth-century French, almost the precise run of an English sentence, that nothing more was needed than care and a small knowledge of the two languages to have produced an adequate translation. And if Miss Lee has failed with Vauvenargues it was not to be expected that she would succeed with La Bruyère. This would have required a special talent, a fine instinct, and a reverent mind; without these qualities it were better to leave untouched one of the great writers of the world, whose perfect French it is nothing less than sacrilege to translate into bad English. Why such an attempt as Miss Lee's should find publicity in print, it is difficult to understand. For those who cannot read the original it is worse than useless—it is a snare—to represent such a sentence as this—'Everything they did was suitable to their circumstances, their expenditure was proportioned to their income, their liveries, equipages, furniture, table, town, and country houses were all in proportion to their revenue and circumstances'—as having anything in common with La Bruyère. It is plain from her Introduction that Miss Lee has no conception of the sanctity upon which she is laying her hands; and the consequences of this ignorance are, in her translation, even plainer. From the beautiful portrait of Arténice the charming sentence—'On ne sait si on l'aime ou si on l'admire' has been wantonly omitted; and into the very midst of the exquisite crescendo of the 'fleuristes' the hideous phrase 'tired with his perambulations' has been inserted, as a translation, one must suppose, of 'il se lasse.' It is melancholy to find this shapeless sentence, 'A fool is an automaton, a machine with springs which turn him about always in one manner and preserve his equilibrium,' standing for the mechanical exactitude of 'Le sot est automate, il est machine, il est ressort; le poids l'emporte, le fait mouvoir, le fait tourner, et toujours, et dans le même sens, et avec la même égalité.' The truth is, that the whole supremacy of La Bruyère's art consists in that absolute precision, that complete finish, that perfect proportion, which give his Characters the quality of a De Hoogh, and his aphorisms the brilliant hardness of a Greek gem. Every detail, every rhythm, every word, is essential to the beauty of the whole; and to destroy a single one of them is to convert perfection into nothing at all. The connoisseur of fruit, in Miss Lee's translation, 'with much ado gathers the exquisite plum'; in La Bruyère 'il cueille artistement cette prune exquise': this is exactly how Miss Lee should have treated her exquisite original.

But La Bruyère was not only a stylist; he was a philosopher. This hardly appears in Miss Lee's selections, which are confined almost entirely to those 'portraits of the more or less trifling eccentricities of men,' which give no true impression of the width and profundity of La Bruyère's mind. He was, in fact, a 'philosophe' out of water, a 'philosophe' in the *Grand Siècle*; his attitude towards the old *régime* was almost exactly the eighteenth-century attitude; and his elaborate picture of the Court of Versailles might have come straight out of the *Lettres Persanes*. Detached enough to recognise the absurdity of rouge and the injustice of torture, he perceived, perhaps more clearly than any other Frenchman before the Revolution, the volcano upon which society reposed. 'Quand le peuple est en mouvement,' he says, 'on ne comprend pas par où le calme peut y rentrer; et quand il est paisible, on ne voit pas par où le calme peut en sortir.' And he goes on, discussing the general theory of political change, 'il y a de certains maux dans la République qui y sont soufferts parce qu'ils préviennent ou empêchent de plus grands maux';

he weighs, like Hamlet, these conflicting evils; 'les plus sages,' he concludes, 'doutent quelquefois s'il est mieux de connaître ces maux que de les ignorer.'

La Bruyère, however, differed from eighteenth-century writers in two respects—he was a Roman Catholic and a poet. His religious bias, which led him to make his one great error in political judgment—his approval of the Revocation of the Edict of Nantes—inspires the entire chapter 'Des Esprits Forts,' where he confounds atheism, and shows how easy it is for a great man to be a small metaphysician. His poetry—that subtle and delicate employment of words, that vivid imagination, that marvellous command of atmosphere—is scattered all through his book; but it is in the chapters which deal with the intercourse of human beings that it reaches its fullest development. 'Il y a du plaisir à rencontrer les yeux de celui à qui l'on vient de donner.' Was anything ever written at once so subtle and so simple as that? Or at once so radiant and so intimate as this: 'Un beau visage est le plus beau de tous les spectacles, et la plus douce harmonie est le son de voix de celle que l'on aime'? Such sentences are nothing less than prose lyrics, as impossible to translate as the rhymed ones of Heine, and upon these heights it is only natural that Miss Lee should fall behind. 'The things we most desire never happen, or if they happen it is neither at the time nor under (*sic*) the circumstances when they would have given most pleasure.' This seems to be nothing more than a platitudinous way of saying something that is hardly true. But La Bruyère has in reality expressed in one sentence the whole dismal fatality of things: 'Les choses les plus souhaitées n'arrivent point: ou si elles arrivent ce n'est ni dans le temps ni dans les circonstances où elles auraient fait un extrême plaisir.' By what magic has he conveyed into these few words the suggestion of his surrender, of his disgust, of his infinite regret?

1903.

VOLTAIRE'S TRAGEDIES

THE historian of Literature is little more than a historian of exploded reputations. What has he to do with Shakespeare, with Dante, with Sophocles? Has he entered into the springs of the sea? Or has he walked in the search of the depth? The great fixed luminaries of the firmament of Letters dazzle his optic glass; and he can hardly hope to do more than record their presence, and admire their splendours with the eyes of an ordinary mortal. His business is with the succeeding ages of men, not with all time; but *Hyperion* might have been written on the morrow of Salamis, and the Odes of Pindar dedicated to George the Fourth. The literary historian must rove in other hunting grounds. He is the geologist of literature, whose study lies among the buried strata of forgotten generations, among the fossil remnants of the past. The great men with whom he must deal are the great men who are no longer great ——mammoths and ichthyosauri kindly preserved to us, among the siftings of so many epochs, by the impartial benignity of Time. It is for him to unravel the jokes of Erasmus, and to be at home among the platitudes of Cicero. It is for him to sit up all night with the spectral heroes of Byron; it is for him to exchange innumerable alexandrines with the faded heroines of Voltaire.

The great potentate of the eighteenth century has suffered cruelly indeed at the hands of posterity. Everyone, it is true, has heard of him; but who has read him? It is by his name that ye shall know him, and not by his works. With the exception of his letters, of *Candide*, of *Akakia*, and of a few other of his shorter pieces, the vast mass of his productions has been already consigned to oblivion. How many persons now living have travelled through *La Henriade* or *La Pucelle*? How many have so much as glanced at the imposing volumes of *L'Esprit des Mœurs*? *Zadig* and *Zaïre*, *Mérope* and *Charles*

XII still linger, perhaps, in the schoolroom; but what has become of *Oreste*, and of *Mahomet*, and of *Alzire*? *Où sont les neiges d'antan?*

Though Voltaire's reputation now rests mainly on his achievements as a precursor of the Revolution, to the eighteenth century he was as much a poet as a reformer. The whole of Europe beheld at Ferney the oracle, not only of philosophy, but of good taste; for thirty years every scribbler, every rising genius, and every crowned head, submitted his verses to the censure of Voltaire; Voltaire's plays were performed before crowded houses; his epic was pronounced superior to Homer's, Virgil's, and Milton's; his epigrams were transcribed by every letter-writer, and got by heart by every wit. Nothing, perhaps, shows more clearly the gulf which divides us from our ancestors of the eighteenth century, than a comparison between our thoughts and their thoughts, between our feelings and their feelings, with regard to one and the same thing—a tragedy by Voltaire. For us, as we take down the dustiest volume in our bookshelf, as we open it vaguely at some intolerable tirade, as we make an effort to labour through the procession of pompous commonplaces which meets our eyes, as we abandon the task in despair, and hastily return the book to its forgotten corner—to us it is well-nigh impossible to imagine the scene of charming brilliance which, five generations since, the same words must have conjured up. The splendid gaiety, the refined excitement, the pathos, the wit, the passion—all these things have vanished as completely from our perceptions as the candles, the powder, the looking-glasses, and the brocades, among which they moved and had their being. It may be instructive, or at least entertaining, to examine one of these forgotten masterpieces a little more closely; and we may do so with the less hesitation, since we shall only be following in the footsteps of Voltaire himself. His examination of *Hamlet* affords a precedent which is particularly applicable, owing to the fact that the same interval of time divided him from Shakespeare as that which divides ourselves from him. One point of difference, indeed, does exist between the relative positions of the two authors. Voltaire, in his study of Shakespeare, was dealing with a living, and a growing force; our interest in the dramas of Voltaire is solely an antiquarian interest. At the present moment,[1] a literal translation of *King Lear* is drawing full houses at the Théâtre Antoine. As a rule it is rash to prophesy; but, if that rule has any exceptions, this is certainly one of them—a hundred years hence a literal translation of *Zaïre* will not be holding the English boards.

It is not our purpose to appreciate the best, or to expose the worst, of Voltaire's tragedies. Our object is to review some specimen of what would have been recognised by his contemporaries as representative of the average flight of his genius. Such a specimen is to be found in *Alzire, ou Les Américains,* first produced with great success in 1736, when Voltaire was forty-two years of age and his fame as a dramatist already well established.

Act I.—The scene is laid in Lima, the capital of Peru, some years after the Spanish conquest of America. When the play opens, Don Gusman, a Spanish grandee, has just succeeded his father, Don Alvarez in the Governorship of Peru. The rule of Don Alvarez had been beneficent and just; he had spent his life in endeavouring to soften the cruelty of his countrymen; and his only remaining wish was to see his son carry on the work which he had begun. Unfortunately, however, Don Gusman's temperament was the very opposite of his father's; he was tyrannical, harsh, headstrong, and bigoted.

> L'Américain farouche est un monstre sauvage
> Qui mord en frémissant le frein de l'esclavage . . .
> Tout pouvoir, en un mot, périt par l'indulgence,
> Et la sévérité produit l'obéissance.

Such were the cruel maxims of his government—maxims which he was only too ready to put into practice. It was in vain that Don Alvarez reminded his son that the true Christian

[1] April, 1905.

returns good for evil, and that, as he epigrammatically put it, 'Le vrai Dieu, mon fils, est un Dieu qui pardonne.' To enforce his argument, the good old man told the story of how his own life had been spared by a virtuous American, who, as he said, 'au lieu de me frapper, embrassa mes genoux.' But Don Gusman remained unmoved by such narratives, though he admitted that there was one consideration which impelled him to adopt a more lenient policy. He was in love with Alzire, Alzire the young and beautiful daughter of Montèze, who had ruled in Lima before the coming of the Spaniards. 'Je l'aime, je l'avoue,' said Gusman to his father, 'et plus que je ne veux.' With these words, the dominating situation of the play becomes plain to the spectator. The wicked Spanish Governor is in love with the virtuous American princess. From such a state of affairs, what interesting and romantic developments may not follow? Alzire, we are not surprised to learn, still fondly cherished the memory of a Peruvian prince, who had been slain in an attempt to rescue his country from the tyranny of Don Gusman. Yet, for the sake of Montèze, her ambitious and scheming father, she consented to give her hand to the Governor. She consented; but, even as she did so, she was still faithful to Zamore. 'Sa foi me fut promise,' she declared to Don Gusman, 'il eut pour moi des charmes.'

> Il m'aima: son trépas me coûte encore des larmes:
> Vous, loin d'oser ici condamner ma douleur,
> Jugez de ma constance, et connaissez mon cœur.

The ruthless Don did not allow these pathetic considerations to stand in the way of his wishes, and gave orders that the wedding ceremony should be immediately performed. But, at the very moment of his apparent triumph, the way was being prepared for the overthrow of all his hopes.

Act II.—It was only natural to expect that a heroine affianced to a villain should turn out to be in love with a hero. The hero adored by Alzire had, it is true, perished; but then what could be more natural than his resurrection? The noble Zamore was not dead; he had escaped with his life from the torture-chamber of Don Gusman, had returned to avenge himself, had been immediately apprehended, and was lying imprisoned in the lowest dungeon of the castle, while his beloved princess was celebrating her nuptials with his deadly foe.

In this distressing situation, he was visited by the venerable Alvarez, who had persuaded his son to grant him an order for the prisoner's release. In the gloom of the dungeon, it was at first difficult to distinguish the features of Zamore; but the old man at last discovered that he was addressing the very American who, so many years ago, instead of hitting him, had embraced his knees. He was overwhelmed by this extraordinary coincidence. 'Approach. O heaven! O Providence! It is he, behold the object of my gratitude. . . . My benefactor! My son!' But let us not pry further into so affecting a passage; it is sufficient to state that Don Alvarez, after promising his protection to Zamore, hurried off to relate this remarkable occurrence to his son, the Governor.

Act III.—Meanwhile, Alzire has been married. But she still could not forget her Peruvian lover. While she was lamenting her fate, and imploring the forgiveness of the shade of Zamore, she was informed that a released prisoner begged a private interview. 'Admit him.' He was admitted. 'Heaven! Such were his features, his gait, his voice: Zamore!' She falls into the arms of her confidante. 'Je succombe: à peine je respire.'

> *Zamore:* Reconnais ton amant.
> *Alzire:*   Zamore aux pieds d'Alzire!
>   Est-ce une illusion?

It was no illusion; and the unfortunate princess was obliged to confess to her lover that she was already married to Don Gusman. Zamore was at first unable to grasp the horrible truth, and, while he was still struggling with his conflicting emotions, the door was flung open, and Don Gusman, accompanied by his father, entered the room.

A double recognition followed. Zamore was no less horrified to behold in Don Gusman the son of the venerable

Alvarez, than Don Gusman was infuriated at discovering that the prisoner to whose release he had consented was no other than Zamore. When the first shock of surprise was over, the Peruvian hero violently insulted his enemy, and upbraided him with the tortures he had inflicted. The Governor replied by ordering the instant execution of the prince. It was in vain that Don Alvarez reminded his son of Zamore's magnanimity; it was in vain that Alzire herself offered to sacrifice her life for that of her lover. Zamore was dragged from the apartment; and Alzire and Don Alvarez were left alone to bewail the fate of the Peruvian hero. Yet some faint hopes still lingered in the old man's breast. 'Gusman fut inhumain,' he admitted, 'je le sais, j'en frémis;

> Mais il est ton époux, il t'aime, il est mon fils:
> Son âme à la pitié se peut ouvrir encore.'

'Hélas!' (replied Alzire), 'que n'êtes-vous le père de Zamore!'

Act IV.—Even Don Gusman's heart was, in fact, unable to steel itself entirely against the prayers and tears of his father and his wife; and he consented to allow a brief respite to Zamore's execution. Alzire was not slow to seize this opportunity of doing her lover a good turn; for she immediately obtained his release by the ingenious stratagem of bribing the warder of the dungeon. Zamore was free. But alas! Alzire was not; was she not wedded to the wicked Gusman? Her lover's expostulations fell on unheeding ears. What mattered it that her marriage vow had been sworn before an alien God? 'J'ai promis; il suffit; il n'importe à quel dieu!'

Zamore: Ta promesse est un crime; elle est ma perte; adieu.
Périssent tes serments et ton Dieu que j'abhorre!
Alzire: Arrête; quels adieux! arrête, cher Zamore!

But the prince tore himself away, with no further farewell upon his lips than an oath to be revenged upon the Governor. Alzire, perplexed, deserted, terrified, tortured by remorse, agitated by passion, turned for comfort to that God, who, she could not but believe, was, in some mysterious way, the Father of All.

Great God, lead Zamore in safety through the desert places. . . . Ah! can it be true that thou art but the Deity of another universe? Have the Europeans alone the right to please thee? Art thou after all the tyrant of one world and the father of another? . . . No! The conquerors and the conquered, miserable mortals as they are, all are equally the work of thy hands. . . .

Her reverie was interrupted by an appalling sound. She heard shrieks; she heard a cry of 'Zamore!' And her confidante, rushing in, confusedly informed her that her lover was in peril of his life.

> Ah, chère Emire [she exclaimed], allons le secourir!
> *Emire:* Que pouvez-vous, Madame? O Ciel!
> *Alzire:*   Je puis mourir.

Hardly was the epigram out of her mouth when the door opened, and an emissary of Don Gusman announced to her that she must consider herself under arrest. She demanded an explanation in vain, and was immediately removed to the lowest dungeon.

Act V.—It was not long before the unfortunate princess learnt the reason of her arrest. Zamore, she was informed, had rushed straight from her apartment into the presence of Don Gusman, and had plunged a dagger into his enemy's breast. The hero had then turned to Don Alvarez and, with perfect tranquillity, had offered him the bloodstained poniard.

> J'ai fait ce que j'ai dû, j'ai vengé mon injure;
> Fais ton devoir, dit-il, et venge la nature.

Before Don Alvarez could reply to this appeal, Zamore had been haled off by the enraged soldiery before the Council of Grandees. Don Gusman had been mortally wounded; and the Council proceeded at once to condemn to death, not only Zamore, but also Alzire, who, they found, had been guilty of complicity in the murder. It was the unpleasant duty of Don Alvarez to announce to the prisoners the Council's sentence. He did so in the following manner:

Good God, what a mixture of tenderness and horror! My own liberator is the assassin of my son. Zamore! . . . Yes, it is to thee that

I owe this life which I detest; how dearly didst thou sell me that fatal gift. . . . I am a father, but I am also a man; and, in spite of thy fury, in spite of the voice of that blood which demands vengeance from my agitated soul, I can still hear the voice of thy benefactions. And thou, who wast my daughter, thou whom in our misery I yet call by a name which makes our tears to flow, ah! how far is it from thy father's wishes to add to the agony which he already feels the horrible pleasure of vengeance. I must lose, by an unheard-of catastrophe, at once my liberator, my daughter, and my son. The Council has sentenced you to death.

Upon one condition, however, and upon one alone, the lives of the culprits were to be spared—that of Zamore's conversion to Christianity. What need is there to say that the noble Peruvians did not hesitate for a moment? 'Death, rather than dishonour!' exclaimed Zamore, while Alzire added some elegant couplets upon the moral degradation entailed by hypocritical conversion. Don Alvarez was in complete despair, and was just beginning to make another speech, when Don Gusman, with the pallor of death upon his features, was carried into the room. The implacable Governor was about to utter his last words. Alzire was resigned; Alvarez was plunged in misery; Zamore was indomitable to the last. But lo! when the Governor spoke, it was seen at once that an extraordinary change had come over his mind. He was no longer proud, he was no longer cruel, he was no longer unforgiving; he was kind, humble, and polite; in short, he had repented. Everybody was pardoned, and everybody recognised the truth of Christianity. And their faith was particularly strengthened when Don Gusman, invoking a final blessing upon Alzire and Zamore, expired in the arms of Don Alvarez. For thus were the guilty punished, and the virtuous rewarded. The noble Zamore, who had murdered his enemy in cold blood, and the gentle Alzire who, after bribing a sentry, had allowed her lover to do away with her husband, lived happily ever afterwards. That they were able to do so was owing entirely to the efforts of the wicked Don Gusman; and the wicked Don Gusman very properly descended to the grave.

Such is the tragedy of *Alzire*, which, it may be well to repeat, was in its day one of the most applauded of its author's productions. It was upon the strength of works of this kind that his contemporaries recognised Voltaire's right to be ranked in a sort of dramatic triumvirate, side by side with his great predecessors, Corneille and Racine. With Racine, especially, Voltaire was constantly coupled; and it is clear that he himself firmly believed that the author of *Alzire* was a worthy successor of the author of *Athalie*. At first sight, indeed, the resemblance between the two dramatists is obvious enough; but a closer inspection reveals an ocean of differences too vast to be spanned by any superficial likeness.

A careless reader is apt to dismiss the tragedies of Racine as mere *tours de force*; and, in one sense, the careless reader is right. For, as mere displays of technical skill, those works are certainly unsurpassed in the whole range of literature. But the notion of 'a mere *tour de force*' carries with it something more than the idea of technical perfection; for it denotes, not simply a work which is technically perfect, but a work which is technically perfect and nothing more. The problem before a writer of a Chant Royal is to overcome certain technical difficulties of rhyme and rhythm; he performs his *tour de force*, the difficulties are overcome, and his task is accomplished. But Racine's problem was very different. The technical restrictions he laboured under were incredibly great; his vocabulary was cribbed, his versification was cabined, his whole power of dramatic movement was scrupulously confined; conventional rules of every conceivable denomination hurried out to restrain his genius, with the alacrity of Lilliputians pegging down a Gulliver; wherever he turned he was met by a hiatus or a pitfall, a blind-alley or a *mot bas*. But his triumph was not simply the conquest of these refractory creatures; it was something much more astonishing. It was the creation, in spite of them, nay, by their very aid, of a glowing, living, soaring, and enchanting work of art. To have brought about this amazing combination, to have erected, upon a structure of Alexandrines, of Unities, of Noble

Personages, of stilted diction, of the whole intolerable para-
phernalia of the Classical stage, an edifice of subtle psychology, of exquisite poetry, of overwhelming passion—that is a
tour de force whose achievement entitles Jean Racine to a
place among the very few consummate artists of the world.

Voltaire, unfortunately, was neither a poet nor a psychologist; and, when he took up the mantle of Racine, he put it,
not upon a human being, but upon a tailor's block. To change
the metaphor, Racine's work resembled one of those elaborate paper transparencies which delighted our grandmothers,
illuminated from within so as to present a charming tinted
picture with varying degrees of shadow and of light. Voltaire
was able to make the transparency, but he never could light
the candle; and the only result of his efforts was some sticky
pieces of paper, cut into curious shapes, and roughly daubed
with colour. To take only one instance, his diction is the very
echo of Racine's. There are the same pompous phrases, the
same inversions, the same stereotyped list of similes, the same
poor bedraggled company of words. It is amusing to note the
exclamations which rise to the lips of Voltaire's characters
in moments of extreme excitement— *Qu'entends-je? Que
vois-je? Où suis-je? Grands Dieux! Ah, c'en est trop, Seigneur!
Juste Ciel! Sauve-toi de ces lieux! Madame, quelle horreur . . .*
&c. And it is amazing to discover that these are the very
phrases with which Racine has managed to express all the
violence of human terror, and rage, and love. Voltaire at his
best never rises above the standard of a sixth-form boy writing
hexameters in the style of Virgil; and, at his worst, he certainly falls within measurable distance of a flogging. He is
capable, for instance, of writing lines as bad as the second of
this couplet—

> C'est ce même guerrier dont la main tutélaire,
> De Gusman, votre époux, sauva, dit-on, le père,

or as

> Qui les font pour un temps rentrer tous en eux-mêmes,

or

> Vous comprenez, seigneur, que je ne comprends pas.

Voltaire's most striking expressions are too often borrowed from his predecessors. Alzire's 'Je puis mourir,' for instance, is an obvious reminiscence of the 'Qu'il mourût!' of le vieil Horace; and the cloven hoof is shown clearly enough by the 'O ciel!' with which Alzire's confidante manages to fill out the rest of the line. Many of these blemishes are, doubtless, the outcome of simple carelessness; for Voltaire was too busy a man to give over-much time to his plays. 'This tragedy was the work of six days,' he wrote to d'Alembert, enclosing *Olympie*. 'You should not have rested on the seventh,' was d'Alembert's reply. But, on the whole, Voltaire's verses succeed in keeping up to a high level of mediocrity; they are the verses, in fact, of a very clever man. It is when his cleverness is out of its depth, that he most palpably fails. A human being by Voltaire bears the same relation to a real human being that stage scenery bears to a real landscape; it can only be looked at from in front. The curtain rises, and his villains and his heroes, his good old men and his exquisite princesses, display for a moment their one thin surface to the spectator; the curtain falls, and they are all put back into their box. The glance which the reader has taken into the little case labelled *Alzire* has perhaps given him a sufficient notion of these queer discarded marionettes.

Voltaire's dramatic efforts were hampered by one further unfortunate incapacity; he was almost completely devoid of the dramatic sense. It is only possible to write good plays without the power of character-drawing, upon one condition —that of possessing the power of creating dramatic situations. The *Oedipus Tyrannus* of Sophocles, for instance, is not a tragedy of character; and its vast crescendo of horror is produced by a dramatic treatment of situation, not of persons. One of the principal elements in this stupendous example of the manipulation of a great dramatic theme has been pointed out by Voltaire himself. The guilt of Oedipus, he says, becomes known to the audience very early in the play; and, when the *dénouement* at last arrives, it comes as a shock, not to the audience, but to the King. There can be no doubt that

Voltaire has put his finger upon the very centre of those underlying causes which make the *Oedipus* perhaps the most awful of tragedies. To know the hideous truth, to watch its gradual dawn upon one after another of the characters, to see Oedipus at last alone in ignorance, to recognise clearly that he too must know, to witness his struggles, his distraction, his growing terror, and, at the inevitable moment, the appalling revelation—few things can be more terrible than this. But Voltaire's comment upon the master-stroke by which such an effect has been obtained illustrates, in a remarkable way, his own sense of the dramatic. 'Nouvelle preuve,' he remarks, 'que Sophocle n'avait pas perfectionné son art.'

More detailed evidence of Voltaire's utter lack of dramatic insight is to be found, of course, in his criticisms of Shakespeare. Throughout these, what is particularly striking is the manner in which Voltaire seems able to get into such intimate contact with his great predecessor, and yet to remain as absolutely unaffected by him as Shakespeare himself was by Voltaire. It is unnecessary to dwell further upon so hackneyed a subject; but one instance may be given of the lengths to which this dramatic insensibility of Voltaire's was able to go—his adaptation of *Julius Caesar* for the French stage. A comparison of the two pieces should be made by anyone who wishes to realise fully, not only the degradation of the copy, but the excellence of the original. Particular attention should be paid to the transmutation of Antony's funeral oration into French alexandrines. In Voltaire's version, the climax of the speech is reached in the following passage; it is an excellent sample of the fatuity of the whole of his concocted rigmarole:—

Antoine: Brutus . . . où suis-je? O ciel! O crime! O barbarie!
　　　　　Chers amis, je succombe; et mes sens interdits . . .
　　　　　Brutus, son assassin! . . . ce monstre était son fils!
Romains: Ah dieux!

If Voltaire's demerits are obvious enough to our eyes, his merits were equally clear to his contemporaries, whose vision of them was not perplexed and retarded by the conventions of

117

another age. The weight of a reigning convention is like the weight of the atmosphere—it is so universal that no one feels it; and an eighteenth-century audience came to a performance of *Alzire* unconscious of the burden of the Classical rules. They found instead an animated procession of events, of scenes just long enough to be amusing and not too long to be dull, of startling incidents, of happy *mots*. They were dazzled by an easy display of cheap brilliance, and cheap philosophy, and cheap sentiment, which it was very difficult to distinguish from the real thing, at such a distance, and under artificial light. When, in *Mérope*, one saw La Dumesnil; 'lorsque,' to quote Voltaire himself, 'les yeux égarés, la voix entrecoupée, levant une main tremblante, elle allait immoler son propre fils; quand Narbas l'arrêta; quand, laissant tomber son poignard, on la vit s'évanouir entre les bras de ses femmes, et qu'elle sortit de cet état de mort avec les transports d'une mère; lorsque, ensuite, s'élançant aux yeux de Polyphonte, traversant en un clin d'œil tout le théâtre, les larmes dans les yeux, la pâleur sur le front, les sanglots à la bouche, les bras étendus, elle s'écria: "Barbare, il est mon fils!" '—how, face to face with splendours such as these, could one question for a moment the purity of the gem from which they sparkled? Alas! to us, who know not La Dumesnil, to us whose *Mérope* is nothing more than a little sediment of print, the precious stone of our forefathers has turned out to be a simple piece of paste. Its glittering was the outcome of no inward fire, but of a certain adroitness in the manufacture; to use our modern phraseology, Voltaire was able to make up for his lack of genius by a thorough knowledge of 'technique,' and a great deal of 'go.'

And to such titles of praise let us not dispute his right. His vivacity, indeed, actually went so far as to make him something of an innovator. He introduced new and imposing spectacular effects; he ventured to write tragedies in which no persons of royal blood made their appearance; he was so bold as to rhyme 'père' with 'terre.' The wild diversity of his incidents shows a trend towards the romantic, which, doubtless, under happier influences, would have led him much further along the primrose path which ended in the bonfire of 1830.

But it was his misfortune to be for ever clogged by a tradition of decorous restraint; so that the effect of his plays is as anomalous as would be——let us say——that of a shilling shocker written by Miss Yonge. His heroines go mad in epigrams, while his villains commit murder in inversions. Amid the hurly-burly of artificiality, it was all his cleverness could do to keep its head to the wind; and he was only able to remain afloat at all by throwing overboard his humour. The Classical tradition has to answer for many sins; perhaps its most infamous achievement was that it prevented Molière from being a great tragedian. But there can be no doubt that its most astonishing one was to have taken——if only for some scattered moments——the sense of the ridiculous from Voltaire.

1905.

THE WRONG TURNING

'ENGLISH Men of Letters: Fanny Burney (Madame D'Arblay).' So runs the title of Mr. Dobson's book[1]; and let none but pedants exclaim against a Man of Letters who is a lady, and a lady who is not one lady, but two. For the Fanny Burney of the novels and the Madame D'Arblay of the Diary has each her separate claim to a literary distinction, and memorial beyond the grave. Though *Camilla* has long since faded from the circulating libraries, though Colonel Digby and Mrs. Schwellenberg may only exist for us in an essay of Macaulay, there is yet good reason to remember, now and then, the works that Johnson praised, that Burke sat up all night to finish, that charmed Sir Joshua, that held Gibbon enthralled, and not to forget altogether the girl who scribbled in Newton's Observatory, who grew up amidst the famous circle of 'the Club,' the friend of Garrick and Warren Hastings and Rogers, who had been paid a compliment by Soame Jenyns and lived long enough to pay one to Walter Scott, the correspondent of 'Daddy' Crisp and of Disraeli, who talked scandal with Mrs. Thrale, and wrote plays for Mrs. Siddons, and discussed Shakespeare with George III.

Mr. Dobson has devoted most of his charming volume to the lady of the Diary, though the fifty pages he has given up to the novels contain nothing that is not admirably happy, discriminating, and just. But it is only natural that the author of *Beau Brocade* should dwell chiefly upon that side of Fanny Burney's life which brings us most into contact with the delightful and brilliant society of eighteenth-century London; for here his unrivalled knowledge and peculiar sympathy have opened out for him opportunities which he can use to the utmost, with rights and powers all his own. Mr. Dobson,

[1] *Fanny Burney.* By Austin Dobson. London: Macmillan and Co. 1903.

indeed, is himself so much at home in that world 'of Drum and Ridotto, of Rake and of Belle,' that he succeeds in transferring to the willing reader his own sense of pleasant familiarity and ease. One wanders with him happily from Poland Street to Queen Square, from Bloomsbury to Leicester Fields; one looks in at Portman Square on Mrs. Montagu amid her feathered walls; one catches glimpses of Horace Walpole or Sheridan or Lady Di; one has the *entrée* at Streatham; one visits Brighton, and takes the waters at Bath. Across this past which has become the present there float visions of a remoter past: Sir Isaac walks once more from St. Martin's Street to visit the Princess Caroline at Leicester House; the ghostly chairs of Lady Worsley and Lady Betty Germaine wait still at the narrow approach from the Fields, as they did in the old days when 'their mistresses "disputed Whig and Tory," with Mrs. Conduit, or were interrupted in a *tête-à-tête* by Gay and the Duchess of Queensberry.'

In laying so little stress on Madame D'Arblay's novels, Mr. Dobson has followed the lead of Macaulay, who, in his metallic way, devoted the greater part of an Essay to a description of her life, and reserved only the fag end of it for a discussion of her place in literature. And even then, his criticism amounts to nothing more than saying, with extraordinary cleverness, that her characters were caricatures, and that her style degenerated from Nature to Johnson, and from Johnson to insufferable affectation. Neither Macaulay nor Mr. Dobson has indeed really solved the enigma of why it happened that writings, pronounced immortal by the greatest intellects of their own day, fell almost at once into insignificance, and eventually into nearly complete oblivion. *Evelina* and *Cecilia* were hailed by Johnson, the greatest contemporary critic, as worthy to rank beside the best work of Richardson and Fielding; and *Evelina* is now read only as a quaint example of eighteenth-century literature, while *Cecilia* is not read at all. 'Tell them,' said Johnson of the latter volume, in a vein of ironic censure, 'how little there is in it of human nature, and how well your knowledge of the world enables you to judge of the failings in that book.' But the words are ironical in a sense undreamt of by the Doctor; for they exactly express the opinion of the modern reader, who inevitably does find in *Cecilia* very little of human nature, and whose knowledge of the world does enable him to judge quite easily of the failings of 'that book.' The difference is complete; and a compromise appears to be impossible. If we are right, Johnson must have been wrong; if we are wrong, Johnson must have been right. But we, *ex hypothesi*, are right; how then did it happen—it is the only question left to ask—that Johnson came to be wrong?

There can be no doubt that, during the last quarter of the eighteenth century, the English novel experienced a remarkable eclipse. From the publication of *The Vicar of Wakefield*, in 1766, to the composition of *Pride and Prejudice*, in 1796, for the whole of that period of thirty years, no novel of the first class was produced at all; and few indeed of the novels which were actually written attained the level even of Miss Burney's second-class work. English prose, it is true, had never flourished more gloriously; but it reserved its magnificent outpourings for History, for Philosophy, for Oratory, for Essays, for Memoirs, for Letters, for everything, in fact, except the particular sort of prose romance which is concerned with the portrayal of human nature. Why this was the case, why, between the great constellation of Richardson, Fielding, and Sterne, and the great constellation of Jane Austen and Walter Scott, there should intervene a vast tract of literature illumined only by stars of the third magnitude— this is a mystery perhaps beyond solution, though it would be partly accounted for, if it were true that the direct study of human nature was, for some unknown reason, not interesting to the English of that generation. At any rate, whether they were (to use Johnson's phrase) 'character-mongers' or no in actual life, it seems clear that at least in literary criticism they were not. It is a standing proof of their innate incapacity for estimating the true value of the characterisation in a work of fiction, their utter lack of *flair* for portraiture, that they left it to the nineteenth century to discover the fact that what makes Sterne immortal is not his sentiment, nor his indecency, nor his asterisks, but his Mr. Shandy and his Uncle Toby.

It was precisely this quality of literary acumen which her contemporaries brought to bear on the novels of Fanny Burney. 'You have,' Burke wrote to her, 'crowded into a few small volumes an incredible variety of characters; most of them well planned, well supported, and well contrasted with each other'; and it is obvious that by 'characters' Burke meant just what he should not have meant—descriptions, that is to say, of persons who might exist. The truth is, that if we had been told that Delvile *père* was ten feet high, and that Mr. Morrice was made of cardboard, we should have had very little reason for astonishment; such peculiarities of form would have been remarkable, no doubt, but not more remarkable than those of their minds, which Burke was so ready to accept as eminently natural. In fact, Miss Burney's characters, to use Macaulay's phrase, are in reality nothing but 'humours,' and not characters at all; and immediately this is recognised, immediately 'humours' is substituted for 'characters' in Burke's appreciation, what he says becomes perfectly just. They are indeed, these humours, 'well planned, well supported, and well contrasted with each other'; Miss Burney displays great cleverness and admirable care in her arrangement of them; and this Burke, as well as Macaulay, thoroughly understood. But such, both for Burke and for his distinguished circle, was the limit of understanding; outside that limit the God of Convention reigned triumphant. Conventional feelings, conventional phrases, conventional situations, conventional oddities, conventional loves,—these were the necessary ingredients of their perfect novel; and all these Miss Burney was able, with supreme correctness, to supply. In the culminating scene of *Cecilia*, where the conflicting passions of affection and family pride at last meet face to face, the dialogue is as wonderfully finished and as superbly orthodox as the dialogue of a second-rate French tragedy; one cannot help seeing Cecilia and Mortimer and Mrs. Delvile, in perruques and togas, delivering their harangues with appropriate gestures from the front of a Louis Quinze stage, with Corinthian columns in the background. Johnson's favourite, the mad philanthropical Albany, does indeed actually burst sometimes into downright blank verse.

> Poor subterfuge of callous cruelty!

he suddenly exclaims,

> You cheat yourselves to shun the fraud of others!
> And yet how better do you use the wealth
> So guarded?
> What nobler purpose can it answer to you,
> Than even a chance to snatch some wretch from sinking?
> Think less how *much* ye save, and more for *what*;

'And then consider how thy full coffers may hereafter make reparation for the empty catalogue of thy virtues.'

'Anan!' cries Mr. Briggs, in reply to these noble sentiments; and that—whatever it may mean—is perhaps the best rejoinder.

But it is to be feared that Miss Burney's friends did worse than misjudge her merits; it seems clear that they encouraged her faults, and turned away her energies from where her true strength lay. For, in her first work, she had succeeded in depicting one character which, though neither elaborate nor profound, was really convincing—Evelina herself. The refined, over-modest girl, around whose perplexities and sufferings and joys the troupe of usual humours dance and tumble, is delicately brought out by a sympathetic hand. Here at last is something that is more than cleverness—a little spark of genius; and it shows itself most clearly in a few little scenes and conversations, of which the following specimen may be taken as a fair example. Lord Orville, who is in love with Evelina, discovers her in the garden at an early hour, talking intimately to Mr. Macartney. Everything points (wrongly, of course) to an assignation. Evelina, who is in love with Lord Orville, returns with him to the house.

'Determined as I was to act honourably by Mr. Macartney,

124

I yet most anxiously wished to be restored to the good opinion of Lord Orville; but his silence, and the thoughtfulness of his air, discouraged me from speaking.

'My situation soon grew disagreeable and embarrassing; and I resolved to return to my chamber till breakfast was ready. To remain longer, I feared, might seem *asking* for his inquiries; and I was sure it would ill become me to be more eager to speak than he was to hear.

'Just as I reached the door, turning to me hastily, he said, "Are you going, Miss Anville?"

' "I am, my lord," answered I; yet I stopped.

' "Perhaps to return to—but I beg your pardon!" He spoke with a degree of agitation that made me readily comprehend he meant to *the garden*; and I instantly said: "To my own room, my lord." And again I would have gone; but, convinced by my answer that I understood him, I believe he was sorry for the insinuation; he approached me with a very serious air, though at the same time he forced a smile, and said: "I know not what evil genius pursues me this morning, but I seem destined to do or say something I ought not; I am so much ashamed of myself, that I can scarce solicit your forgiveness." '

That is a small picture, perhaps, of a small affair; it describes hardly more than a turn to and from a door; but it possesses qualities of beauty, of restraint, of quick imagination, of charming feeling, of real atmosphere, that make it approach, in its tiny way, close to perfection. But this quiet sort of miniature analysis Miss Burney repeated in none of her later books. Cecilia is a burlesque Evelina, a wax figure whose refinement has become a settled affectation, whose modesty is an obsession, who blushes every time her lover's name is mentioned, who is scandalised when he proposes, and is too maidenly to be married. Henceforward Miss Burney had no time for the subtleties of art; at all hazards she must be creating 'well supported' characters, and putting them into 'well planned' situations; and, her work thus cut out for her, she carried it through with credit. But it is impossible not to think that perhaps, if she had written in a more discriminating age, she would have developed her own peculiar vein as it deserved, instead of working others of inferior ore with implements too heavy for her strength. Fortunately for us indeed, she was left to herself in one domain; for her Diary flourished beyond the reach of criticism, deep-rooted in her own most private nature, and fed with truth. No one can doubt that Mr. Dobson is right to place it high above the novels, and to rank it with the great diaries of literature. It is here that Madame D'Arblay appears at full length; it is here that she shows us her mirror of the world, gives us the relish of real persons, real intimacies, real conversations. Who would not be willing to abolish for ever the whole elaborate waste of *Cecilia*, for the sake of those few pages in the Diary, where, looking down upon the crowded benches of Westminster Hall, we can see distinct before us the pale face of Hastings, and watch the Managers in their box and the Duchesses in their gallery, while we listen alternately to the tedious droning of the lawyers, to the whispered flatteries of Mr. Windham, and the stupendous oratory of Burke?

1904.

'A SIMPLE STORY' [1]

A Simple Story is one of those books which, for some reason
or other, have failed to come down to us, as they deserved,
along the current of time, but have drifted into a literary
backwater where only the professional critic or the curious
discoverer can find them out. 'The iniquity of oblivion
blindly scattereth her poppy'; and nowhere more blindly than
in the republic of letters. If we were to inquire how it has
happened that the true value of Mrs. Inchbald's achievement
has passed out of general recognition, perhaps the answer to
our question would be found to lie in the extreme difficulty
with which the mass of readers detect and appreciate mere
quality in literature. Their judgment is swayed by a hundred
side-considerations which have nothing to do with art, but
happen easily to impress the imagination, or to fit in with the
fashion of the hour. The reputation of Mrs. Inchbald's contemporary, Fanny Burney, is a case in point. Every one has
heard of Fanny Burney's novels, and *Evelina* is still widely
read. Yet it is impossible to doubt that, so far as quality alone
is concerned, *Evelina* deserves to be ranked considerably
below *A Simple Story*. But its writer was the familiar friend
of the greatest spirits of her age; she was the author of one
of the best of diaries; and her work was immediately and
immensely popular. Thus it has happened that the name of
Fanny Burney has maintained its place upon the roll of
English novelists, while that of Mrs. Inchbald is forgotten.

But the obscurity of Mrs. Inchbald's career has not, of
course, been the only reason for the neglect of her work. The
merits of *A Simple Story* are of a kind peculiarly calculated
to escape the notice of a generation of readers brought up on
the fiction of the nineteenth century. That fiction, infinitely

[1] [Originally published as an introduction to a re-issue of *A Simple
Story*. By Mrs. Inchbald. Henry Frowde. 1908.]

various as it is, possesses at least one characteristic common to
the whole of it—a breadth of outlook upon life, which can
be paralleled by no other body of literature in the world save
that of the Elizabethans. But the comprehensiveness of view
shared by Dickens and Tolstoy, by Balzac and George Eliot,
finds no place in Mrs. Inchbald's work. Compared with *A
Simple Story* even the narrow canvases of Jane Austen seem
spacious pictures of diversified life. Mrs. Inchbald's novel is
not concerned with the world at large, or with any section of
society, hardly even with the family; its subject is a group of
two or three individuals whose interaction forms the whole
business of the book. There is no local colour in it, no complexity of detail nor violence of contrast; the atmosphere is
vague and neutral, the action passes among ill-defined sitting-
rooms, and the most poignant scene in the story takes place
upon a staircase which has never been described. Thus the
reader of modern novels is inevitably struck, in *A Simple
Story*, by a sense of emptiness and thinness, which may well
blind him to high intrinsic merits. The spirit of the eighteenth
century is certainly present in the book, but it is the eighteenth
century of France rather than of England. Mrs. Inchbald no
doubt owed much to Richardson; her view of life is the indoor
sentimental view of the great author of *Clarissa*; but her
treatment of it has very little in common with his method of
microscopic analysis and vast accumulation. If she belongs to
any school, it is among the followers of the French classical
tradition that she must be placed. *A Simple Story* is, in its small
way, a descendant of the Tragedies of Racine; and Miss
Milner may claim relationship with Madame de Clèves.

Besides her narrowness of vision, Mrs. Inchbald possesses
another quality, no less characteristic of her French predecessors, and no less rare among the novelists of England.
She is essentially a stylist—a writer whose whole conception
of her art is dominated by stylistic intention. Her style, it is
true, is on the whole poor; it is often heavy and pompous,
sometimes clumsy and indistinct; compared with the style of
such a master as Thackeray it sinks at once into insignificance.

But the interest of her style does not lie in its intrinsic merit so much as in the use to which she puts it. Thackeray's style is mere ornament, existing independently of what he has to say; Mrs. Inchbald's is part and parcel of her matter. The result is that when, in moments of inspiration, she rises to the height of her opportunity, when, mastering her material, she invests her expression with the whole intensity of her feeling and her thought, then she achieves effects of the rarest beauty—effects of a kind for which one may search through Thackeray in vain. The most triumphant of these passages is the scene on the staircase of Elmwood House—a passage which would be spoilt by quotation and which no one who has ever read it could forget. But the same quality is to be found throughout her work. 'Oh, Miss Woodley!' exclaims Miss Milner, forced at last to confess to her friend what she feels towards Dorriforth, 'I love him with all the passion of a mistress, and with all the tenderness of a wife.' No young lady, even in the eighteenth century, ever gave utterance to such a sentence as that. It is the sentence, not of a speaker, but of a writer; and yet, for that very reason, it is delightful, and comes to us charged with a curious sense of emotion, which is none the less real for its elaboration. In *Nature and Art*, Mrs. Inchbald's second novel, the climax of the story is told in a series of short paragraphs, which, for bitterness and concentration of style, are almost reminiscent of Stendhal:

'The jury consulted for a few minutes. The verdict was "Guilty."'

'She heard it with composure.'

'But when William placed the fatal velvet on his head and rose to pronounce sentence, she started with a kind of convulsive motion, retreated a step or two back, and, lifting up her hands with a scream, exclaimed—

' "Oh, not from *you*!"'

'The piercing shriek which accompanied these words prevented their being heard by part of the audience; and those who heard them thought little of their meaning, more than that they expressed her fear of dying.

'Serene and dignified, as if no such exclamation had been uttered, William delivered the fatal speech, ending with "Dead, dead, dead."

'She fainted as he closed the period, and was carried back to prison in a swoon; while he adjourned the court to go to dinner.'

Here, no doubt, there is a touch of melodrama; but it is the melodrama of a rhetorician, and, in that fine 'She heard it with composure,' genius has brushed aside the forced and the obvious, to express, with supreme directness, the anguish of a soul.

For, in spite of Mrs. Inchbald's artificialities, in spite of her lack of that kind of realistic description which seems to modern readers the very blood and breath of a good story, she has the power of doing what, after all, only a very few indeed of her fellow-craftsmen have ever been able to do—she can bring into her pages the living pressure of a human passion, she can invest, if not with realism, with something greater than realism—with the sense of reality itself—the pains, the triumphs, and the agitations of the human heart. 'The heart,' to use the old-fashioned phrase—there is Mrs. Inchbald's empire, there is the sphere of her glory and her command. Outside of it, her powers are weak and fluctuating. She has no firm grasp of the masculine elements in character: she wishes to draw a rough man, Sandford, and she draws a rude one; she tries her hand at a hero, Rushbrook, and she turns out a prig. Her humour is not faulty, but it is exceedingly slight. What an immortal figure the dim Mrs. Horton would have become in the hands of Jane Austen! In *Nature and Art* her attempts at social satire are superficial and overstrained. But weaknesses of this kind—and it would be easy to prolong the list—are what every reader of the following pages will notice without difficulty, and what no wise one will regard. 'Il ne faut point juger des hommes par ce qu'ils ignorent, mais par ce qu'ils savent'; and Mrs. Inchbald's knowledge was as profound as it was limited. Her Miss Milner is an original and brilliant creation, compact of charm and life. She is a flirt, and a flirt not only adorable, but worthy of adoration. Did Mrs. Inchbald take the suggestion of a heroine with imperfections from the little masterpiece which, on more sides than one, closely touches hers—*Manon Lescaut*? Perhaps; and yet, if this was so, the borrowing was of the slightest, for it is only in the fact that she *is* imperfect that Miss Milner bears to Manon any resemblance at all. In every other respect the English heroine is the precise contrary of the French one: she is a creature of fiery will, of high bearing, of noble disposition; and her shortcomings are born, not of weakness, but of excess of strength. Mrs. Inchbald has taken this character, she has thrown it under the influence of a violent and absorbing passion, and, upon that theme, she has written her delicate, sympathetic, and artificial book.

As one reads it, one cannot but feel that it is, if not directly and circumstantially, at least in essence, autobiographical. One finds oneself speculating over the author, wondering what was her history, and how much of it was Miss Milner's. Unfortunately, the greater part of what we should most like to know of Mrs. Inchbald's life has vanished beyond recovery. She wrote her Memoirs, and she burnt them; and who can tell whether even there we should have found a self-revelation? Confessions are sometimes curiously discreet, and, in the case of Mrs. Inchbald, we may be sure that it is only what was indiscreet that would really be worth the hearing. Yet her life is not devoid of interest. A brief sketch of it may be welcome to her readers.

Elizabeth Inchbald was born on the 15th of October, 1753, at Standingfield, near Bury St. Edmunds in Suffolk,[1] one of the numerous offspring of John and Mary Simpson. The Simpsons, who were Roman Catholics, held a moderate farm in Standingfield, and ranked among the gentry of the neighbourhood. In Elizabeth's eighth year her father died;

---

[1] The following account is based upon the *Memoirs of Mrs. Inchbald, including her familiar correspondence with the most distinguished persons of her time*, edited by James Boaden, Esq.—a discursive, vague, and not unamusing book.

but the family continued at the farm, the elder daughters marrying and settling in London, while Elizabeth grew up into a beautiful and charming girl. One misfortune, however, interfered with her happiness—a defect of utterance which during her early years rendered her speech so indistinct as to be unintelligible to strangers. She devoted herself to reading and to dreams of the great world. At thirteen, she declared she would rather die than live longer without seeing the world; she longed to go to London; she longed to go upon the stage. When, in 1770, one of her brothers became an actor at Norwich, she wrote secretly to his manager, Mr. Griffith, begging for an engagement. Mr. Griffith was encouraging, and, though no definite steps were taken, she was sufficiently charmed with him to write out his name at length in her diary, with the inscription 'Each dear letter of thy name is harmony.' Was Mr. Griffith the hero of the company as well as its manager? That, at any rate, was clearly Miss Simpson's opinion; but she soon had other distractions. In the following year she paid a visit to her married sisters in London, where she met another actor, Mr. Inchbald, who seems immediately to have fallen in love with her, and to have proposed. She remained cool. 'In spite of your eloquent pen,' she wrote to him, with a touch of that sharp and almost bitter sense that was always hers, 'matrimony still appears to me with less charms than terrors; the bliss arising from it, I doubt not, is superior to any other—but best not to be ventured for (in my opinion), till some little time have proved the emptiness of all other; which it seldom fails to do.' Nevertheless, the correspondence continued, and, early in 1772, some entries in her diary give a glimpse of her state of mind:

Jan. 22. Saw Mr. Griffith's picture.

Jan. 28. Stole it.

Jan. 29. Rather disappointed at not receiving a letter from Mr. Inchbald.

A few months later she did the great deed of her life: she stepped secretly into the Norwich coach, and went to London. The days that followed were full of hazard and adventure, but the details of them are uncertain. She was a girl of eighteen absolutely alone, and astonishingly attractive—'tall,' we are told, 'slender, straight, of the purest complexion, and most beautiful features; her hair of a golden auburn, her eyes full at once of spirit and sweetness'; and it was only to be expected that, in such circumstances, romance and daring would soon give place to discomfort and alarm. She attempted in vain to obtain a theatrical engagement; she found herself, more than once, obliged to shift her lodging; and at last, after ten days of trepidation, she was reduced to apply for help to her married sisters. This put an end to her difficulties, but, in spite of her efforts to avoid notice, her beauty had already attracted attention, and she had received a letter from a stranger, with whom she immediately entered into correspondence. She had all the boldness of innocence, and, in addition, a force of character which brought her safely through the risks she ran. While she was still in her solitary lodging, a theatrical manager, named Dodd, attempted to use his position as a cover for seduction. She had several interviews with him alone, and the story goes that, in the last, she snatched up a basin of hot water and dashed it in his face. But she was not to go unprotected for long; for within two months of her arrival in London she had married Mr. Inchbald.

The next twelve years of Mrs. Inchbald's life were passed amid the rough-and-tumble of the eighteenth-century stage. Her husband was thirty-seven when she married him, a Roman Catholic like herself, and an actor who depended for his living upon ill-paid and uncertain provincial engagements. Mrs. Inchbald conquered her infirmity of speech and threw herself into her husband's profession. She accompanied him to Bristol, to Scotland, to Liverpool, to Birmingham, appearing in a great variety of rôles, but never with any very conspicuous success. The record of these journeys throws an interesting light upon the conditions of the provincial companies of those days. Mrs. Inchbald and her companions would set out to walk from one Scotch town to another: they would think themselves lucky if they could climb on to a

passing cart, to arrive at last, drenched with rain perhaps, at
some wretched hostelry. But this kind of barbarism did not
stand in the way of an almost childish gaiety. In Yorkshire,
we find the Inchbalds, the Siddonses, and Kemble retiring
to the moors, in the intervals of business, to play blind man's
buff or puss-in-the-corner. Such were the pastimes of Mrs.
Siddons before the days of her fame. No doubt this kind of
lightheartedness was the best antidote to the experience of
being 'saluted with volleys of potatoes and broken bottles,'
as the Siddonses were by the citizens of Liverpool, for having
ventured to appear on their stage without having ever played
before the King. On this occasion the audience, according to
a letter from Kemble to Mrs. Inchbald, 'extinguished all the
lights round the house; then jumped upon the stage; brushed
every lamp out with their hats; took back their money; left
the theatre, and determined themselves to repeat this till they
have another company.' These adventures were diversified by
a journey to Paris, undertaken in the hope that Mr. Inchbald,
who found himself without engagements, might pick up a
livelihood as a painter of miniatures. The scheme came to
nothing, and the Inchbalds eventually went to Hull, where
they returned to their old profession. Here, in 1779, suddenly
and somewhat mysteriously, Mr. Inchbald died. To his
widow the week that followed was one of 'grief, horror, and
almost despair'; but soon, with her old pertinacity, she was
back at her work, settling at last in London, and becoming a
member of the Covent Garden company. Here, for the next
five years, she earned for herself a meagre living, until, quite
unexpectedly, deliverance came. In her moments of leisure
she had been trying her hand upon dramatic composition; she
had written some farces, and, in 1784, one of them, *A Mogul
Tale*, was accepted, acted, and obtained a great success. This
was the turning-point of her career. She followed up her farce
with a series of plays, either original or adapted, which, almost
without exception, were well received, so that she was soon
able to retire from the stage with a comfortable competence.
She had succeeded in life; she was happy, respected, free.

Mrs. Inchbald's plays are so bad that it is difficult to believe that they brought her a fortune. But no doubt it was their faults that made them popular—their sentimentalities, their melodramatic absurdities, their strangely false and high-pitched moral tone. They are written in a jargon which resembles, if it resembles anything, an execrable prose translation from very flat French verse. 'Ah, Manuel!' exclaims one of her heroines, 'I am now amply punished by the Marquis for all my cruelty to Duke Cordunna—he to whom my father in my infancy betrothed me, and to whom I willingly pledged my faith, hoping to wed; till Romono, the Marquis of Romono, came from the field of glory, and with superior claims of person as of fame, seized on my heart by force, and perforce made me feel I had never loved till then.' Which is the more surprising—that actors could be found to utter such speeches, or that audiences could be collected to applaud them? Perhaps, for us, the most memorable fact about Mrs. Inchbald's dramatic work is that one of her adaptations (from the German of Kotzebue) was no other than that *Lovers' Vows* which, as every one knows, was rehearsed so brilliantly at Ecclesford, the seat of the Right Hon. Lord Ravenshaw, in Cornwall, and which, after all, was *not* performed at Sir Thomas Bertram's. But that is an interest *sub specie aeternitatis*; and, from the temporal point of view, Mrs. Inchbald's plays must be regarded merely as means—means towards her own enfranchisement, and that condition of things which made possible *A Simple Story*. That novel had been sketched as early as 1777; but it was not completely written until 1790, and not published until the following year. A second edition was printed immediately, and several more followed; the present reprint is taken from the fourth, published in 1799—but with the addition of the characteristic preface, which, after the second edition, was dropped. The four small volumes of these early editions—with their large type, their ample spacing, their charming flavour of antiquity, delicacy, and rest—may be met with often enough in secluded corners of second-hand bookshops, or on some neglected shelf in the library of a country house. For their own generation, they represented a distinguished title to fame. Mrs. Inchbald—to use the expression of her biographer—'was ascertained to be one of the greatest ornaments of her sex.' She was painted by Lawrence, she was eulogised by Miss Edgeworth, she was complimented by Madame de Staël herself. She had, indeed, won for herself a position which can hardly be paralleled among the women of the eighteenth century—a position of independence and honour, based upon talent, and upon talent alone. In 1796 she published *Nature and Art*, and ten years later appeared her last work—a series of biographical and critical notices prefixed to a large collection of acting plays. During the greater part of the intervening period she lived in lodgings in Leicester Square—or 'Leicester Fields,' as the place was still often called—in a house opposite that of Sir Joshua Reynolds. The economy which she had learnt in her early days she continued to practise, dressing with extraordinary plainness, and often going without a fire in winter, so that she was able, through her self-sacrifice, to keep from want a large band of poor relatives and friends. The society she mixed with was various, but, for the most part, obscure. There were occasional visits from the now triumphant Mrs. Siddons; there were incessant propositions—but, alas! they were equivocal—from Sir Charles Bunbury; for the rest, she passed her life among actor-managers and humble playwrights and unremembered medical men. One of her friends was William Godwin, who described her to Mrs. Shelley as a 'piquante mixture between a lady and a milkmaid,' and who, it is said, suggested part of the plot of *A Simple Story*. But she quarrelled with him when he married Mary Wollstonecraft, after whose death she wrote to him thus: 'With the most sincere sympathy in all you have suffered—with the most perfect forgiveness of all you have said to me, there must nevertheless be an end to our acquaintance *for ever*. I respect your prejudices, but I also respect my own.' Far more intimate were her relations with Dr. Gisborne—a mysterious figure, with whom, in some tragic manner that we can only just discern, was enacted her final romance. His name—often in company with that of another physician, Dr. Warren, for whom, too, she had a passionate affection—occurs frequently among her papers; and her diary for December 17, 1794, has this entry: 'Dr. Gisborne drank tea here, and staid very late: he talked seriously of marrying—but not *me*.' Many years later, one September, she amused herself by making out a list of all the Septembers since her marriage, with brief notes as to her state of mind during each. The list has fortunately survived, and some of the later entries are as follows:

1791. London; after my novel, *Simple Story* . . . very happy.
1792. London; in Leicester Square . . . cheerful, content, and sometimes rather happy. . . .
1794. Extremely happy, but for poor Debby's death.
1795. My brother George's death, and an intimate acquaintance with Dr. Gisborne—not happy. . . .
1797. After an alteration in my teeth, and the death of Dr. Warren—yet far from unhappy.
1798. Happy, but for suspicion amounting almost to certainty of a rapid appearance of age in my face. . . .
1802. After feeling wholly indifferent about Dr. Gisborne—very happy but for ill health, ill looks, &c.
1803. After quitting Leicester Square probably for ever—after caring scarce at all or thinking of Dr. Gisborne . . . very happy. . . .
1806. . . . After the death of Dr. Gisborne, too, often very unhappy, yet mostly cheerful, and on my return to London nearly happy.

The record, with all its quaintness, produces a curious impression of stoicism—of a certain grim acceptance of the facts of life. It would have been a pleasure, certainly, but an alarming pleasure, to have known Mrs. Inchbald.

In the early years of the century she gradually withdrew from London, establishing herself in suburban boarding-houses, often among sisters of charity, and devoting her days to the practice of her religion. In her early and middle life she had been an indifferent Catholic: 'Sunday. Rose late, dressed, and read in the Bible about David, &c.'—this is one of the very few references in her diary to anything approaching a religious observance during many years. But, in her old age, her views changed; her devotions increased with her retirement; and her retirement was at last complete. She died, in an obscure Kensington boarding-house, on August 1, 1821. She was buried in Kensington churchyard. But, if her ghost lingers anywhere, it is not in Kensington: it is in the heart of the London that she had always loved. Yet, even there, how much now would she find to recognise? Mrs. Inchbald's world has passed away from us for ever; and, as we walk there to-day amid the press of the living, it is hard to believe that she too was familiar with Leicester Square.

1908.

THE POETRY OF BLAKE[1]

THE new edition of Blake's poetical works, published by the Clarendon Press, will be welcomed by every lover of English poetry. The volume is worthy of the great university under whose auspices it has been produced, and of the great artist whose words it will help to perpetuate. Blake has been, hitherto, singularly unfortunate in his editors. With a single exception, every edition of his poems up to the present time has contained a multitude of textual errors which, in the case of any other writer of equal eminence, would have been well-nigh inconceivable. The great majority of these errors were not the result of accident: they were the result of deliberate falsification. Blake's text has been emended and corrected and 'improved,' so largely and so habitually, that there was a very real danger of its becoming permanently corrupted; and this danger was all the more serious, since the work of mutilation was carried on to an accompaniment of fervent admiration of the poet. 'It is not a little bewildering,' says Mr. Sampson, the present editor, 'to find one great poet and critic extolling Blake for the "glory of metre" and "the sonorous beauty of lyrical work" in the two opening lyrics of the *Songs of Experience*, while he introduces into the five short stanzas quoted no less than seven emendations of his own, involving additions of syllables and important changes of meaning.' This is Procrustes admiring the exquisite proportions of his victim. As one observes the countless instances accumulated in Mr. Sampson's notes, of the clippings and filings to which the free and spontaneous expression of Blake's genius has been

[1] *The Poetical Works of William Blake. A new and verbatim text from the manuscript, engraved, and letter-press originals, with variorum readings and bibliographical notes and prefaces.* By John Sampson, Librarian in the University of Liverpool. Oxford: At the Clarendon Press, 1905.

The Lyrical Poems of William Blake. Text by John Sampson, with an Introduction by Walter Raleigh. Oxford: At the Clarendon Press, 1905.

subjected, one is reminded of a verse in one of his own lyrics, where he speaks of the beautiful garden in which—

> Priests in black gowns were walking their rounds,
> And binding with briers my joys and desires;

and one cannot help hazarding the conjecture, that Blake's prophetic vision recognised, in the lineaments of the 'priests in black gowns,' most of his future editors. Perhaps, though, if Blake's prescience had extended so far as this, he would have taken a more drastic measure; and we shudder to think of the sort of epigram with which the editorial efforts of his worshippers might have been rewarded. The present edition, however, amply compensates for the past. Mr. Sampson gives us, in the first place, the correct and entire text of the poems, so printed as to afford easy reading to those who desire access to the text and nothing more. At the same time, in a series of notes and prefaces, he has provided an elaborate commentary, containing, besides all the variorum readings, a great mass of bibliographical and critical matter; and, in addition, he has enabled the reader to obtain a clue through the labyrinth of Blake's mythology, by means of ample quotations from those passages in the *Prophetic Books*, which throw light upon the obscurities of the poems. The most important Blake document—the Rossetti MS.—has been freshly collated, with the generous aid of the owner, Mr. W. A. White, to whom the gratitude of the public is due in no common measure; and the long-lost Pickering MS.—the sole authority for some of the most mystical and absorbing of the poems—was, with deserved good fortune, discovered by Mr. Sampson in time for collation in the present edition. Thus there is hardly a line in the volume which has not been reproduced from an original, either written or engraved by the hand of Blake. Mr. Sampson's minute and ungrudging care, his high critical acumen, and the skill with which he has brought his wide knowledge of the subject to bear upon the difficulties of the text, combine to make his edition a noble and splendid monument of English scholarship. It will be long indeed before the poems of Blake cease to afford matter for fresh discussions and commentaries and interpretations; but it is safe to predict that, so far as their form is concerned, they will henceforward remain unchanged. There will be no room for further editing. The work has been done by Mr. Sampson, once and for all.

In the case of Blake, a minute exactitude of text is particularly important, for more than one reason. Many of his effects depend upon subtle differences of punctuation and of spelling, which are too easily lost in reproduction. 'Tiger, tiger, burning bright,' is the ordinary version of one of his most celebrated lines. But in Blake's original engraving the words appear thus—'Tyger! Tyger! burning bright'; and who can fail to perceive the difference? Even more remarkable is the change which the omission of a single stop has produced in the last line of one of the succeeding stanzas of the same poem.

> And what shoulder, and what art,
> Could twist the sinews of thy heart?
> And when thy heart began to beat,
> What dread hand? and what dread feet?

So Blake engraved the verse; and, as Mr. Sampson points out, 'the terrible, compressed force' of the final line vanishes to nothing in the 'languid punctuation' of subsequent editions:— 'What dread hand and what dread feet?' It is hardly an exaggeration to say, that the re-discovery of this line alone would have justified the appearance of the present edition.

But these considerations of what may be called the mechanics of Blake's poetry are not—important as they are— the only justification for scrupulous adherence to his autograph text. Blake's use of language was not guided by the ordinarily accepted rules of writing; he allowed himself to be trammelled neither by prosody nor by grammar; he wrote, with an extraordinary audacity, according to the mysterious dictates of his own strange and intimate conception of the beautiful and the just. Thus his compositions, amenable to no other laws than those of his own making, fill a unique place in the poetry of the world. They are the rebels and atheists of literature, or rather, they are the sanctuaries of an Unknown God; and to invoke that deity by means of orthodox incantations is to run the risk of hell fire. Editors may punctuate afresh the text of Shakespeare with impunity, and perhaps even with advantage; but add a comma to the text of Blake, and you put all Heaven in a rage. You have laid your hands upon the Ark of the Covenant. Nor is this all. When once, in the case of Blake, the slightest deviation has been made from the authoritative version, it is hardly possible to stop there. The emendator is on an inclined plane which leads him inevitably from readjustments of punctuation to corrections of grammar, and from corrections of grammar to alterations of rhythm; if he is in for a penny, he is in for a pound. The first poem in the Rossetti MS. may be adduced as one instance— out of the enormous number which fill Mr. Sampson's notes —of the dangers of editorial laxity.

> I told my love, I told my love,
>   I told her all my heart;
> Trembling, cold, in ghastly fears,
>   Ah! she doth depart.

This is the first half of the poem; and editors have been contented with an alteration of stops, and the change of 'doth' into 'did.' But their work was not over; they had, as it were, tasted blood; and their version of the last four lines of the poem is as follows:

> Soon after she was gone from me,
>   A traveller came by,
> Silently, invisibly:
>   He took her with a sigh.

Reference to the MS., however, shows that the last line had been struck out by Blake, and another substituted in its place —a line which is now printed for the first time by Mr. Sampson. So that the true reading of the verse is:

> Soon as she was gone from me,
>   A traveller came by,
> Silently, invisibly—
>   O! was no deny.

After these exertions, it must have seemed natural enough to Rossetti and his successors to print four other expunged lines as part of the poem, and to complete the business by clapping a title to their decoction—'Love's Secret'—a title which there is no reason to suppose had ever entered the poet's mind.

Besides illustrating the shortcomings of his editors, this little poem is an admirable instance of Blake's most persistent quality—his triumphant freedom from conventional restraints. His most characteristic passages are at once so unexpected and so complete in their effect, that the reader is moved by them, spontaneously, to some conjecture of 'inspiration.' Sir Walter Raleigh, indeed, in his interesting Introduction to a smaller edition of the poems, protests against such attributions of peculiar powers to Blake, or indeed to any other poet. 'No man,' he says, 'destitute of genius, could live for a day.' But even if we all agree to be inspired together, we must still admit that there are degrees of inspiration; if Mr. F's Aunt was a woman of genius, what are we to say of Hamlet? And Blake, in the hierarchy of the inspired, stands very high indeed. If one could strike an average among poets, it would probably be true to say that, so far as inspiration is concerned, Blake is to the average poet, as the average poet is to the man in the street. All poetry, to be poetry at all, must have the power of making one, now and then, involuntarily ejaculate: 'What made him think of that?' With Blake, one is asking the question all the time.

Blake's originality of manner was not, as has sometimes been the case, a cloak for platitude. What he has to say belongs no less distinctly to a mind of astonishing self-dependence than his way of saying it. In English literature, as Sir Walter Raleigh observes, he 'stands outside the regular line of succession.' All that he had in common with the great leaders of the Romantic Movement was an abhorrence of the conventionality and the rationalism of the eighteenth century; for the eighteenth century itself was hardly more alien to his spirit than that exaltation of Nature—the 'Vegetable Universe,' as he called it—from which sprang the pantheism of Wordsworth and the paganism of Keats. 'Nature is the work of the Devil,' he exclaimed one day; 'the Devil is in us as far as we are Nature.' There was no part of the sensible world which, in his philosophy, was not impregnated with vileness. Even the 'ancient heavens' were not, to his uncompromising vision, 'fresh and strong'; they were 'writ with Curses from Pole to Pole,' and destined to vanish into nothingness with the triumph of the Everlasting Gospel.

There are doubtless many to whom Blake is known simply as a charming and splendid lyrist, as the author of *Infant Joy*, and *The Tyger*, and the rest of the *Songs of Innocence and Experience*. These poems show but faint traces of any system of philosophy; but, to a reader of the Rossetti and Pickering MSS., the presence of a hidden and symbolic meaning in Blake's words becomes obvious enough—a meaning which receives its fullest expression in the *Prophetic Books*. It was only natural that the extraordinary nature of Blake's utterance in these latter works should have given rise to the belief that he was merely an inspired idiot—a madman who happened to be able to write good verses. That belief, made finally impossible by Mr. Swinburne's elaborate Essay, is now, happily, nothing more than a curiosity of literary history; and indeed signs are not wanting that the whirligig of Time, which left Blake for so long in the Paradise of Fools, is now about to place him among the Prophets. Anarchy is the most fashionable of creeds; and Blake's writings, according to Sir Walter Raleigh, contain a complete exposition of its doctrines. The same critic asserts that Blake was 'one of the most consistent of English poets and thinkers.' This is high praise indeed; but there seems to be some ambiguity in it. It is one thing to give Blake credit for that sort of consistency which lies in the repeated enunciation of the same body of beliefs throughout a large mass of compositions and over a long period of time, and which could never be possessed by a madman or an incoherent charlatan. It is quite another thing to assert that his doctrines form in themselves a consistent whole, in the sense in which that quality would be ordinarily attributed to a system of philosophy. Does Sir Walter mean to assert that Blake is, in this sense too, 'consistent'? It is a little difficult to discover. Referring, in his Introduction, to Blake's abusive notes on Bacon's *Essays*, he speaks of—

The sentimental enthusiast, who worships all great men indifferently, [and who] finds himself in a distressful position when his gods fall out among themselves. His case [Sir Walter wittily adds] is not much unlike that of Terah, the father of Abraham, who (if the legend be true) was a dealer in idols among the Chaldees, and, coming home to his shop one day, after a brief absence, found that the idols had quarrelled, and the biggest of them had smashed the rest to atoms. Blake is a dangerous idol for any man to keep in his shop.

We wonder very much whether he is kept in Sir Walter Raleigh's.

It seems clear, at any rate, that no claim for a 'consistency' which would imply freedom from self-contradiction can be validly made for Blake. His treatment of the problem of evil is enough to show how very far he was from that clarity of thought without which even prophets are liable, when the time comes, to fall into disrepute. 'Plato,' said Blake, 'knew of nothing but the virtues and vices, and good and evil. There is nothing in all that. Everything is good in God's eyes.' And this is the perpetual burden of his teaching. 'Satan's empire is the empire of nothing'; there is no such thing as evil—it is a mere 'negation.' And the 'moral virtues,' which attempt to discriminate between right and wrong, are the idlest of delusions; they are merely 'allegories and dissimulations,' they 'do not exist.' Such was one of the most fundamental of Blake's doctrines; but it requires only a superficial acquaintance with his writings to recognise that their whole tenour is an implicit contradiction of this very belief. Every page he wrote contains a moral exhortation; bad thoughts and bad feelings raised in him a fury of rage and indignation which the bitterest of satirists never surpassed. His epigrams on Reynolds are masterpieces of virulent abuse; the punishment which he devised for Klopstock—his impersonation of 'flaccid fluency

10

and devout sentiment'—is unprintable; as for those who attempt to enforce moral laws, they shall be 'cast out,' for they 'crucify Christ with the head downwards.' The contradiction is indeed glaring. 'There is no such thing as wickedness,' Blake says in effect, 'and you are wicked if you think there is.' If it is true that evil does not exist, all Blake's denunciations are so much empty chatter; and, on the other hand, if there is a real distinction between good and bad, if everything, in fact, is *not* good in God's eyes—then why not say so? Really Blake, as politicians say, 'cannot have it both ways.'

But of course, his answer to all this is simple enough. To judge him according to the light of reason is to make an appeal to a tribunal whose jurisdiction he had always refused to recognise as binding. In fact, to Blake's mind, the laws of reason were nothing but a horrible phantasm deluding and perplexing mankind, from whose clutches it is the business of every human soul to free itself as speedily as possible. Reason is the 'Spectre' of Blake's mythology, that Spectre, which, he says,

> Around me night and day
> Like a wild beast guards my way.

It is a malignant spirit, for ever struggling with the 'Emanation,' or imaginative side of man, whose triumph is the supreme end of the universe. Ever since the day when, in his childhood, Blake had seen God's forehead at the window, he had found in imaginative vision the only reality and the only good. He beheld the things of this world 'not with, but through, the eye':

> With my inward Eye, 'tis an old Man grey,
> With my outward, a Thistle across my way

It was to the imagination, and the imagination alone, that Blake yielded the allegiance of his spirit. His attitude towards reason was the attitude of the mystic; and it involved an inevitable dilemma. He never could, in truth, quite shake himself free of his 'Spectre'; struggle as he would, he could not

escape altogether from the employment of the ordinary forms
of thought and speech; he is constantly arguing, as if argument
were really a means of approaching the truth; he was subdued
to what he worked in. As in his own poem, he had, somehow
or other, been locked into a crystal cabinet—the world of the
senses and of reason—a gilded, artificial, gimcrack dwelling,
after 'the wild' where he had danced so merrily before.

> I strove to seize the inmost Form
> > With ardour fierce and hands of flame,
> But burst the Crystal Cabinet,
> > And like a Weeping Babe became—

> A weeping Babe upon the wild. . . .

To be able to lay hands upon 'the inmost form,' one must
achieve the impossible; one must be inside and outside the
crystal cabinet at the same time. But Blake was not to be
turned aside by such considerations. He would have it both
ways; and whoever demurred was crucifying Christ with the
head downwards.

Besides its unreasonableness, there is an even more serious
objection to Blake's mysticism—and indeed to all mysticism:
its lack of humanity. The mystic's creed—even when arrayed
in the wondrous and ecstatic beauty of Blake's verse—comes
upon the ordinary man, in the rigidity of its uncompromising
elevation, with a shock which is terrible, and almost cruel.
The sacrifices which it demands are too vast, in spite of the
divinity of what it has to offer. What shall it profit a man, one
is tempted to exclaim, if he gain his own soul, and lose the
whole world? The mystic ideal is the highest of all; but it has
no breadth. The following lines express, with a simplicity and
an intensity of inspiration which he never surpassed, Blake's
conception of that ideal:

> And throughout all Eternity
> I forgive you, you forgive me.
> As our dear Redeemer said:
> 'This the Wine, & this the Bread.'

It is easy to imagine the sort of comments to which Voltaire, for instance, with his 'wracking wheel' of sarcasm and common-sense, would have subjected such lines as these. His criticism would have been irrelevant, because it would never have reached the heart of the matter at issue; it would have been based upon no true understanding of Blake's words. But that they do admit of a real, an unanswerable criticism, it is difficult to doubt. Charles Lamb, perhaps, might have made it; incidentally, indeed, he has. 'Sun, and sky, and breeze, and solitary walks, and summer holidays, and the greenness of fields, and the delicious juices of meats and fishes, and society, and the cheerful glass, and candle-light, and fireside conversations, and innocent vanities, and jests, and *irony itself*'— do these things form no part of your Eternity?

The truth is plain: Blake was an intellectual drunkard. His words come down to us in a rapture of broken fluency from impossible intoxicated heights. His spirit soared above the empyrean; and, even as it soared, it stumbled in the gutter of Felpham. His lips brought forth, in the same breath, in the same inspired utterance, the *Auguries of Innocence* and the epigrams on Sir Joshua Reynolds. He was in no condition to chop logic, or to take heed of the existing forms of things. In the imaginary portrait of himself, prefixed to Sir Walter Raleigh's volume, we can see him, as he appeared to his own 'inward eye,' staggering between the abyss and the star of Heaven, his limbs cast abroad, his head thrown back in an ecstasy of intoxication, so that, to the frenzy of his rolling vision, the whole universe is upside down. We look, and, as we gaze at the strange image and listen to the marvellous melody, we are almost tempted to go and do likewise.

But it is not as a prophet, it is as an artist, that Blake deserves the highest honours and the most enduring fame. In spite of his hatred of the 'vegetable universe,' his poems possess the inexplicable and spontaneous quality of natural objects; they are more like the works of Heaven than the works of man. They have, besides, the two most obvious characteristics of Nature—loveliness and power. In some of his lyrics there is an exquisite simplicity, which seems, like a flower or a child, to be unconscious of itself. In his poem of *The Birds*—to mention, out of many, perhaps a less known instance—it is not the poet that one hears, it is the birds themselves.

> O thou summer's harmony,
> I have lived and mourned for thee;
> Each day I mourn along the wood,
> And night hath heard my sorrows loud.

In his other mood—the mood of elemental force—Blake produces effects which are unique in literature. His mastery of the mysterious suggestions which lie concealed in words is complete.

> He who torments the Chafer's Sprite
> Weaves a Bower in endless Night.

What dark and terrible visions the last line calls up! And, with the aid of this control over the secret springs of language, he is able to produce in poetry those vast and vague effects of gloom, of foreboding, and of terror, which seem to be proper to music alone. Sometimes his words are heavy with the doubtful horror of an approaching thunderstorm:

> The Guests are scattered thro' the land,
> For the Eye altering alters all;
> The Senses roll themselves in fear,
> And the flat Earth becomes a Ball;

> The Stars, Sun, Moon, all shrink away,
> A desart vast without a bound,
> And nothing left to eat or drink,
> And dark desart all around.

And sometimes Blake invests his verses with a sense of name-less and infinite ruin, such as one feels when the drum and the violin mysteriously come together, in one of Beethoven's Symphonies, to predict the annihilation of worlds:

> On the shadows of the Moon,
> Climbing through Night's highest noon:
> In Time's Ocean falling, drowned:
> In Aged Ignorance profound,

Holy and cold, I clipp'd the Wings
Of all Sublunary Things:
But when once I did descry
The Immortal Man that cannot Die,
Thro' evening shades I haste away
To close the Labours of my Day.
The Door of Death I open found,
And the Worm Weaving in the Ground:
Thou'rt my Mother, from the Womb;
Wife, Sister, Daughter, to the Tomb:
Weaving to Dreams the Sexual strife,
And weeping over the Web of Life.

Such music is not to be lightly mouthed by mortals; for us, in our weakness, a few strains of it, now and then, amid the murmur of ordinary converse, are enough. For Blake's words will always be strangers on this earth; they could only fall with familiarity from the lips of his own Gods:

above Time's troubled fountains,
On the great Atlantic Mountains,
In my Golden House on high.

They belong to the language of Los and Rahab and Enitharmon; and their mystery is revealed for ever in the land of the Sunflower's desire.

1906.

HENRI BEYLE

In the whole of French literature it would be difficult to point to a figure at once so important, so remarkable, and so little known to English readers as Henri Beyle. Most of us are, no doubt, fairly familiar with his pseudonym of 'Stendhal'; some of us have read *Le Rouge et Le Noir* and *La Chartreuse de Parme*; but how many of us have any further knowledge of a man whose works are at the present moment appearing in Paris in all the pomp of an elaborate and complete edition, every scrap of whose manuscripts is being collected and deciphered with enthusiastic care, and in honour of whose genius the literary periodicals of the hour are filling entire numbers with exegesis and appreciation? The eminent critic, M. André Gide, when asked lately to name the novel which stands in his opinion first among the novels of France, declared that since, without a doubt, the place belongs to one or other of the novels of Stendhal, his only difficulty was in making his choice among these; and he finally decided upon *La Chartreuse de Parme*. According to this high authority, Henri Beyle was indisputably the creator of the greatest work of fiction in the French language, yet on this side of the Channel we have hardly more than heard of him! Nor is it merely as a writer that Beyle is admired in France. As a man, he seems to have come in, sixty or seventy years after his death, for a singular devotion. There are 'Beylistes,' or 'Stendhaliens,' who dwell with rapture upon every detail of the master's private life, who extend with pious care the long catalogue of his amorous adventures, who discuss the shades of his character with the warmth of personal friendship, and register his opinions with a zeal which is hardly less than sectarian. But indeed it is precisely in these extremes of his French devotees that we shall find a clue to the explanation of our own indifference. Beyle's mind contained, in a highly exaggerated form, most of the peculiarly distinctive elements of the French character. This does not mean that he was a typical Frenchman; far from it. He did not, like Voltaire or Hugo, strike a note to which the whole national genius vibrated in response. He has never been, it is unlikely that he ever will be, a popular writer. His literary reputation in France has been confined, until perhaps quite lately, to a small distinguished circle. 'On me lira,' he was fond of saying, 'vers 1880'; and the 'Beylistes' point to the remark in triumph as one further proof of the almost divine prescience of the great man. But in truth Beyle was always read by the *élite* of French critics and writers—'the happy few,' as he used to call them; and among these he has never been without enthusiastic admirers. During his lifetime Balzac, in an enormous eulogy of *La Chartreuse de Parme*, paid him one of the most magnificent compliments ever received by a man of letters from a fellow craftsman. In the next generation Taine declared himself his disciple; a little later—'vers 1880,' in fact—we find Zola describing him as 'notre père à tous,' and M. Bourget followed with elaborate incense. To-day we have writers of such different tendencies as M. Barrès and M. Gide acclaiming him as a supreme master, and the fashionable idolatry of the 'Beylistes.' Yet, at the same time, running parallel to this stream of homage, it is easy to trace a line of opinion of a totally different kind. It is the opinion of the more solid, the more middle-class elements of French life. Thus Sainte-Beuve, in two characteristic 'Lundis,' poured a great deal of very tepid water upon Balzac's flaming panegyric. Then Flaubert—'vers 1880,' too—confessed that he could see very little in Stendhal. And, only a few years ago, M. Chuquet, of the Institute, took the trouble to compose a thick book in which he has collected with scrupulous detail all the known facts concerning the life and writings of a man whom he forthwith proceeds to damn through five hundred pages of faint praise. These discrepancies are curious: how can we account for such odd differences of taste? How are we to reconcile the admiration of Balzac with the dislike of Flaubert, the raptures of M. Bourget and M. Barrès with the sniffs of Sainte-Beuve and M. Chuquet of the Institute? The explanation seems to be that Beyle occupies a position in France analogous to that of Shelley in England. Shelley is not a national hero, not because he lacked the distinctive qualities of an Englishman, but for the opposite reason—because he possessed so many of them in an extreme degree. The idealism, the daring, the imagination, and the unconventionality which give Shakespeare, Nelson, and Dr. Johnson their place in our pantheon —all these were Shelley's, but they were his in too undiluted and intense a form, with the result that, while he will never fail of worshippers among us, there will also always be Englishmen unable to appreciate him at all. Such, *mutatis mutandis*—and in this case the proviso is a very large one—is the position of Beyle in France. After all, when Bunthorne asked for a not-too-French French bean he showed more commonsense than he intended. Beyle is a too-French French writer—too French even for the bulk of his own compatriots; and so for us it is only natural that he should be a little difficult. Yet this very fact is in itself no bad reason for giving him some attention. An understanding of this very Gallic individual might give us a new insight into the whole strange race. And besides, the curious creature is worth looking at for his own sake too.

But, when one tries to catch him and pin him down on the dissecting-table, he turns out to be exasperatingly elusive. Even his most fervent admirers cannot agree among themselves as to the true nature of his achievements. Balzac thought of him as an artist, Taine was captivated by his conception of history, M. Bourget adores him as a psychologist, M. Barrès lays stress upon his 'sentiment d'honneur,' and the 'Beylistes' see in him the embodiment of modernity. Certainly very few writers have had the good fortune to appeal at once so constantly and in so varied a manner to succeeding generations as Henri Beyle. The circumstances of his life no doubt in part account for the complexity of his genius. He was born in 1783, when the *ancien régime* was still in full swing; his early manhood was spent in the turmoil of the Napoleonic wars; he lived to see the Bourbon reaction, the Romantic revival, the revolution of 1830, and the establishment of Louis Philippe; and when he died, at the age of sixty, the nineteenth century was nearly half-way through. Thus his life exactly spans the interval between the old world and the new. His family, which belonged to the magistracy of Grenoble, preserved the living tradition of the eighteenth century. His grandfather was a polite, amiable, periwigged sceptic after the manner of Fontenelle, who always spoke of 'M. de Voltaire' with a smile 'mélangé de respect et d'affection'; and when the Terror came, two representatives of the people were sent down to Grenoble, with the result that Beyle's father was pronounced (with a hundred and fifty others) 'notoirement suspect' of disaffection to the Republic, and confined to his house. At the age of sixteen Beyle arrived in Paris, just after the *coup d'état* of the 18th Brumaire had made Bonaparte First Consul, and he immediately came under the influence of his cousin Daru, that extraordinary man to whose terrific energies was due the organisation of Napoleon's greatest armies, and whose leisure moments—for apparently he had leisure moments—were devoted to the composition of idylls in the style of Tibullus and to an enormous correspondence on literary topics with the poetasters of the day. It was as a subordinate to this remarkable personage that Beyle spent nearly the whole of the next fifteen years of his life—in Paris, in Italy, in Germany, in Russia—wherever the whirling tempest of the Napoleonic policy might happen to carry him. His actual military experience was considerably slighter than what, in after years, he liked to give his friends to understand it had been. For hardly more than a year, during the Italian campaign, he was in the army as a lieutenant of dragoons: the rest of his public service was spent in the commissariat department. The descriptions which he afterwards delighted to give of his adventures at Marengo, at Jéna, at Wagram, or at the crossing of the Niémen have been shown by M. Chuquet's unkind researches to have been imaginary. Beyle was present at only one great battle—Bautzen. 'Nous voyons fort bien,' he wrote in his journal on the following day, 'de midi à trois heures, tout ce qu'on peut voir d'une bataille, c'est à dire rien.' He was, however, at Moscow in 1812, and he accompanied the army through the horrors of the retreat. When the conflagration had broken out in the city he had abstracted from one of the deserted palaces a finely bound copy of the *Facéties* of Voltaire; the book helped to divert his mind as he lay crouched by the campfire through the terrible nights that followed; but, as his companions showed their disapproval of anyone who could smile over Akakia and Pompignan in such a situation, one day he left the red-morocco volume behind him in the snow.

The fall of Napoleon threw Beyle out of employment, and the period of his literary activity began. His books were not successful; his fortune gradually dwindled; and he drifted in Paris and Italy, and even in England, more and more disconsolately, with thoughts of suicide sometimes in his head. But in 1830 the tide of his fortunes turned. The revolution of July, by putting his friends into power, brought him a competence in the shape of an Italian consulate; and in the same year he gained for the first time some celebrity by the publication of *Le Rouge et Le Noir*. The rest of his life was spent in the easy discharge of his official duties at Civita Vecchia, alternating with periods of leave—one of them lasted for three years—spent in Paris among his friends, of whom the most distinguished was Prosper Mérimée. In 1839 appeared his last published work—*La Chartreuse de Parme*; and three years later he died suddenly in Paris. His epitaph, composed by himself with the utmost care, was as follows:

QUI GIACE
ARRIGO BEYLE MILANESE
VISSE, SCRISSE, AMO.

The words, read rightly, indicate many things—his adoration of Italy and Milan, his eccentricity, his scorn of the conventions of society and the limits of nationality, his adventurous life, his devotion to literature, and, lastly, the fact that, through all the varieties of his experience—in the earliest years of his childhood, in his agitated manhood, in his calm old age—there had never been a moment when he was not in love.

Beyle's work falls into two distinct groups—the first consisting of his novels, and the second of his miscellaneous writings, which include several biographies, a dissertation on Love, some books of criticism and travel, his letters and various autobiographical fragments. The bulk of the latter group is large; much of it has only lately seen the light; and more of it, at present in MS. at the library of Grenoble, is promised us by the indefatigable editors of the new complete edition which is now appearing in Paris. The interest of this portion of Beyle's writings is almost entirely personal: that of his novels is mainly artistic. It was as a novelist that Beyle first gained his celebrity, and it is still as a novelist—or rather as the author of *Le Rouge et Le Noir* and *La Chartreuse de Parme* (for an earlier work, *Armance*, some short stories, and some later posthumous fragments may be left out of account) —that he is most widely known to-day. These two remarkable works lose none of their significance if we consider the time at which they were composed. It was in the full flood of the Romantic revival, that marvellous hour in the history of French literature when the tyranny of two centuries was shattered for ever, and a boundless wealth of inspirations, possibilities, and beauties before undreamt-of suddenly burst upon the view. It was the hour of Hugo, Vigny, Musset, Gautier, Balzac, with their new sonorities and golden cadences, their new lyric passion and dramatic stress, their new virtuosities, their new impulse towards the strange and the magnificent, their new desire for diversity and the manifold comprehension of life. But, if we turn to the contemporaneous pages of Stendhal, what do we find? We find a succession of colourless, unemphatic sentences; we find cold reasoning and exact narrative; we find polite irony and dry wit. The spirit of the eighteenth century is everywhere; and if the old gentleman with the perruque and the 'M. de

Voltaire' could have taken a glance at his grandson's novels, he would have rapped his snuff-box and approved. It is true that Beyle joined the ranks of the Romantics for a moment with a *brochure* attacking Racine at the expense of Shakespeare; but this was merely one of those contradictory changes of front which were inherent in his nature; and in reality the whole Romantic movement meant nothing to him. There is a story of a meeting in the house of a common friend between him and Hugo, in which the two men faced each other like a couple of cats with their backs up and their whiskers bristling. No wonder! But Beyle's true attitude towards his great contemporaries was hardly even one of hostility: he simply could not open their books. As for Chateaubriand, the god of their idolatry, he loathed him like poison. He used to describe how, in his youth, he had been on the point of fighting a duel with an officer who had ventured to maintain that a phrase in *Atala*—'la cime indéterminée des forêts'—was not intolerable. Probably he was romancing (M. Chuquet says so); but at any rate the story sums up symbolically Beyle's attitude towards his art. To him the whole apparatus of 'fine writing'—the emphatic phrase, the picturesque epithet, the rounded rhythm—was anathema. The charm that such ornaments might bring was in reality only a cloak for loose thinking and feeble observation. Even the style of the eighteenth century was not quite his ideal; it was too elegant; there was an artificial neatness about the form which imposed itself upon the substance, and degraded it. No, there was only one example of the perfect style, and that was the *Code Napoléon*; for there alone everything was subordinated to the exact and complete expression of what was to be said. A statement of law can have no place for irrelevant beauties, or the vagueness of personal feeling; by its very nature, it must resemble a sheet of plate glass through which every object may be seen with absolute distinctness, in its true shape. Beyle declared that he was in the habit of reading several paragraphs of the Code every morning after breakfast 'pour prendre le ton.' This again was for long supposed to be one of his little jokes; but quite lately the searchers among the MSS. at Grenoble have discovered page after page copied out from the Code in Beyle's handwriting. No doubt, for that wayward lover of paradoxes, the real joke lay in everybody taking for a joke what *he* took quite seriously.

This attempt to reach the exactitude and the detachment of an official document was not limited to Beyle's style; it runs through the whole tissue of his work. He wished to present life dispassionately and intellectually, and if he could have reduced his novels to a series of mathematical symbols, he would have been charmed. The contrast between his method and that of Balzac is remarkable. That wonderful art of materialisation, of the sensuous evocation of the forms, the qualities, the very stuff and substance of things, which was perhaps Balzac's greatest discovery, Beyle neither possessed nor wished to possess. Such matters were to him of the most subordinate importance, which it was no small part of the novelist's duty to keep very severely in their place. In the earlier chapters of *Le Rouge et Le Noir*, for instance, he is concerned with almost the same subject as Balzac in the opening of *Les Illusions Perdues*—the position of a young man in a provincial town, brought suddenly from the humblest surroundings into the midst of the leading society of the place through his intimate relations with a woman of refinement. But while in Balzac's pages what emerges is the concrete vision of provincial life down to the last pimple on the nose of the lowest footman, Beyle concentrates his whole attention on the personal problem, hints in a few rapid strokes at what Balzac has spent all his genius in describing, and reveals to us instead, with the precision of a surgeon at an operation, the inmost fibres of his hero's mind. In fact, Beyle's method is the classical method—the method of selection, of omission, of unification, with the object of creating a central impression of supreme reality. Zola criticises him for disregarding 'le milieu.'

Il y a [he says] un épisode célèbre dans 'Le Rouge et Le Noir,' a scène où Julien, assis un soir à côté de Mme. de Rénal, sous les branches noires d'un arbre, se fait un devoir de lui prendre la main, pendant qu'elle cause avec Mme. Derville. C'est un petit drame muet d'une grande puissance, et Stendhal y a analysé merveilleusement les états d'âme de ses deux personnages. Or, le milieu n'apparaît pas une seule fois. Nous pourrions être n'importe où dans n'importe quelles conditions, la scène resterait la même pourvu qu'il fît noir ... Donnez l'épisode à un écrivain pour qui les milieux existent, et dans la défaite de cette femme, il fera entrer la nuit, avec ses odeurs, avec ses voix, avec ses voluptés molles. Et cet écrivain sera dans la vérité, son tableau sera plus complet.

More complete, perhaps; but would it be more convincing? Zola, with his statistical conception of art, could not understand that you could tell a story properly unless you described in detail every contingent fact. He could not see that Beyle was able, by simply using the symbol 'nuit,' to suggest the 'milieu' at once to the reader's imagination. Everybody knows all about the night's accessories—'ses odeurs, ses voix, ses voluptés molles'; and what a relief it is to be spared, for once in a way, an elaborate expatiation upon them! And Beyle is perpetually evoking the gratitude of his readers in this way. 'Comme il insiste peu!' as M. Gide exclaims. Perhaps the best test of a man's intelligence is his capacity for making a summary. Beyle knew this, and his novels are full of passages which read like nothing so much as extraordinarily able summaries of some enormous original narrative which has been lost.

It was not that he was lacking in observation, that he had no eye for detail, or no power of expressing it; on the contrary his vision was of the sharpest, and his pen could call up pictorial images of startling vividness, when he wished. But he very rarely did wish: it was apt to involve a tiresome insistence. In his narratives he is like a brilliant talker in a sympathetic circle, skimming swiftly from point to point, taking for granted the intelligence of his audience, not afraid here and there to throw out a vague 'etc.' when the rest of the sentence is too obvious to state; always plain of speech, never self-assertive, and taking care above all things never to force the note. His famous description of the Battle of Waterloo in *La Chartreuse de Parme* is certainly the finest example of this side of his art. Here he produces an indelible impression by a series of light touches applied with unerring skill. Unlike Zola, unlike Tolstoy, he shows us neither the loathsomeness nor the devastation of a battlefield, but its insignificance, its irrelevant detail, its unmeaning grotesquenesses and indignities, its incoherence, and its empty weariness. Remembering his own experience at Bautzen, he has made his hero—a young Italian impelled by Napoleonic enthusiasm to join the French army as a volunteer on the eve of the battle—go through the great day in such a state of vague perplexity that in the end he can never feel quite certain that he really *was* at Waterloo. He experiences a succession of trivial and unpleasant incidents, culminating in his being hoisted off his horse by two of his comrades, in order that a general, who has had his own shot from under him, might be supplied with a mount; for the rest, he crosses and recrosses some fields, comes upon a dead body in a ditch, drinks brandy with a *vivandière*, gallops over a field covered with dying men, has an indefinite skirmish in a wood—and it is over. At one moment, having joined the escort of some generals, the young man allows his horse to splash into a stream, thereby covering one of the generals with muddy water from head to foot. The passage that follows is a good specimen of Beyle's narrative style:

En arrivant sur l'autre rive, Fabrice y avait trouvé les généraux tout seuls; le bruit du canon lui sembla redoubler; ce fut à peine s'il entendit le général, par lui si bien mouillé, qui criait à son oreille:

Où as-tu pris ce cheval?

Fabrice était tellement troublé, qu'il répondit en Italien: *l'ho comprato poco fa.* (Je viens de l'acheter à l'instant.)

Que dis-tu? lui cria le général.

Mais le tapage devint tellement fort en ce moment, que Fabrice ne put lui répondre. Nous avouerons que notre héros était fort peu héros en ce moment. Toutefois, la peur ne venait chez lui qu'en seconde ligne; il était surtout scandalisé de ce bruit qui lui faisait mal aux oreilles. L'escorte prit le galop; on traversait une grande pièce de terre labourée, située au delà du canal, et ce champ était jonché de cadavres.

How unemphatic it all is! What a paucity of epithet, what a reticence in explanation! How a Romantic would have lingered over the facial expression of the general, and how a Naturalist would have analysed that 'tapage'! And yet, with all their efforts, would they have succeeded in conveying that singular impression of disturbance, of cross-purposes, of hurry, and of ill-defined fear, which Beyle with his quiet terseness has produced?

It is, however, in his psychological studies that the detached and intellectual nature of Beyle's method is most clearly seen. When he is describing, for instance, the development of Julien Sorel's mind in *Le Rouge et Le Noir*, when he shows us the soul of the young peasant with its ignorance, its ambition, its pride, going step by step into the whirling vortex of life— then we seem to be witnessing not so much the presentment of a fiction as the unfolding of some scientific fact. The procedure is almost mathematical: a proposition is established, the inference is drawn, the next proposition follows, and so on until the demonstration is complete. Here the influence of the eighteenth century is very strongly marked. Beyle had drunk deeply of that fountain of syllogism and analysis that flows through the now forgotten pages of Helvétius and Condillac; he was an ardent votary of logic in its austerest form—'la lo-gique' he used to call it, dividing the syllables in a kind of awe-inspired emphasis; and he considered the ratiocinative style of Montesquieu almost as good as that of the *Code Civil*.

If this had been all, if we could sum him up simply as an acute and brilliant writer who displays the scientific and prosaic sides of the French genius in an extreme degree, Beyle's position in literature would present very little difficulty. He would take his place at once as a late—an abnormally late—product of the eighteenth century. But he was not that. In his blood there was a virus which had never tingled in the veins of Voltaire. It was the virus of modern life—that new sensibility, that new passionateness, which Rousseau had first made known to the world, and which had won its way over Europe behind the thunder of Napoleon's artillery. Beyle had passed his youth within earshot of that mighty roar, and his inmost spirit could never lose the echo of it. It was in vain that he studied Condillac and modelled his style on the Code; in vain that he sang the praises of *la lo-gique*, shrugged his shoulders at the Romantics, and turned the cold eye of a scientific investigator upon the phenomena of life; he remained essentially a man of feeling. His unending series of *grandes passions* was one unmistakable sign of this; another was his intense devotion to the Fine Arts. Though his taste in music and painting was the taste of his time—the literary and sentimental taste of the age of Rossini and Canova —he nevertheless brought to the appreciation of works of art a kind of intimate gusto which reveals the genuineness of his emotion. The 'jouissances d'ange,' with which at his first entrance into Italy he heard at Novara the *Matrimonio Segreto* of Cimarosa, marked an epoch in his life. He adored Mozart: 'I can imagine nothing more distasteful to me,' he said, 'than a thirty-mile walk through the mud; but I would take one at this moment if I knew that I should hear a good performance of *Don Giovanni* at the end of it.' The Virgins of Guido Reni sent him into ecstasies and the Goddesses of Correggio into rapture. In short, as he himself admitted, he never could resist 'le Beau' in whatever form he found it. *Le Beau!* The phrase is characteristic of the peculiar species of ingenuous sensibility which so oddly agitated this sceptical man of the world. His whole vision of life was coloured by it. His sense of values was impregnated with what he called his 'espagnolisme'—his immense admiration for the noble and the high-sounding in speech or act or character—an admiration which landed him often enough in hysterics and absurdity. Yet this was the soil in which a temperament of caustic reasonableness had somehow implanted itself. The contrast is surprising, because it is so extreme. Other men have been by turns sensible and enthusiastic: but who before or since has combined the emotionalism of a schoolgirl with the cold penetration of a judge on the bench? Beyle, for instance, was capable of writing, in one of those queer epitaphs of himself which he was constantly composing, the high-falutin' words 'Il respecta un seul homme: Napoléon'; and yet, as he wrote them, he must have remembered well enough that when he met Napoleon face to face his unabashed scrutiny had detected swiftly that the man was a play-actor, and a vulgar one at that. Such were the contradictions of his double nature, in which the elements, instead of being mixed, came together, as it were, in layers, like superimposed strata of chalk and flint.

In his novels this cohabitation of opposites is responsible both for what is best and what is worst. When the two forces work in unison the result is sometimes of extraordinary value —a product of a kind which it would be difficult to parallel in any other author. An eye of icy gaze is turned upon the tumultuous secrets of passion, and the pangs of love are recorded in the language of Euclid. The image of the surgeon inevitably suggests itself—the hand with the iron nerve and the swift knife laying bare the trembling mysteries within. It is the intensity of Beyle's observation, joined with such an exactitude of exposition, that makes his dry pages sometimes more thrilling than the wildest tale of adventure or all the marvels of high romance. The passage in *La Chartreuse de Parme* describing Count Mosca's jealousy has this quality, which appears even more clearly in the chapters of *Le Rouge et Le Noir* concerning Julien Sorel and Mathilde de la Mole. Here Beyle has a subject after his own heart. The loves of the peasant youth and the aristocratic girl, traversed and agitated by their overweening pride, and triumphing at last rather over themselves than over each other—these things make up a gladiatorial combat of 'espagnolismes,' which is displayed to the reader with a supreme incisiveness. The climax is reached when Mathilde at last gives way to her passion, and throws herself into the arms of Julien, who forces himself to make no response:

Ses bras se roidirent, tant l'effort imposé par la politique était pénible. Je ne dois pas même me permettre de presser contre mon cœur ce corps souple et charmant; ou elle me méprise, ou elle me maltraite. Quel affreux caractère!

Et en maudissant le caractère de Mathilde, il l'en aimait cent fois plus; il lui semblait avoir dans ses bras une reine.

L'impassible froideur de Julien redoubla le malheur de Mademoiselle de la Mole. Elle était loin d'avoir le sang-froid nécessaire pour chercher à deviner dans ses yeux ce qu'il sentait pour elle en cet instant. Elle ne put se résoudre à le regarder; elle tremblait de rencontrer l'expression du mépris.

Assise sur le divan de la bibliothèque, immobile et la tête tournée du côté opposé à Julien, elle était en proie aux plus vives douleurs que l'orgueil et l'amour puissent faire éprouver à une âme humaine. Dans quelle atroce démarche elle venait de tomber!

Il m'était réservé, malheureuse que je suis! de voir repoussées les avances les plus indécentes! Et repoussées par qui? ajoutait l'orgueil fou de douleur, repoussées par un domestique de mon père.

C'est ce que je ne souffrirai pas, dit-elle à haute voix.

At that moment she suddenly sees some unopened letters addressed to Julien by another woman.

—Ainsi, s'écria-t-elle hors d'elle-même, non seulement vous êtes bien avec elle, mais encore vous la méprisez. Vous, un homme de rien, mépriser Madame la Maréchale de Fervaques!

—Ah! pardon, mon ami, ajouta-t-elle en se jetant à ses genoux, méprise-moi si tu veux, mais aime-moi, je ne puis plus vivre privée de ton amour. Et elle tomba tout à fait évanouie.

—La voilà donc, cette orgueilleuse, à mes pieds! se dit Julien.

Such is the opening of this wonderful scene, which contains the concentrated essence of Beyle's genius, and which, in its combination of high passion, intellectual intensity, and dramatic force, may claim comparison with the great dialogues of Corneille.

'Je fais tous les efforts possibles pour être *sec*,' he says of himself. 'Je veux imposer silence à mon cœur, qui croit avoir beaucoup à dire. Je tremble toujours de n'avoir écrit qu'un

soupir, quand je crois avoir noté une vérité.' Often he succeeds, but not always. At times his desire for dryness becomes
a mannerism and fills whole pages with tedious and obscure
argumentation. And, at other times, his sensibility gets the
upper hand, throws off all control, and revels in an orgy of
melodrama and 'espagnolisme.' Do what he will, he cannot
keep up a consistently critical attitude towards the creatures
of his imagination: he depreciates his heroes with extreme
care, but in the end they get the better of him and sweep him
off his feet. When, in *La Chartreuse de Parme*, Fabrice kills
a man in a duel, his first action is to rush to a looking-glass to
see whether his beauty has been injured by a cut in the face;
and Beyle does not laugh at this; he is impressed by it. In the
same book he lavishes all his art on the creation of the brilliant,
worldly, sceptical Duchesse de Sanseverina, and then, not
quite satisfied, he makes her concoct and carry out the murder
of the reigning Prince in order to satisfy a desire for amorous
revenge. This really makes her perfect. But the most striking
example of Beyle's inability to resist the temptation of sacri-
ficing his head to his heart is in the conclusion of *Le Rouge et
Le Noir*, where Julien, to be revenged on a former mistress
who defames him, deliberately goes down into the country,
buys a pistol, and shoots the lady in church. Not only is Beyle
entranced by the *bravura* of this senseless piece of brutality,
but he destroys at a blow the whole atmosphere of impartial
observation which fills the rest of the book, lavishes upon his
hero the blindest admiration, and at last, at the moment of
Julien's execution, even forgets himself so far as to write a
sentence in the romantic style: 'Jamais cette tête n'avait été
aussi poétique qu'au moment où elle allait tomber.' Just as
Beyle, in his contrary mood, carries to an extreme the French
love of logical precision, so in these rhapsodies he expresses in
an exaggerated form a very different but an equally characteristic quality of his compatriots—their instinctive responsiveness
to fine poses. It is a quality that Englishmen in particular find
it hard to sympathise with. They remain stolidly unmoved
when their neighbours are in ecstasies. They are repelled by

the 'noble' rhetoric of the French Classical Drama; they find the tirades of Napoleon, which animated the armies of France to victory, pieces of nauseous clap-trap. And just now it is this side—to us the obviously weak side—of Beyle's genius that seems to be most in favour with French critics. To judge from M. Barrès, writing dithyrambically of Beyle's 'sentiment d'honneur,' that is his true claim to greatness. The sentiment of honour is all very well, one is inclined to mutter on this side of the Channel; but oh, for a little sentiment of humour too!

The view of Beyle's personality which his novels give us may be seen with far greater detail in his miscellaneous writings. It is to these that his most modern admirers devote their main attention—particularly to his letters and his autobiographies; but they are all of them highly characteristic of their author, and—whatever the subject may be, from a guide to Rome to a life of Napoleon—one gathers in them, scattered up and down through their pages, a curious, dimly adumbrated philosophy—an ill-defined and yet intensely personal point of view—*le Beylisme*. It is in fact almost entirely in this secondary quality that their interest lies; their ostensible subject-matter is unimportant. An apparent exception is the book in which Beyle has embodied his reflections upon Love. The volume, with its meticulous apparatus of analysis, definition, and classification, which gives it the air of being a parody of *L'Esprit des Lois*, is yet full of originality, of lively anecdote and keen observation. Nobody but Beyle could have written it; nobody but Beyle could have managed to be at once so stimulating and so jejune, so clear-sighted and so exasperating. But here again, in reality, it is not the question at issue that is interesting—one learns more of the true nature of Love in one or two of La Bruyère's short sentences than in all Beyle's three hundred pages of disquisition; but what is absorbing is the sense that comes to one, as one reads it, of the presence, running through it all, of a restless and problematical spirit. 'Le Beylisme' is certainly not susceptible of any exact definition; its author was too capricious, too unmethodical, in spite of his *lo-gique*, ever to have framed a coherent philosophy; it is essentially a thing of shreds and patches, of hints, suggestions, and quick visions of flying thoughts. M. Barrès says that what lies at the bottom of it is a 'passion de collectionner les belles énergies.' But there are many kinds of 'belles énergies,' and some of them certainly do not fit into the framework of 'le Beylisme.' 'Quand je suis arrêté par des voleurs, ou qu'on me tire des coups de fusil, je me sens une grande colère contre le gouvernement et le curé de l'endroit. Quand au voleur, il me plaît, s'il est énergique, car il m'amuse.' It was the energy of self-assertiveness that pleased Beyle; that of self-restraint did not interest him. The immorality of the point of view is patent, and at times it appears to be simply based upon the common selfishness of an egotist. But in reality it was something more significant than that. The 'chasse au bonheur' which Beyle was always advocating was no respectable epicureanism; it had about it a touch of the fanatical. There was anarchy in it—a hatred of authority, an impatience with custom, above all a scorn for the commonplace dictates of ordinary morality. Writing his memoirs at the age of fifty-two, Beyle looked back with pride on the joy that he had felt, as a child of ten, amid his royalist family at Grenoble, when the news came of the execution of Louis XVI. His father announced it:

—C'en est fait, dit-il avec un gros soupir, ils l'ont assassiné.
Je fus saisi d'un des plus vifs mouvements de joie que j'ai éprouvé en ma vie. Le lecteur pensera peut-être que je suis cruel, mais tel j'étais à 5×2, tel je suis à $10 \times 5 + 2 \ldots$ Je puis dire que l'approbation des êtres, que je regarde comme faibles, m'est absolument indifférente.

These are the words of a born rebel, and such sentiments are constantly recurring in his books. He is always discharging his shafts against some established authority; and, of course, he reserved his bitterest hatred for the proudest and most insidious of all authorities—the Roman Catholic Church. It is odd to find some of the 'Beylistes' solemnly hailing the man whom the power of the Jesuits haunted like a nightmare, and whose account of the seminary in *Le Rouge et Le Noir* is one of the most scathing pictures of religious tyranny ever drawn, as a prophet of the present Catholic movement in France. For in truth, if Beyle was a prophet of anything he was a prophet of that spirit of revolt in modern thought which first reached a complete expression in the pages of Nietzsche. His love of power and self-will, his aristocratic outlook, his scorn of the Christian virtues, his admiration of the Italians of the Renaissance, his repudiation of the herd and the morality of the herd—these qualities, flashing strangely among his observations on Rossini and the Coliseum, his reflections on the memories of the past and his musings on the ladies of the present, certainly give a surprising foretaste of the fiery potion of Zarathustra. The creator of the Duchesse de Sanseverina had caught more than a glimpse of the transvaluation of all values. Characteristically enough, the appearance of this new potentiality was only observed by two contemporary forces in European society—Goethe and the Austrian police. It is clear that Goethe alone among the critics of the time understood that Beyle was something more than a novelist, and discerned an uncanny significance in his pages. 'I do not like reading M. de Stendhal,' he observed to Winckelmann, 'but I cannot help doing so. He is extremely free and extremely impertinent, and . . . I recommend you to buy all his books.' As for the Austrian police they had no doubt about the matter. Beyle's book of travel, *Rome, Naples et Florence*, was, they decided, pernicious and dangerous in the highest degree; and the poor man was hunted out of Milan in consequence.

It would be a mistake to suppose that Beyle displayed in his private life the qualities of the superman. Neither his virtues nor his vices were on the grand scale. In his own person he never seems to have committed an 'espagnolisme.' Perhaps his worst sin was that of plagiarism: his earliest book, a life of Haydn, was almost entirely 'lifted' from the work of a learned German; and in his next he embodied several choice extracts culled from the *Edinburgh Review*. On this occasion he was particularly delighted, since the *Edinburgh*, in reviewing the book, innocently selected for special approbation the very passages which he had stolen. It is singular that so original a writer should have descended to pilfering. But Beyle was nothing if not inconsistent. With all his Classicism he detested Racine; with all his love of music he could see nothing in Beethoven; he adored Italy, and, so soon as he was given his Italian consulate, he was usually to be found in Paris. As his life advanced he grew more and more wayward, capricious, and eccentric. He indulged in queer mystifications, covering his papers with false names and anagrams—for the police, he said, were on his track, and he must be careful. His love-affairs became less and less fortunate; but he was still sometimes successful, and when he was he registered the fact —upon his braces. He dreamed and drifted a great deal. He went up to San Pietro in Montorio, and looking over Rome, wrote the initials of his past mistresses in the dust. He tried to make up his mind whether Napoleon after all *was* the only being he respected; no—there was also Mademoiselle de Lespinasse. He went to the opera at Naples and noted that 'la musique parfaite, comme la pantomime parfaite, me fait songer à ce qui forme actuellement l'objet de mes rêveries et me fait venir des idées excellentes: ... or, ce soir, je ne puis me dissimuler que j'ai le malheur *of being too great an admirer of Lady L. . . .*' He abandoned himself to 'les charmantes visions du Beau qui souvent encore remplissent ma tête à l'âge de *fifty-two.*' He wondered whether Montesquieu would have thought his writings worthless. He sat scribbling his reminiscences by the fire till the night drew on and the fire went out, and still he scribbled, more and more illegibly, until at last the paper was covered with hieroglyphics undecipherable even by M. Chuquet himself. He wandered among the ruins of ancient Rome, playing to perfection the part of cicerone to such travellers as were lucky enough to fall in with him; and often his stout and jovial form, with the satyric look in the sharp eyes and the compressed lips, might be seen by the wayside in the Campagna, as he stood and jested with the reapers or the vine-dressers or with the girls coming out, as they had come since the days of Horace, to draw water from the fountains of Tivoli. In more cultivated society he was apt to be nervous; for his philosophy was never proof against the terror of being laughed at. But sometimes, late at night, when the surroundings were really sympathetic, he could be very happy among his friends. 'Un salon de huit ou dix personnes,' he said, 'dont toutes les femmes ont eu des amants, où la conversation est gaie, anecdotique, et où l'on prend du punch léger à minuit et demie, est l'endroit du monde où je me trouve le mieux.'

And in such a Paradise of Frenchmen we may leave Henri Beyle.

1914.

THE LAST ELIZABETHAN

THE shrine of Poetry is a secret one; and it is fortunate that this should be the case; for it gives a sense of security. The cult is too mysterious and intimate to figure upon census papers; there are no turnstiles at the temple gates; and so, as all inquiries must be fruitless, the obvious plan is to take for granted a good attendance of worshippers, and to pass on. Yet, if Apollo were to come down (after the manner of deities) and put questions—must we suppose to the Laureate?—as to the number of the elect, would we be quite sure of escaping wrath and destruction? Let us hope for the best; and perhaps, if we were bent upon finding out the truth, the simplest way would be to watch the sales of the new edition of the poems of Beddoes, which Messrs. Routledge have lately added to the 'Muses' Library.' How many among Apollo's pew-renters, one wonders, have ever read Beddoes, or, indeed, have ever heard of him? For some reason or another, this extraordinary poet has not only never received the recognition which is his due, but has failed almost entirely to receive any recognition whatever. If his name is known at all, it is known in virtue of the one or two of his lyrics which have crept into some of the current anthologies. But Beddoes' highest claim to distinction does not rest upon his lyrical achievements, consummate as those achievements are; it rests upon his extraordinary eminence as a master of dramatic blank verse. Perhaps his greatest misfortune was that he was born at the beginning of the nineteenth century, and not at the end of the sixteenth. His proper place was among that noble band of Elizabethans, whose strong and splendid spirit gave to England, in one miraculous generation, the most glorious heritage of drama that the world has known. If Charles Lamb had discovered his tragedies among the folios of the British Museum, and had given extracts from them in the *Specimens of Dramatic*

Poets, Beddoes' name would doubtless be as familiar to us now as those of Marlowe and Webster, Fletcher and Ford. As it happened, however, he came as a strange and isolated phenomenon, a star which had wandered from its constellation, and was lost among alien lights. It is to very little purpose that Mr. Ramsay Colles, his latest editor, assures us that 'Beddoes is interesting as marking the transition from Shelley to Browning'; it is to still less purpose that he points out to us a passage in *Death's Jest Book* which anticipates the doctrines of *The Descent of Man*. For Beddoes cannot be hoisted into line with his contemporaries by such methods as these; nor is it in the light of such after-considerations that the value of his work must be judged. We must take him on his own merits, 'unmixed with seconds'; we must discover and appraise his peculiar quality for its own sake.

> He hath skill in language;
> And knowledge is in him, root, flower, and fruit,
> A palm with winged imagination in it,
> Whose roots stretch even underneath the grave;
> And on them hangs a lamp of magic science
> In his soul's deepest mine, where folded thoughts
> Lie sleeping on the tombs of magi dead.

If the neglect suffered by Beddoes' poetry may be accounted for in more ways than one, it is not so easy to understand why more curiosity has never been aroused by the circumstances of his life. For one reader who cares to concern himself with the intrinsic merit of a piece of writing there are a thousand who are ready to explore with eager sympathy the history of the writer; and all that we know both of the life and the character of Beddoes possesses those very qualities of peculiarity, mystery, and adventure, which are so dear to the hearts of subscribers to circulating libraries. Yet only one account of his career has ever been given to the public; and that account, fragmentary and incorrect as it is, has long been out of print. It was supplemented some years ago by Mr. Gosse, who was able to throw additional light upon one important circumstance, and who has also published a small collection of

Beddoes' letters. The main biographical facts, gathered from these sources, have been put together by Mr. Ramsay Colles, in his introduction to the new edition; but he has added nothing fresh; and we are still in almost complete ignorance as to the details of the last twenty years of Beddoes' existence —full as those years certainly were of interest and even excitement. Nor has the veil been altogether withdrawn from that strange tragedy which, for the strange tragedian, was the last of all.

Readers of Miss Edgeworth's letters may remember that her youngest sister Anne, married a distinguished Clifton physician, Dr. Thomas Beddoes. Their eldest son, born in 1803, was named Thomas Lovell, after his father and grandfather, and grew up to be the author of *The Brides' Tragedy* and *Death's Jest Book*. Dr. Beddoes was a remarkable man, endowed with high and varied intellectual capacities and a rare independence of character. His scientific attainments were recognised by the University of Oxford, where he held the post of Lecturer in Chemistry, until the time of the French Revolution, when he was obliged to resign it, owing to the scandal caused by the unconcealed intensity of his liberal opinions. He then settled at Clifton as a physician, established a flourishing practice, and devoted his leisure to politics and scientific research. Sir Humphry Davy, who was his pupil, and whose merit he was the first to bring to light, declared that 'he had talents which would have exalted him to the pinnacle of philosophical eminence, if they had been applied with discretion.' The words are curiously suggestive of the history of his son; and indeed the poet affords a striking instance of the hereditary transmission of mental qualities. Not only did Beddoes inherit his father's talents and his father's inability to make the best use of them; he possessed in a no less remarkable degree his father's independence of mind. In both cases, this quality was coupled with a corresponding eccentricity of conduct, which occasionally, to puzzled onlookers, wore the appearance of something very near insanity. Many stories are related of the queer behaviour of Dr.

Beddoes. One day he astonished the ladies of Clifton by appearing at a tea-party with a packet of sugar in his hand; he explained that it was East Indian sugar, and that nothing would induce him to eat the usual kind, which came from Jamaica and was made by slaves. More extraordinary were his medical prescriptions; for he was in the habit of ordering cows to be conveyed into his patients' bedrooms, in order, as he said, that they might 'inhale the animals' breath.' It is easy to imagine the delight which the singular spectacle of a cow climbing upstairs into an invalid's bedroom must have given to the future author of *Harpagus* and *The Oviparous Tailor*. But 'little Tom,' as Miss Edgeworth calls him, was not destined to enjoy for long the benefit of parental example; for Dr. Beddoes died in the prime of life, when the child was not yet six years old.

The genius at school is usually a disappointing figure, for, as a rule, one must be commonplace to be a successful boy. In that preposterous world, to be remarkable is to be overlooked; and nothing less vivid than the white-hot blaze of a Shelley will bring with it even a distinguished martyrdom. But Beddoes was an exception, though he was not a martyr. On the contrary, he dominated his fellows as absolutely as if he had been a dullard and a dunce. He was at Charterhouse; and an entertaining account of his existence there has been preserved to us in a paper of school reminiscences, written by Mr. C. D. Bevan, who had been his fag. Though his place in the school was high, Beddoes' interests were devoted not so much to classical scholarship as to the literature of his own tongue. Cowley, he afterwards told a friend, had been the first poet he had understood; but no doubt he had begun to understand poetry many years before he went to Charterhouse; and, while he was there, the reading which he chiefly delighted in was the Elizabethan drama. 'He liked acting,' says Mr. Bevan, 'and was a good judge of it, and used to give apt though burlesque imitations of the popular actors, particularly Kean and Macready. Though his voice was harsh and his enunciation offensively conceited, he read with so much propriety of expression and manner, that I was always glad to listen: even when I was pressed into the service as his accomplice, his enemy, or his love, with a due accompaniment of curses, caresses, or kicks, as the course of his declamation required. One play in particular, Marlowe's *Tragedy of Dr. Faustus*, excited my admiration in this way; and a liking for the old English drama, which I still retain, was created and strengthened by such recitations.' But Beddoes' dramatic performances were not limited to the works of others; when the occasion arose he was able to supply the necessary material himself. A locksmith had incurred his displeasure by putting a bad lock on his bookcase; Beddoes vowed vengeance; and when next the man appeared he was received by a dramatic interlude, representing his last moments, his horror and remorse, his death, and the funeral procession, which was interrupted by fiends, who carried off body and soul to eternal torments. Such was the realistic vigour of the performance that the locksmith, according to Mr. Bevan, 'departed in a storm of wrath and execrations, and could not be persuaded, for some time, to resume his work.'

Besides the interlude of the wicked locksmith, Beddoes' school compositions included a novel in the style of Fielding (which has unfortunately disappeared), the beginnings of an Elizabethan tragedy, and much miscellaneous verse. In 1820 he left Charterhouse, and went to Pembroke College, Oxford, where, in the following year, while still a freshman, he published his first volume, *The Improvisatore*, a series of short narratives in verse. The book had been written in part while he was at school; and its immaturity is obvious. It contains no trace of the nervous vigour of his later style; the verse is weak, and the sentiment, to use his own expression, 'Moorish.' Indeed, the only interest of the little work lies in the evidence which it affords that the singular pre-occupation which eventually dominated Beddoes' mind had, even in these days, made its appearance. The book is full of death. The poems begin on battle-fields and end in charnel-houses; old men are slaughtered in cold blood, and lovers are struck by lightning into mouldering heaps of corruption. The boy, with his elaborate exhibitions of physical horror, was doing his best to make his readers' flesh creep. But the attempt was far too crude; and in after years, when Beddoes had become a pastmaster of that difficult art, he was very much ashamed of his first publication. So eager was he to destroy every trace of its existence, that he did not spare even the finely bound copies of his friends. The story goes that he amused himself by visiting their libraries with a penknife, so that, when next they took out the precious volume, they found the pages gone.

Beddoes, however, had no reason to be ashamed of his next publication, *The Brides' Tragedy*, which appeared in 1822. In a single bound, he had reached the threshold of poetry, and was knocking at the door. The line which divides the best and most accomplished verse from poetry itself—that subtle and momentous line which every one can draw, and no one can explain—Beddoes had not yet crossed. But he had gone as far as it was possible to go by the aid of mere skill in the art of writing, and he was still in his twentieth year. Many passages in *The Brides' Tragedy* seem only to be waiting for the breath of inspiration which will bring them into life; and indeed, here and there, the breath has come, the warm, the true, the vital breath of Apollo. No one, surely, whose lips had not tasted of the waters of Helicon, could have uttered such words as these:

> Here's the blue violet, like Pandora's eye,
> When first it darkened with immortal life

or a line of such intense imaginative force as this:

> I've huddled her into the wormy earth;

or this splendid description of a stormy sunrise:

> The day is in its shroud while yet an infant;
> And Night with giant strides stalks o'er the world,
> Like a swart Cyclops, on its hideous front
> One round, red, thunder-swollen eye ablaze.

The play was written on the Elizabethan model, and, as a

play, it is disfigured by Beddoes' most characteristic faults:
the construction is weak, the interest fluctuates from character
to character, and the motives and actions of the characters
themselves are for the most part curiously remote from the
realities of life. Yet, though the merit of the tragedy depends
almost entirely upon the verse, there are signs in it that,
while Beddoes lacked the gift of construction, he nevertheless
possessed one important dramatic faculty—the power of
creating detached scenes of interest and beauty. The scene
in which the half-crazed Leonora imagines to herself, beside
the couch on which her dead daughter lies, that the child is
really living after all, is dramatic in the highest sense of the
word; the situation, with all its capabilities of pathetic irony,
is conceived and developed with consummate art and absolute
restraint. Leonora's speech ends thus:

> ... Speak, I pray thee, Floribel,
> Speak to thy mother; do but whisper 'aye';
> Well, well, I will not press her; I am sure
> She has the welcome news of some good fortune,
> And hoards the telling till her father comes;
> ... Ah! She half laughed. I've guessed it then;
> Come tell me, I'll be secret. Nay, if you mock me,
> I must be very angry till you speak.
> Now this is silly; some of these young boys
> Have dressed the cushions with her clothes in sport.
> 'Tis very like her. I could make this image
> Act all her greetings; she shall bow her head:
> 'Good-morrow, mother'; and her smiling face
> Falls on my neck.—Oh, heaven, 'tis she indeed!
> I know it all—don't tell me.

The last seven words are a summary of anguish, horror, and
despair, such as Webster himself might have been proud to
write.

The Brides' Tragedy was well received by critics; and a
laudatory notice of Beddoes in the *Edinburgh*, written by
Bryan Waller Procter—better known then than now under
his pseudonym of Barry Cornwall—led to a lasting friendship

between the two poets. The connection had an important result, for it was through Procter that Beddoes became acquainted with the most intimate of all his friends—Thomas Forbes Kelsall, then a young lawyer at Southampton. In the summer of 1823 Beddoes stayed at Southampton for several months, and, while ostensibly studying for his Oxford degree, gave up most of his time to conversations with Kelsall and to dramatic composition. It was a culminating point in his life: one of those moments which come, even to the most fortunate, once and once only—when youth, and hope, and the high exuberance of genius combine with circumstance and opportunity to crown the marvellous hour. The spadework of *The Brides' Tragedy* had been accomplished; the seed had been sown; and now the harvest was beginning. Beddoes, 'with the delicious sense,' as Kelsall wrote long afterwards, 'of the laurel freshly twined around his head,' poured out, in these Southampton evenings, an eager stream of song. 'His poetic composition,' says his friend, 'was then exceedingly facile: more than once or twice has he taken home with him at night some unfinished act of a drama, in which the editor [Kelsall] had found much to admire, and, at the next meeting, has produced a new one, similar in design, but filled with other thoughts and fancies, which his teeming imagination had projected, in its sheer abundance, and not from any feeling, right or fastidious, of unworthiness in its predecessor. Of several of these very striking fragments, large and grand in their aspect as they each started into form,

Like the red outline of beginning Adam,

. . . the only trace remaining is literally the impression thus deeply cut into their one observer's mind. The fine verse just quoted is the sole remnant, indelibly stamped on the editor's memory, of one of these extinct creations.' Fragments survive of at least four dramas, projected, and brought to various stages of completion, at about this time. Beddoes was impatient of the common restraints; he was dashing forward in the spirit of his own advice to another poet:

Creep not nor climb,
As they who place their topmost of sublime
On some peak of this planet, pitifully.
Dart eaglewise with open wings, and fly
Until you meet the gods!

Eighteen months after his Southampton visit, Beddoes took
his degree at Oxford, and, almost immediately, made up his
mind to a course of action which had the profoundest effect
upon his future life. He determined to take up the study of
medicine; and with that end in view established himself, in
1825, at the University at Göttingen. It is very clear, however, that he had no intention of giving up his poetical work.
He took with him to Germany the beginnings of a new play
—'a very Gothic-style tragedy,' he calls it, 'for which I have
a jewel of a name—DEATH'S JEST-BOOK; of course,' he adds,
'no one will ever read it'; and, during his four years at Göttingen, he devoted most of his leisure to the completion of
this work. He was young; he was rich; he was interested in
medical science; and no doubt it seemed to him that he could
well afford to amuse himself for half-a-dozen years, before he
settled down to the poetical work which was to be the serious
occupation of his life. But, as time passed, he became more
and more engrossed in the study of medicine, for which he
gradually discovered he had not only a taste but a gift; so that
at last he came to doubt whether it might not be his true
vocation to be a physician, and not a poet after all. Engulfed
among the students of Göttingen, England and English ways
of life, and even English poetry, became dim to him; 'dir,
dem Anbeter der seligen Gottheiten der Musen, u.s.w.,' he
wrote to Kelsall, 'was Unterhaltendes kann der Liebhaber
von Knochen, der fleissige Botaniker und Phisiolog mit-
theilen?' In 1830 he was still hesitating between the two
alternatives. 'I sometimes wish,' he told the same friend,
'to devote myself exclusively to the study of anatomy and
physiology in science, of languages, and dramatic poetry';
his pen had run away with him; and his 'exclusive' devotion
turned out to be a double one, directed towards widely

different ends. While he was still in this state of mind, a new interest took possession of him—an interest which worked havoc with his dreams of dramatic authorship and scientific research: he became involved in the revolutionary movement which was at that time beginning to agitate Europe. The details of his adventures are unhappily lost to us, for we know nothing more of them than can be learnt from a few scanty references in his rare letters to English friends; but it is certain that the part he played was an active, and even a dangerous one. He was turned out of Würzburg by 'that ingenious Jackanapes,' the King of Bavaria; he was an intimate friend of Hegetschweiler, one of the leaders of liberalism in Switzerland; and he was present in Zurich when a body of six thousand peasants, 'half unarmed, and the other half armed with scythes, dungforks and poles, entered the town and overturned the liberal government.' In the tumult Hegetschweiler was killed, and Beddoes was soon afterwards forced to fly the canton. During the following years we catch glimpses of him, flitting mysteriously over Germany and Switzerland, at Berlin, at Baden, at Giessen, a strange solitary figure, with tangled hair and meerschaum pipe, scribbling lampoons upon the King of Prussia, translating Grainger's *Spinal Cord* into German, and Schoenlein's *Diseases of Europeans* into English, exploring Pilatus and the Titlis, evolving now and then some ghostly lyric or some rabelaisian tale, or brooding over the scenes of his 'Gothic-styled tragedy,' wondering if it were worthless or inspired, and giving it—as had been his wont for the last twenty years—just one more touch before he sent it to the press. He appeared in England once or twice, and in 1846 made a stay of several months, visiting the Procters in London, and going down to Southampton to be with Kelsall once again. Eccentricity had grown on him; he would shut himself for days in his bedroom, smoking furiously; he would fall into fits of long and deep depression. He shocked some of his relatives by arriving at their country house astride a donkey; and he amazed the Procters by starting out one evening to set fire to Drury Lane Theatre with a lighted five-pound note.

After this last visit to England, his history becomes even more obscure than before. It is known that in 1847 he was in Frankfort, where he lived for six months in close companionship with a young baker called Degen—'a nice-looking young man, nineteen years of age,' we are told, 'dressed in a blue blouse, fine in expression, and of a natural dignity of manner'; and that, in the spring of the following year, the two friends went off to Zurich, where Beddoes hired the theatre for a night in order that Degen might appear on the stage in the part of Hotspur. At Basel, however, for some unexplained reason, the friends parted, and Beddoes fell immediately into the profoundest gloom. 'Il a été misérable,' said the waiter at the Cigogne Hotel, where he was staying, 'il a voulu se tuer.' It was true. He inflicted a deep wound in his leg with a razor, in the hope, apparently, of bleeding to death. He was taken to the hospital, where he constantly tore off the bandages, until at last it was necessary to amputate the leg below the knee. The operation was successful, Beddoes began to recover, and, in the autumn, Degen came back to Basel. It seemed as if all were going well; for the poet, with his books around him, and the blue-bloused Degen by his bedside, talked happily of politics and literature, and of an Italian journey in the spring. He walked out twice; was he still happy? Who can tell? Was it happiness, or misery, or what strange impulse, that drove him, on his third walk, to go to a chemist's shop in the town, and to obtain there a phial of deadly poison? On the evening of that day—the 26th of January, 1849—Dr. Ecklin, his physician, was hastily summoned, to find Beddoes lying insensible upon the bed. He never recovered consciousness, and died that night. Upon his breast was found a pencil note, addressed to one of his English friends. 'My dear Philips,' it began, 'I am food for what I am good for—worms.' A few testamentary wishes followed. Kelsall was to have the manuscripts; and—'W. Beddoes must have a case (50 bottles) of Champagne Moet, 1847 growth, to drink my death in . . . I ought to have been, among other things,' the gruesome document concluded, 'a good poet.

Life was too great a bore on one peg, and that a bad one. Buy for Dr. Ecklin one of Reade's best stomach-pumps.' It was the last of his additions to Death's Jest Book, and the most *macabre* of all.

Kelsall discharged his duties as literary executor with exemplary care. The manuscripts were fragmentary and confused. There were three distinct drafts of *Death's Jest Book*, each with variations of its own; and from these Kelsall compiled his first edition of the drama, which appeared in 1850. In the following year he brought out the two volumes of poetical works, which remained for forty years the only record of the full scope and power of Beddoes' genius. They contain reprints of *The Brides' Tragedy* and *Death's Jest Book*, together with two unfinished tragedies, and a great number of dramatic fragments and lyrics; and the poems are preceded by Kelsall's memoir of his friend. Of these rare and valuable volumes the Muses' Library edition is almost an exact reprint, except that it omits the memoir and revives *The Improvisatore*. Only one other edition of Beddoes exists—the limited one brought out by Mr. Gosse in 1890, and based upon a fresh examination of the manuscripts. Mr. Gosse was able to add ten lyrics and one dramatic fragment to those already published by Kelsall; he made public for the first time the true story of Beddoes' suicide, which Kelsall had concealed; and, in 1893, he followed up his edition of the poems by a volume of Beddoes' letters. It is clear, therefore, that there is no one living to whom lovers of Beddoes owe so much as to Mr. Gosse. He has supplied most important materials for the elucidation of the poet's history: and, among the lyrics which he has printed for the first time, are to be found one of the most perfect specimens of Beddoes' command of unearthly pathos—*The Old Ghost*—and one of the most singular examples of his vein of grotesque and ominous humour—*The Oviparous Tailor*. Yet it may be doubted whether even Mr. Gosse's edition is the final one. There are traces in Beddoes' letters of unpublished compositions which may still come to light. What has happened, one would like to know, to *The Ivory Gate*, that 'volume of prosaic poetry and poetical prose,' which Beddoes talked of publishing in 1837? Only a few fine stanzas from it have ever appeared. And, as Mr. Gosse himself tells us, the variations in *Death's Jest Book* alone would warrant the publication of a variorum edition of that work—'if,' he wisely adds, for the proviso contains the gist of the matter—'if the interest in Beddoes should continue to grow.'

'Say what you will, I am convinced the man who is to awaken the drama must be a bold, trampling fellow—no creeper into worm-holes—no reviver even—however good. These reanimations are vampire-cold.' The words occur in one of Beddoes' letters, and they are usually quoted by critics, on the rare occasions on which his poetry is discussed, as an instance of the curious incapacity of artists to practise what they preach. But the truth is that Beddoes was not a 'creeper into worm-holes,' he was not even a 'reviver'; he was a re-incarnation. Everything that we know of him goes to show that the laborious and elaborate effort of literary reconstruction was quite alien to his spirit. We have Kelsall's evidence as to the ease and abundance of his composition; we have the character of the man, as it shines forth in his letters and in the history of his life—records of a 'bold, trampling fellow,' if ever there was one; and we have the evidence of his poetry itself. For the impress of a fresh and vital intelligence is stamped unmistakably upon all that is best in his work. His mature blank verse is perfect. It is not an artificial concoction galvanised into the semblance of life; it simply lives. And, with Beddoes, maturity was precocious, for he obtained complete mastery over the most difficult and dangerous of metres at a wonderfully early age. Blank verse is like the Djin in the Arabian Nights; it is either the most terrible of masters, or the most powerful of slaves. If you have not the magic secret, it will take your best thoughts, your bravest imaginations, and change them into toads and fishes; but, if the spell be yours, it will turn into a flying carpet and lift your simplest utterance into the highest heaven. Beddoes had mastered the 'Open, Sesame' at an age when most poets are still mouthing ineffectual wheats and barleys. In his twenty-second year, his thoughts filled and moved and animated his blank verse as easily and familiarly as a hand in a glove. He wishes to compare, for instance, the human mind, with its knowledge of the past, to a single eye receiving the light of the stars; and the object of the comparison is to lay stress upon the concentration on one point of a vast multiplicity of objects. There could be no better exercise for a young verse-writer than to attempt his own expression of this idea, and then to examine these lines by Beddoes—lines where simplicity and splendour have been woven together with the ease of accomplished art.

> How glorious to live! Even in one thought
> The wisdom of past times to fit together,
> And from the luminous minds of many men
> Catch a reflected truth; as, in one eye,
> Light, from unnumbered worlds and farthest planets
> Of the star-crowded universe, is gathered
> Into one ray.

The effect is, of course, partly produced by the diction; but the diction, fine as it is, would be useless without the phrasing —that art by which the two forces of the metre and the sense are made at once to combat, to combine with, and to heighten each other. It is, however, impossible to do more than touch upon this side—the technical side—of Beddoes' genius. But it may be noticed that in his mastery of phrasing—as in so much besides—he was a true Elizabethan. The great artists of that age knew that without phrasing dramatic verse was a dead thing; and it is only necessary to turn from their pages to those of an eighteenth-century dramatist—Addison, for instance—to understand how right they were.

Beddoes' power of creating scenes of intense dramatic force, which had already begun to show itself in *The Brides' Tragedy*, reached its full development in his subsequent work. The opening act of *The Second Brother*—the most nearly complete of his unfinished tragedies—is a striking example of a powerful and original theme treated in such a way that, while the whole of it is steeped in imaginative poetry, yet not one ounce of its dramatic effectiveness is lost. The duke's next brother, the heir to the dukedom of Ferrara, returns to the city, after years of wandering, a miserable and sordid beggar —to find his younger brother, rich, beautiful, and reckless, leading a life of gay debauchery, with the assurance of succeeding to the dukedom when the duke dies. The situation presents possibilities for just those bold and extraordinary contrasts which were so dear to Beddoes' heart. While Marcello, the second brother, is meditating over his wretched fate, Orazio, the third, comes upon the stage, crowned and glorious, attended by a train of singing revellers, and with a courtesan upon either hand. 'Wine in a ruby!' he exclaims, gazing into his mistress's eyes:

> I'll solemnize their beauty in a draught
> Pressed from the summer of an hundred vines.

Meanwhile Marcello pushes himself forward, and attempts to salute his brother.

Orazio.   Insolent beggar!
Marcello.   Prince! But we must shake hands.
> Look you, the round earth's like a sleeping serpent,
> Who drops her dusky tail upon her crown
> Just here. Oh, we are like two mountain peaks
> Of two close planets, catching in the air:
> You, King Olympus, a great pile of summer,
> Wearing a crown of gods; I, the vast top
> Of the ghosts' deadly world, naked and dark,
> With nothing reigning on my desolate head
> But an old spirit of a murdered god,
> Palaced within the corpse of Saturn's father.

They begin to dispute, and at last Marcello exclaims—

> Aye, Prince, you have a brother—
Orazio.   The Duke—he'll scourge you.
Marcello.   Nay, *the second*, sir,
> Who, like an envious river, flows between
> Your footsteps and Ferrara's throne. . . .

Orazio.   Stood he before me there,
By you, in you, as like as you're unlike,
Straight as you're bowed, young as you are old,
And many years nearer than him to Death,
The falling brilliancy of whose white sword
Your ancient locks so silverly reflect,
I would deny, outswear, and overreach,
And pass him with contempt, as I do you.
Jove! How we waste the stars: set on, my friends.

And so the revelling band pass onward, singing still, as they
vanish down the darkened street:

> Strike, you myrtle-crownèd boys,
> Ivied maidens, strike together! . . .

and Marcello is left alone:

                                   I went forth
Joyfully, as the soul of one who closes
His pillowed eyes beside an unseen murderer,
And like its horrible return was mine,
To find the heart, wherein I breathed and beat,
Cold, gashed, and dead. Let me forget to love,
And take a heart of venom: let me make
A staircase of the frightened breasts of men,
And climb into a lonely happiness!
And thou, who only art alone as I,
Great solitary god of that one sun,
I charge thee, by the likeness of our state,
Undo these human veins that tie me close
To other men, and let your servant griefs
Unmilk me of my mother, and pour in
Salt scorn and steaming hate!

A moment later he learnt that the duke has suddenly died,
and that the dukedom is his. The rest of the play affords an
instance of Beddoes' inability to trace out a story, clearly and
forcibly, to an appointed end. The succeeding acts are
crowded with beautiful passages, with vivid situations, with
surprising developments, but the central plot vanishes away
into nothing, like a great river dissipating itself among a

thousand streams. It is, indeed, clear enough that Beddoes was embarrassed with his riches, that his fertile mind conceived too easily, and that he could never resist the temptation of giving life to his imaginations, even at the cost of killing his play. His conception of Orazio, for instance, began by being that of a young Bacchus, as he appears in the opening scene. But Beddoes could not leave him there; he must have a romantic wife, whom he has deserted; and the wife, once brought into being, must have an interview with her husband. The interview is an exquisitely beautiful one, but it shatters Orazio's character, for, in the course of it, he falls desperately in love with his wife; and meanwhile the wife herself has become so important and interesting a figure that she must be given a father, who in his turn becomes the central character in more than one exciting scene. But, by this time, what has happened to the second brother? It is easy to believe that Beddoes was always ready to begin a new play rather than finish an old one. But it is not so certain that his method was quite as inexcusable as his critics assert. To the reader, doubtless, his faulty construction is glaring enough; but Beddoes wrote his plays to be acted, as a passage in one of his letters very clearly shows. 'You are, I think,' he writes to Kelsall, 'disinclined to the stage: now I confess that I think this is the highest aim of the dramatist, and should be very desirous to get on it. To look down on it is a piece of impertinence, as long as one chooses to write in the form of a play, and is generally the result of one's own inability to produce anything striking and affecting in that way.' And it is precisely upon the stage that such faults of construction as those which disfigure Beddoes' tragedies matter least. An audience, whose attention is held and delighted by a succession of striking incidents clothed in splendid speech, neither cares nor knows whether the effect of the whole, as a whole, is worthy of the separate parts. It would be foolish, in the present melancholy condition of the art of dramatic declamation, to wish for the public performance of *Death's Jest Book*; but it is impossible not to hope that the time may come when an adequate representation of that strange and great work may be something more than 'a possibility more thin than air.' Then, and then only, shall we be able to take the true measure of Beddoes' genius.

Perhaps, however, the ordinary reader finds Beddoes' lack of construction a less distasteful quality than his disregard of the common realities of existence. Not only is the subject-matter of the greater part of his poetry remote and dubious; his very characters themselves seem to be infected by their creator's delight in the mysterious, the strange, and the unreal. They have no healthy activity; or, if they have, they invariably lose it in the second act; in the end, they are all hypochondriac philosophers, puzzling over eternity and dissecting the attributes of Death. The central idea of *Death's Jest Book*—the resurrection of a ghost—fails to be truly effective, because it is difficult to see any clear distinction between the phantom and the rest of the characters. The duke, saved from death by the timely arrival of Wolfram, exclaims, 'Blest hour!' and then, in a moment, begins to ponder, and agonise, and dream:

> And yet how palely, with what faded lips
> Do we salute this unhoped change of fortune!
> Thou art so silent, lady; and I utter
> Shadows of words, like to an ancient ghost,
> Arisen out of hoary centuries
> Where none can speak his language.

Orazio, in his brilliant palace, is overcome with the same feelings:

> Methinks, these fellows, with their ready jests,
> Are like to tedious bells, that ring alike
> Marriage or death.

And his description of his own revels applies no less to the whole atmosphere of Beddoes' tragedies:

> Voices were heard, most loud, which no man owned:
> There were more shadows too than there were men;
> And all the air more dark and thick than night
> Was heavy, as 'twere made of something more
> Than living breaths.

It would be vain to look, among such spectral imaginings as these, for guidance in practical affairs, or for illuminating views on men and things, or for a philosophy, or, in short, for anything which may be called a 'criticism of life.' If a poet must be a critic of life, Beddoes was certainly no poet. He belongs to the class of writers of which, in English literature, Spenser, Keats, and Milton are the dominant figures—the writers who are great merely because of their art. Sir James Stephen was only telling the truth when he remarked that Milton might have put all that he had to say in *Paradise Lost* into a prose pamphlet of two or three pages. But who cares about what Milton had to say? It is his way of saying it that matters; it is his expression. Take away the expression from the *Satires* of Pope, or from *The Excursion*, and, though you will destroy the poems, you will leave behind a great mass of thought. Take away the expression from *Hyperion*, and you will leave nothing at all. To ask which is the better of the two styles is like asking whether a peach is better than a rose, because, both being beautiful, you can eat the one and not the other. At any rate, Beddoes is among the roses: it is in his expression that his greatness lies. His verse is an instrument of many modulations, of exquisite delicacy, of strange suggestiveness, of amazing power. Playing on it, he can give utterance to the subtlest visions, such as this:

> Just now a beam of joy hung on his eyelash;
> But, as I looked, it sunk into his eye,
> Like a bruised worm writhing its form of rings
> Into a darkening hole.

Or to the most marvellous of vague and vast conceptions, such as this:

> I begin to hear
> Strange but sweet sounds, and the loud rocky dashing
> Of waves, where time into Eternity
> Falls over ruined worlds.

Or he can evoke sensations of pure loveliness, such as these:

So fair a creature! of such charms compact
As nature stints elsewhere: which you may find
Under the tender eyelid of a serpent,
Or in the gurge of a kiss-coloured rose,
By drops and sparks: but when she moves, you see,
Like water from a crystal overfilled,
Fresh beauty tremble out of her and lave
Her fair sides to the ground.

Or he can put into a single line all the long memories of
adoration:

My love was much;
My life but an inhabitant of his.

Or he can pass in a moment from tiny sweetness to colossal
turmoil:

I should not say
How thou art like the daisy in Noah's meadow,
On which the foremost drop of rain fell warm
And soft at evening: so the little flower
Wrapped up its leaves, and shut the treacherous water
Close to the golden welcome of its breast,
Delighting in the touch of that which led
The shower of oceans, in whose billowy drops
Tritons and lions of the sea were warring,
And sometimes ships on fire sunk in the blood,
Of their own inmates; others were of ice,
And some had islands rooted in their waves,
Beasts on their rocks, and forest-powdering winds,
And showers tumbling on their tumbling self,
And every sea of every ruined star
Was but a drop in the world-melting flood.

He can express alike the beautiful tenderness of love, and the
hectic, dizzy, and appalling frenzy of extreme rage:—

... What shall I do? I speak all wrong,
And lose a soul-full of delicious thought
By talking. Hush! Let's drink each other up
By silent eyes. Who lives, but thou and I,
My heavenly wife? ...
I'll watch thee thus, till I can tell a second
By thy cheek's change.

In that, one can almost feel the kisses; and, in this, one can almost hear the gnashing of the teeth. 'Never!' exclaims the duke to his son Torrismond:

> There lies no grain of sand between
> My loved and my detested! Wing thee hence,
> Or thou dost stand to-morrow on a cobweb
> Spun o'er the well of clotted Acheron,
> Whose hydrophobic entrails stream with fire!
> And may this intervening earth be snow,
> And my step burn like the mid coal of Ætna,
> Plunging me, through it all, into the core,
> Where in their graves the dead are shut like seeds,
> If I do not—O, but he is my son!

Is not that tremendous? But, to find Beddoes in his most characteristic mood, one must watch him weaving his mysterious imagination upon the woof of mortality. One must wander with him through the pages of *Death's Jest Book*, one must grow accustomed to the dissolution of reality, and the opening of the nettled lips of graves; one must learn that 'the dead are most and merriest,' one must ask—'Are the ghosts eaves-dropping?'—one must realise that 'murder is full of holes.' Among the ruins of his Gothic cathedral, on whose cloister walls the Dance of Death is painted, one may speculate at ease over the fragility of existence, and, within the sound of that dark ocean,

> Whose tumultuous waves
> Are heaped, contending ghosts,

one may understand how it is that

> Death is mightier, stronger, and more faithful
> To man than Life.

Lingering there, one may watch the Deaths come down from their cloister, and dance and sing amid the moonlight; one may laugh over the grotesque contortions of skeletons; one may crack jokes upon corruption; one may sit down with phantoms, and drink to the health of Death.

In private intercourse Beddoes was the least morbid of human beings. His mind was like one of those Gothic cathedrals of which he was so fond—mysterious within, and filled with a light at once richer and less real than the light of day; on the outside, firm, and towering, and immediately impressive; and embellished, both inside and out, with grinning gargoyles. His conversation, Kelsall tells us, was full of humour and vitality, and untouched by any trace of egoism or affectation. He loved discussion, plunging into it with fire, and carrying it onward with high dexterity and good-humoured force. His letters are excellent: simple, spirited, spicy, and as original as his verse; flavoured with that vein of rattling open-air humour which had produced his school-boy novel in the style of Fielding. He was a man whom it would have been a rare delight to know. His character, so eminently English, compact of courage, of originality, of imagination, and with something coarse in it as well, puts one in mind of Hamlet: not the melodramatic sentimentalist of the stage; but the real Hamlet, Horatio's Hamlet, who called his father's ghost old truepenny, who forged his uncle's signature, who fought Laertes, and ranted in a grave, and lugged the guts into the neighbour room. His tragedy, like Hamlet's, was the tragedy of an overpowerful will—a will so strong as to recoil upon itself, and fall into indecision. It is easy for a weak man to be decided—there is so much to make him so; but a strong man, who can do anything, sometimes leaves everything undone. Fortunately Beddoes, though he did far less than he might have done, possessed so rich a genius that what he did, though small in quantity, is in quality beyond price. 'I might have been among other things, a good poet,' were his last words. 'Among other things'! Aye, there's the rub. But, in spite of his own 'might have been,' a good poet he was. Perhaps for him, after all, there was very little to regret; his life was full of high nobility; and what other way of death would have befitted the poet of death? There is a thought constantly recurring throughout his writings—in his childish as in his most mature work—the thought of the

beauty and the supernal happiness of soft and quiet death. He
had visions of 'rosily dying,' of 'turning to daisies gently in the
grave,' of a 'pink reclining death,' of death coming like a
summer cloud over the soul. 'Let her deathly life pass into
death,' says one of his earliest characters, 'like music on the
night wind.' And, in *Death's Jest Book*, Sibylla has the same
thoughts:

> O Death! I am thy friend,
> I struggle not with thee, I love thy state:
> Thou canst be sweet and gentle, be so now;
> And let me pass praying away into thee,
> As twilight still does into starry night.

Did his mind, obsessed and overwhelmed by images of death,
crave at last for the one thing stranger than all these—the
experience of it? It is easy to believe so, and that, ill, wretched,
and abandoned by Degen at the miserable Cigogne Hotel, he
should seek relief in the gradual dissolution which attends
upon loss of blood. And then, when he had recovered, when
he was almost happy once again, the old thoughts, perhaps,
came crowding back upon him—thoughts of the futility of
life, and the supremacy of death and the mystical whirlpool of
the unknown, and the long quietude of the grave. In the end,
Death had grown to be something more than Death to him—
it was, mysteriously and transcendentally, Love as well.

> Death's darts are sometimes Love's. So Nature tells,
> When laughing waters close o'er drowning men;
> When in flowers' honied corners poison dwells;
> When Beauty dies: and the unwearied ken
> Of those who seek a cure for long despair
> Will learn . . .

What learning was it that rewarded him? What ghostly knowledge of eternal love?

> If there are ghosts to raise,
>   What shall I call,
> Out of hell's murky haze,
>   Heaven's blue pall?

—Raise my loved long-lost boy
To lead me to his joy.—
    There are no ghosts to raise;
    Out of death lead no ways;
      Vain is the call.

    —Know'st thou not ghosts to sue?
      No love thou hast.
    Else lie, as I will do,
      And breathe thy last.
So out of Life's fresh crown
Fall like a rose-leaf down.
    Thus are the ghosts to woo;
    Thus are all dreams made true,
      Ever to last!

1907.

MACAULAY

IN Apollo's house there are many mansions; there is even one (unexpectedly enough) for the Philistine. So complex and various are the elements of literature that no writer can be damned on a mere enumeration of faults. He may always possess merits which make up for everything; if he loses on the swings, he may win on the roundabouts. Macaulay—whatever the refined and the sublime may say to the contrary—is an example of this. A coarse texture of mind—a metallic style—an itch for the obvious and the emphatic—a middle-class, Victorian complacency—it is all too true; Philistine is, in fact, the only word to fit the case; and yet, by dint of sheer power of writing, the Philistine has reached Parnassus. It is a curious occurrence, and deserves a closer examination.

What are the qualities that make a historian? Obviously these three—a capacity for absorbing facts, a capacity for stating them, and a point of view. The two latter are connected, but not necessarily inseparable. The late Professor Samuel Gardiner, for instance, could absorb facts, and he could state them; but he had no point of view; and the result is that his book on the most exciting period of English history resembles nothing so much as a very large heap of sawdust. But a point of view, it must be remembered, by no means implies sympathy. One might almost say that it implies the reverse. At any rate it is curious to observe how many instances there are of great historians who have been at daggers drawn with their subjects. Gibbon, a highly civilised scoffer, spent twenty years of his life writing about barbarism and superstition. Michelet was a romantic and a republican; but his work on mediæval France and the Revolution is far inferior to his magnificent delineation of the classic and despotic centuries. Macaulay's great-nephew, Professor

Trevelyan, has, it is true, written a delightful account of the Italian Risorgimento, of which he is an enthusiastic devotee. But, even here, the rule seems to apply; one cannot but feel that Professor Trevelyan's epic would have been still more delightful if it had contained a little of the salt of criticism— if, in fact, he had not swallowed Garibaldi whole.

As for Macaulay's point of view, everyone knows it was the Whig one. In reality this is simplifying too much; but, however we may describe it, there can be no doubt that Macaulay's vision was singularly alien to the England of the latter years of the seventeenth century. Like Gibbon, like Michelet, like the later Carlyle, he did not—to put it succinctly—understand what he was talking about. Charles II, James II—that whole strange age in which religion, debauchery, intellect, faction, wit and brutality seethed and bubbled together in such an extraordinary *olla podrida*— escaped him. He could see parts of it; but he could not see into the depths; and so much the better: he had his point of view. The definiteness, the fixity, of his position is what is remarkable. He seems to have been created *en bloc*. His manner never changed; as soon as he could write at all—at the age of eight—he wrote in the style of his History. The three main factors in his mental growth—the Clapham sect, Cambridge, Holland House—were not so much influences as suitable environments for the development of a predetermined personality. Whatever had happened to him, he would always have been a middle-class intellectual with Whig views. It is possible, however, that he may actually have gained something from Holland House. The modern habit of gently laughing at Whigs and Whiggery is based on a misconception. A certain *a priori* stuffiness which seems to hang about that atmosphere is in reality a Victorian innovation. The true pre-Reform Bill Whig was a tremendous aristocrat—the heir to a great tradition of intellectual independence and spiritual pride. When the Hollands' son travelled as a youth in Italy he calmly noted in his diary that someone he had met had a face 'almost as stupid as the Duke of Wellington's'; the young

Fox was a chip of the old block. Such surroundings must have been good for Macaulay. It was not only that they supported his self-confidence—he had enough of that already—but that they brought him into touch with the severity, the grandeur, and the amenity of an old civilisation. Without them he might have been provincial or academic; but he was not so; on every page of his work one sees the manifest signs of the culture and the traffic of the great world.

Thus Macaulay's Whiggism was a composite affair—it was partly eighteenth century and partly Victorian. But the completeness with which it dominated him gave him his certainty of attitude and his clarity of vision. It enabled him to stand up against the confusion and frenzy of the seventeenth century and say, very loudly and very distinctly, what he thought of it. So far so good. The misfortune is that what he thought was not of a finer quality. The point of view is distinct enough, but it is without distinction; and Macaulay in consequence remains an excellent but not a supreme historian. His Whiggism was in itself a very serious drawback—not because it was a cause of bias, but because it was a symptom of crudity. The bias was of the wrong kind; it was the outcome of party politics, and the sad truth is that, in the long run, party politics become a bore. They did not, indeed, succeed in making Macaulay a bore; that was impossible; but, though he is never dull, one constantly feels that he might have been much more interesting. Too often he misses the really exciting, the really fascinating, point. And how can one fail to miss a great deal if one persists in considering the world from one side or other of the House of Commons?

A certain crudity, a certain coarseness of fibre—the marks of a party politician—are particularly obvious in those character sketches of great persons which form so important a part of Macaulay's History. Within their limits they are admirably done; but their limits are too narrow. They lack colour; they are steel engravings—unsatisfactory compromises between a portrait in oils and a realistic snapshot. One has

only to compare them with Clarendon's splendid presentments to realise their inadequacy. With what a gorgeous
sinuosity, with what a grandiose delicacy, the older master
elaborates, through his enormous sentences, the lineaments
of a soul! Beside them the skimpy lines and cheap contrasts
of Macaulay's black and white are all too obvious.

But the Whig politician was not only crude; he was also,
to a strange degree, ingenuous and complacent. A preposterous optimism fills his pages. The Revolution of 1688
having succeeded, all was well; Utopia was bound to follow;
and it actually had followed—in the reign of Victoria. Thus
he contrasts with delight, almost with awe, the state of Torbay
at the time of William's landing and its condition in 1850. In
1688 'the huts of ploughmen and fishermen were thinly
scattered over what is now the site of crowded marts and of
luxurious pavilions.' A description of the modern Torquay
becomes irresistible. 'The inhabitants are about ten thousand
in number. The newly-built churches and chapels, the baths
and libraries, the hotels and public gardens, the infirmary and
the museum, the white streets, rising terrace above terrace,
the gay villas peeping from the midst of shrubberies and flower
beds, present a spectacle widely different from any that in
the seventeenth century England could show.' They do
indeed.

The style is the mirror of the mind, and Macaulay's style
is that of a debater. The hard points are driven home like
nails with unfailing dexterity; it is useless to hope for subtlety
or refinement; one cannot hammer with delicacy. The repetitions, the antitheses, resemble revolving cog-wheels; and indeed the total result produces an effect which suggests the
operations of a machine more than anything else—a comparison which, no doubt, would have delighted Macaulay.
The descriptive passages are the most deplorable. In a set-
piece, such as the account of Westminster Hall at the impeachment of Hastings, all the horrors of a remorseless
rhetoric are made manifest. From the time of Cicero downwards, the great disadvantage of oratory has been that it never

lets one off. One must hear everything, however well one knows it, and however obvious it is. For such writers a dose of Stendhal is to be recommended. Macaulay, however, would not have benefited by the prescription, for he was a hopeless case. The tonic pages of the *Chartreuse de Parme* would have had no effect on him whatever. When he wished to state that Schomberg was buried in Westminster Abbey, he *had* to say that 'the illustrious warrior' was laid in 'that venerable abbey, hallowed by the dust of many generations of princes, heroes and poets.' There is no escaping it; and the incidental drawback that Schomberg was not buried at Westminster at all, but in Dublin, is, in comparison with the platitude of the style, of very small importance.

The curiously metallic quality in Macaulay's writing—its hardness of outline, its slightly hollow ring—is so characteristic that it is difficult not to see in it the indication of some profound psychological state. The stout, square man with the prodigious memory and the inexhaustible capacity for conversation, was apparently a normal human being, except in one direction: he never married, and there seems no reason to suppose that he was ever in love. An entertaining essay might perhaps be written on the sexlessness of historians; but it would be entertaining and nothing more: we do not know enough either about the historians or sex. Yet, in Macaulay's case, one cannot resist the conclusion that the absence from his make-up of intense physical emotion brought a barrenness upon his style. His sentences have no warmth and no curves; the embracing fluidity of love is lacking. And it is noticeable how far more effective he is in his treatment of those whom he dislikes than of those whom he admires. His Marlborough is a fine villain. His James II is a caricature, with a queer vitality of its own—the vitality of a marionette. But his William of Orange is a failure—a lifeless image of waxwork perfection. Macaulay's inability to make his hero live—his refusal to make any attempt to illuminate the mysteries of that most obscure and singular character—epitomises all that is weakest in his work.

Probably the futility of his æsthetic judgments was another effect of the same cause. Whenever he writes of pure poetry—in the essay on Byron, for instance—he is plainly at sea; his lack of sensibility becomes painfully obvious. A true child of his age, he had a profound distrust, amounting at times to an actual hatred, of art. That Queen Mary should have ruined her father, turned him out of his kingdom, and seized his throne for herself—all that was no blemish at all on her character: was she not acting upon strictly Whig principles? But one fault she did have. She was responsible for 'a frivolous and inelegant fashion.' She was the first person in England to form 'a vast collection of hideous images, and of vases on which houses, trees, bridges and mandarins were depicted in outrageous defiance of all the laws of perspective.' Queen Mary, in fact, liked china; and that could not be forgiven her.

The weaknesses are obvious, and the strength, suitably enough, is obvious too. History is primarily a narrative, and in power of narration no one has ever surpassed Macaulay. In that he is a genius. When it comes to telling a story, his faults disappear or change into virtues. Narrowness becomes clarity, and crudity turns into force. The rhetoric of the style, from being the ornament of platitude, becomes the servant of excitement. Every word is valuable: there is no hesitation, no confusion, and no waste. It is clear from his journal that Macaulay realised the dominating importance of this side of his work. He laboured at his purely narrative passages for weeks at a time, with the result that they are masterpieces. Nobody who has once read them can ever forget his account of the trial of the Bishops, the siege of Derry, and the battle of Killiecrankie. To write so is to write magnificently, and if one has to be a Philistine to bring off those particular effects one can only say, so much the better for the Philistine. But it is not only in certain passages that Macaulay triumphs. His whole History is conditioned by a supreme sense of the narrative form. It presses on, with masterly precipitation, from start to finish. Everything falls into place. Unsatisfying characters, superficial descriptions, jejune reflections, are seen to be no longer of importance in themselves—they are merely stages in the development of the narrative. They are part of the pattern—the enthralling, ever-shifting pattern of the perfect kaleidoscope. A work of art? Yes, there is no denying it: the Philistine was also an artist. And there he is—squat, square and perpetually talking—on Parnassus.

1928.

THE FIRST EARL OF LYTTON

THE two volumes of letters[1] which Lady Betty Balfour has put together from the private correspondence of her father, the late Lord Lytton, cannot fail to appeal to a large body of readers. The letters themselves are full of interest; they deal, in a masterly and brilliant way, with a vast variety of topics; and they are set before the reader with an admirable skill and an unerring sympathy. Lady Betty Balfour has succeeded not only in the difficult task of selecting and arranging a mass of material whose very richness was embarrassing; she has invested the whole with a living unity, and breathed into it a spirit which is the true commentary of the life which the letters reveal. For there is something more in these volumes than a succession of good things: there is also—what is present in every collection of letters worthy of notice—the portrait of a man. To open the book is to strike at once into the orbit of a new personality. One feels, when one has read it, that one has almost made a friend.

A remarkable range of interests, and a wide catholicity of tastes—these are perhaps the most obvious characteristics of Lord Lytton's correspondence. The letters flow on, naturally and copiously, into a multitude of unbidden channels; they pass without an effort from poetry to politics, from hypnotism to Wagner, from a string of anecdotes to reflections upon the destiny of man. Nor is their versatility merely of the dilettante kind; it is the versatility of an enthusiast—of one of those rare enthusiasts whose province is the whole world. *Humani nihil a me alienum puto :* the old sentence, so often thrown out at random, would have been a peculiarly fitting motto for these letters. And the variety of their subject matter is reflected in the diversity of the correspondents to whom they are addressed.

[1] *Personal and Literary Letters of Robert, First Earl of Lytton.* Edited by Lady Betty Balfour. In two volumes. Longmans, Green & Co. 1906.

Few men of his generation could have had so various an acquaintance as Lord Lytton. He discussed literature with the Brownings, he wrote state papers to Lord Salisbury, he speculated on life and death with Theodor Gomperz, he exchanged epigrams with Lady Dorothy Nevill, he gossiped with Mr. John Morley, and some of his most charming letters are those addressed, when he was Viceroy of India, to the late Queen. He had, too, a genius for friendship, so that his acquaintances very soon became his friends. One of his most intimate correspondents was Sir James Stephen, whom he met for the first time on the eve of his departure to India, and with whom he immediately struck up a lasting friendship. 'India,' says Lady Betty, 'was of course the subject of their talk. Lytton was not more eager to hear than Stephen to tell all that he knew of the conditions of that great empire'; and the two men 'did not part till they had spent half the night walking each other home, too absorbed in their subject to feel fatigue or the wish to separate.' Stephen went home to write for his new friend a pamphlet on the government of India, which Lord Lytton declared had given him 'the master key to the magnificent system of Indian administration.' During the four succeeding years Stephen wrote to the Viceroy by every mail. The friendship is remarkable for something more than its swift beginning: it was a mingling of opposites such as it is a rare delight to think upon. Sir James Stephen was eminently unromantic. His qualities were those of solidity and force; he preponderated with a character of formidable grandeur, with a massive and rugged intellectual sanity, a colossal commonsense. The contrast is complete between this monolithic nature and the mercurial temperament of Lord Lytton, with his ardent imagination, his easy brilliance, his passionate sympathy, his taste for the elaborate and the coloured and the rococo. Such characteristics offended some of his stiff countrymen; they could not tolerate a man to whom conventions were 'incomprehensible things,' who felt at home 'in the pure light air of foreign life,' whose dress 'was original, as nearly all about him,' and who was not afraid to express his feelings in public. But the great lawyer judged differently. 'I never knew a man,' he wrote after Lord Lytton's death, 'towards whom I felt so warmly and to whom I owed so much. . . . I shall always regard it as one of the most fortunate circumstances of my life that I was for many years one of his most intimate friends.'

The story which the letters tell has much of the atractive-ness of a romance. But it is one of those romances which state and amplify a problem, only to leave one, at last, still in doubt. Was the hero a statesman of genius whose true faculties the world misunderstood? Or was he a poet, diverted by the pres-sure of circumstances from a great achievement in art? Different readers will answer the question differently; but, in either case, the reply must involve an admission of failure or perhaps rather of defeat. Lord Lytton's rule in India was at the time the object of unparalleled obloquy, and is now almost forgotten; his poetry blossomed early and blossomed late, but it never bore the fruit which brings immortality. Thus, be-hind all the sparkling movement of the letters, one may per-ceive a sense of melancholy, which at moments deepens into the actual expression of gloom. 'Whether I look forward or backward, an immense despair always comes over me. If I were younger—but it is all too late now; I know that as a poet I shall never do or be what I feel that I might have done and been.' It is difficult to speculate on unfulfilled possibilities; but one may well believe that a writer who trembled so often on the verge of greatness might, if fortune had so willed it, have crossed the perilous line. As it is, one is constantly wondering why Lytton's verse never does quite 'soar above the Aonian mount.' Was Mrs. Browning right when she told her friend 'You *sympathise* too much'? Perhaps his father came nearer the mark in his protests to John Forster: 'He is doing that which the richest mind and the richest soil cannot do long with impunity. He is always taking white crops off his glebe. He never allows poetry to lie fallow.' In truth, diamonds are not made in a day; and, though a Shakespeare or a Coleridge may give you, in a moment, a handful of jewels, who knows how many years of superhuman concentration may have gone to the making of them? One may imagine, at Lord Lytton's poetical christening, a bad fairy gliding in among the rest. The good ones were lavish with their gifts of charm, and distinction, and imagination, and humour, and feeling; and then, after them all, came the witch with her deceitful present: 'Yes, my dear, and may you always write with ease!' The child grew up endowed with a fatal facility. He could put his thoughts into verse as easily as he could pick pebbles out of a brook. The pebbles, wet and glowing in his hand, were beautiful to look upon; and then in a little while, unaccountably, they seemed to be common stones after all. In this world, a glamour caught too easily fades too soon; it turns out to be an illusion. And an illusion is the one thing that a poet should never have.

A brief note from Disraeli, offering the Viceroyalty of India, dramatically shattered Lord Lytton's dreams of ease and poetry. He accepted the great office with an acute sense of all that it involved. 'Oh, the change—the *awful* change!' he exclaims to Forster; and he assured Disraeli 'that if, with the certainty of leaving my life behind me in India, I had a reasonable chance of also leaving there a reputation comparable to Lord Mayo's, I would still, without a moment's hesitation, embrace the high destiny you place within my grasp.' This is not the place for a discussion of the still controversial questions surrounding Lord Lytton's Indian rule. But no reference to the man or to his life could be even superficially complete without some notice of his political capacity. There is enough in the present volumes—there is far more in Lady Betty Balfour's previous work (*Lord Lytton's Indian Administration*)—to make it clear to the most careless reader that the popular conception of Lord Lytton as a minor poet masquerading as a Viceroy, who scribbled verses when he should have been composing dispatches, is a glaring travesty of the facts. The antithesis, however, is delightful, like all antitheses; and, in this case, it is supported by that curious English prejudice which has always—since the days when Rochester libelled the most astute of monarchs—refused to allow that a witty man could be a wise one. The ignorance, too, with which the ordinary Englishman habitually seasons his judgments on Indian affairs has done much to obscure the true character of Lytton's statesmanship. Besides the Afghan war, there is one event, and one alone, which 'the man in the street' connects with Lytton's Indian administration—the proclamation of the Queen as Empress of India. Important as that event was, it is little short of ludicrous that it should be the one remembered act of the administration which gave free trade to India, which accomplished the great reform of the equalisation of the inland duties on salt, which finally established the grand and far-reaching principle of decentralisation, and which instituted the Famine Insurance Fund. The truth is that Lytton's internal administration must take rank as one of the most pregnant and beneficent known in India since the great Governor-Generalship of Dalhousie. It is a curious irony that the Viceroy who carried, in the face of the opposition of a majority of his Council, the measure which opened the door to free trade in India, should labour under the imputation of political flippancy; but, after all, he was a Viceroy who had written love-poems, who wore unusual waistcoats, and who smoked cigarettes. Whether his Afghan policy did or did not deserve the virulent denunciation which it received is a question which does not concern us here; what does concern us is the obvious fact that Lytton's financial and administrative work was the work of a statesman endowed with no mean share of courage, of wisdom, of energy, and of determination. Unfortunately his opponents failed to notice the distinction. In the heat of party, he was declared by one politician to be 'everything which a Viceroy ought not to be'; by a second to be guilty of 'financial dishonesty, trickery, treachery, tyranny and cruelty'; by a third to have shown 'a deliberate desire to shed blood, systematic fraud, violence and inveracity of the vilest kind.' Lytton, though it is clear that he suffered keenly, never let his dignity desert him. To a friend, who had associated himself with these attacks, he wrote: 'I confess I have sometimes fancied that had our positions been reversed—you placed in mine, and I in yours—my confidence in your character and intelligence would have sufficed to satisfy my judgement that there was more honesty and wisdom in your action than in the denunciation of it by persons who could not be fully acquainted with the causes and conditions of it. But no man dare say of himself how he would feel, or what he would do, in a position he has never occupied.' Such words as these have something in them of the old Roman *æquanimitas*—they might have come from the pen of a Pliny or a Trajan, calm in their great government and their mighty toil. And it was in the same spirit that, when the time came for relinquishing his task, Lord Lytton wrote to Stephen:

'Were you ever in the Forest of Arden? I have always fancied it must be the most charming place in the world, more especially in summer-time. I shall shortly be on my way to it, I think, and I hasten to give you rendez-vous at the court of the Banished Duke. If you meet our friend, the melancholy Jaques, greet him from me most lovingly, and tell him—Ducdame!—that all the fools are now in the circle and he need pipe to them no more. . . . And tell your own great heart, dear and good friend, that the joy I take from the prospect of seeing you is more precious to me than all that Providence has taken from the fancy prospect I had painted on the blank wall of the Future of bequeathing to India the supremacy of Central Asia and the revenues of a first-class Power.'

These are fine words; and, in their wit, their fancy, their ornate elaboration, their half-hidden sadness, their noble wealth of feeling, they are supremely characteristic of their author. One is reminded of the beautiful portrait by Watts, where the rich bright colours—the auburn hair and beard, the blue eyes, the turquoise on the finger—blend so wonderfully into the mysterious melancholy of the face. It is easy to talk of defeat and failure. But if one turns back from the portrait to the book, and then back again from the book to the portrait, if one considers those records of achievement and of thought, one begins to wonder whether such things can be measured by such terms. One seems to discern in them something less unfortunate than failure, and something, perchance, more splendid than success.

1907.

A VICTORIAN CRITIC

To the cold and youthful observer there is a strange fascination about the Age of Victoria. It has the odd attractiveness of
something which is at once very near and very far off; it is
like one of those queer fishes that one sees behind glass at an
aquarium, before whose grotesque proportions and sombre
menacing agilities one hardly knows whether to laugh or to
shudder; when once it has caught one's eye, one cannot tear
oneself away. Probably its reputation will always be worse
than it deserves. Reputations, in the case of ages no less than
of individuals, depend, in the long run, upon the judgments of
artists; and artists will never be fair to the Victorian Age. To
them its incoherence, its pretentiousness, and its incurable
lack of detachment will always outweigh its genuine qualities
of solidity and force. They will laugh and they will shudder,
and the world will follow suit. The Age of Victoria was,
somehow or other, unæsthetic to its marrow-bones; and so we
may be sure it will never loom through history with the
glamour that hangs about the Age of Pericles or the brilliance
that sparkles round the eighteenth century. But if men of
science and men of action were not inarticulate, we should
hear a different story.

The case of Matthew Arnold is a case in point. And who
has not heard of Matthew Arnold? Certainly, out of every
hundred who have, you would not find more than forty who
could tell you anything of his contemporary, Lyell, for instance, who revolutionised geology, or more than twenty who
would attach any meaning whatever to the name of another
of his contemporaries, Dalhousie, who laid the foundations
of modern India. Yet, compared to the work of such men as
these, how feeble, how insignificant was Matthew Arnold's
achievement! But he was a literary man; he wrote poetry, and
he wrote essays discussing other poets and dabbling in general

reflections. And so his fame has gone out to the ends of the earth, and now the Clarendon Press have done him the honour of bringing out a cheap collection of his essays,[1] so that even the working-man may read him and find out the heights that could be reached, in the way of criticism, during the golden years of the 'sixties. Surely, before it is too late, a club should be started—an Old Victorian Club—the business of whose members would be to protect the reputation of their Age and give it a fair chance with the public. Perhaps such a club exists already—in some quiet corner of Pimlico; but if so, it has sadly neglected one of its most pressing duties—the hushing-up of Matthew Arnold.

For here in this collection of essays there lies revealed what was really the essential and fatal weakness of the Victorian Age—its incapability of criticism. If we look at its criticism of literature alone, was there ever a time when the critic's functions were more grievously and shamelessly mishandled? When Dryden or Johnson wrote of literature, they wrote of it as an art; but the Victorian critic had a different notion of his business. To him literature was always an excuse for talking about something else. From Macaulay, who used it as a convenient peg for historical and moral disquisitions, to Leslie Stephen, who frankly despised the whole business, this singular tradition holds good. In what other age would it have been possible for a literary critic to begin an essay on Donne, as Leslie Stephen once did, with the cool observation that, as he was not interested in Donne's poetry, he would merely discuss his biography? An historian might as well preface an account of Columbus with the remark that, as he was not interested in Columbus's geographical discoveries, he would say nothing about that part of his career. It was their ineradicable Victorian instinct for action and utility which drove these unfortunate writers into so strangely self-contradictory a position. 'No one in his senses,' they always seem to be saying, 'would discuss anything so impalpable and frivolous as a work of art; and yet it is our painful duty to do so; therefore

[1] *Essays by Matthew Arnold.* Oxford University Press.

we shall tell you all we can about the moral lessons we can draw from it, and the period at which it was produced, and the curious adventures of the man who produced it; and so, as you must admit, we shall have done our duty like the Englishmen that we are.'

This was not quite Matthew Arnold's way; he went about his business with more subtlety. He was a man, so he keeps assuring us, of a refined and even fastidious taste; it was his mission to correct and enlighten the barbarism of his age; he introduced the term 'philistine' into England, and laughed at Lord Macaulay. Yet it is curious to observe the flagrant ineptitudes of judgment committed by a writer of his pretensions directly he leaves the broad flat road of traditional appreciation. On that road he is safe enough. He has an unbounded admiration for Shakespeare, Dante, and Sophocles; he considers Virgil a very fine writer, though marred by melancholy; and he has no doubt that Milton was a master of the grand style. But when he begins to wander on to footpaths of his own, how extraordinary are his discoveries! He tells us that Molière was one of the five or six supreme *poets* of the world; that Shelley will be remembered for his essays and letters rather than for his poetry; that Byron was a greater poet than Coleridge or Shelley or Keats; that the French alexandrine is an inefficient poetical instrument; that Heine was an 'incomparably more important figure' in European poetry than Victor Hugo. As to his taste, a remarkable instance of it occurs in his Lectures on translating Homer. Describing the Trojan encampments by night on the plains of Troy, with their blazing watch-fires as numerous as the stars, Homer concludes with one of those astonishingly simple touches which, for some inexplicable reason, seem to evoke an immediate vision of thrilling and magical romance: 'A thousand fires were kindled in the plain; and by each one there sat fifty men in the light of the blazing fire. And the horses, munching white barley and rye, and standing by the chariots, waited for the bright-throned Morning.' Such was Homer's conception —it was the horses who were waiting for the morning. But

Matthew Arnold will not have it so. 'I want to show you,' he says, 'that it is possible in a plain passage of this sort to keep Homer's simplicity without being heavy and dull'; and accordingly he renders the passage thus:

> By their chariots stood the steeds, and champ'd the white barley,
> While their masters sate by the fire and waited for Morning.

'I prefer,' he explains, 'to attribute this expectation of Morning to the master and not to the horse.' *I prefer!* Surely, if ever the word 'philistine' were applicable, this is the occasion for it. And, indeed, Arnold himself seems to have felt a twinge of conscience. 'Very likely,' he adds, with a charming ingenuousness, 'in this particular, as in any other particular, I may be wrong.'

One of the surest signs of a man's taste being shaky is his trying to prop it up by artificial supports. Matthew Arnold was always doing this. He had a craving for Academies. He thought that if we could only have a Literary Academy in England we should all be able to tell what was good and what was bad without any difficulty; for, of course, the Academy would tell us. He had a profound reverence for the French Academy—a body which has consistently ignored every manifestation of original genius; and no doubt the annual exhibitions of the Royal Academy gave him exquisite satisfaction. He even had dreams of a vast international Academy; carried away by the vision, he seemed almost to imagine that it was already in existence. 'To be recognised by the verdict of such a confederation,' he exclaims, 'is indeed glory; a glory which it would be difficult to rate too highly. For what could be more beneficent, more salutary? The world is forwarded by having its attention fixed on the best things; and here is a tribunal, free from all suspicion of national and provincial partiality, putting a stamp on the best things, and recommending them for general honour and acceptance.' But, failing this, failing the impartial tribunal which shall put 'a stamp on the best things,' one can fall back upon other devices. If one is in doubt as to the merit of a writer, the best course one can take is to make him, so to speak, run the gauntlet of 'the great masters.' We must 'lodge well in our minds' lines and expressions of the great masters—'short passages, even single lines will serve our turn quite sufficiently'—and these we shall find 'an infallible touchstone' for testing the value of all other poetry. The plan is delightfully simple; there is, indeed, only one small difficulty about it: it cannot come into operation until we have decided the very question which it is intended to solve—namely, who 'the great masters' are.

'The world is forwarded by having its attention fixed on the best things.' Yes; *the world is forwarded*. Here, plainly enough, is the tip of the Victorian ear peeping forth from under the hide of the æsthetic lion; the phrase might have come straight from Mr. Roebuck or the *Daily Telegraph*—those perpetual targets for Matthew Arnold's raillery. But when he proceeds to suggest yet another test for literature, when he asserts that, in order to decide upon the value of any piece of writing, what we must do is to ask ourselves whether or not it is a 'Criticism of Life'—then, indeed, all concealment is over; the whole head of the animal is out. There is something pathetic about the eager persistence with which Matthew Arnold enunciates this doctrine. How pleased with himself he must have been when he thought of it! How beautifully it fitted in with all his needs! How wonderfully it smoothed away all the difficulties of his situation! For, of course, he was nothing if not a critic, a man whose nature it was to look at literature from the detached and disinterested standpoint of a refined—a fastidious—æsthetic appreciation; and yet . . . and yet . . . well, after all (but please don't say so), how *could* anyone, at this time of day, in the 'sixties, be expected to take literature seriously, on its own merits, as if it were a thing to be talked about for its own sake? The contradiction was obvious, and it was reconciled by that ingenious godsend, the theory of the Criticism of Life. By means of that theory it became possible to serve God and Mammon at the same time. Life, as everyone knew, was the one serious affair in the world—active, useful life; but then literature, it turned out—or rather, all literature that was worth anything—was a criticism of life; and so, after all, Matthew Arnold was justified in writing about it, and the public were justified in reading what Matthew Arnold wrote, for they were not merely reading about literature—who would do that?—they were reading about the Criticism of Life. And it is singular to see the shifts to which Matthew Arnold was put in order to carry out this theory consistently. He had somehow to bring all 'the great masters' into line with it. Shakespeare was easy enough, for he will fit into any theory; and Sophocles, of course, saw life steadily and saw it whole; but Dante and Milton—a queer kind of criticism of life they give us, surely! But they were so elevated, so extremely elevated, that they would pass; as for Sappho and Catullus, it was convenient not to mention them. Of course Matthew Arnold was careful to give no very exact explanation of his famous phrase, and one is always being puzzled by his use of it. Pope, one would have thought, with those palpitating psychological portraits of his, in which are concentrated the experience and passion of one of the sharpest and most sensitive observers who ever lived—Pope might well be considered a critic of life; but for some reason or other Pope would not do. Byron, on the other hand—not the Byron of *Don Juan*, but the Byron of *Childe Harold* and *Manfred*—did very well indeed. But we must remember that Byron was still fashionable in the 'sixties, and that Pope was not.

Certainly it is a curious and instructive case, that of Matthew Arnold: all the more so since no one could suppose that he was a stupid man. On the contrary, his intelligence was above the average, and he could write lucidly, and he got up his subjects with considerable care. Unfortunately, he mistook his vocation. He might, no doubt, if he had chosen, have done some excellent and lasting work upon the movements of glaciers or the fertilisation of plants, or have been quite a satisfactory collector in an up-country district in India. But no; he *would* be a critic.

1914.

A RUSSIAN HUMORIST

'Look well at the face of Dostoievsky, half a Russian peasant's face, half a criminal physiognomy, flat nose, small penetrating eyes beneath lids that quiver with a nervous affection; look at the forehead, lofty, thoroughly well formed; the expressive mouth, eloquent of numberless torments, of abysmal melancholy, of infinite compassion and envy!—An epileptic genius, whose exterior speaks of the mild milk of human kindness, with which his temperament was flooded, and of the depth of an almost maniacal acuteness which mounted to his brain.' These words of Dr. Brandes, which occur in a letter to Nietzsche, written in 1888, express with force and precision the view of Dostoievsky, both as a man and as a writer, which probably every reader of the extraordinary works now being translated by Mrs. Garnett[1] would naturally be inclined to take. To the English reader, no less than to the Norwegian critic, what must first be apparent in those works is the strange and poignant mixture which they contain of 'an almost maniacal acuteness' with 'the mild milk of human kindness'—of the terrible, febrile agitations reflected in those penetrating eyes and their quivering lids, with the serene nobility and 'infinite compassion' which left their traces in the expressive mouth and the lofty brow. These conflicting and mingling qualities are, in fact, so obvious wherever Dostoievsky's genius reveals itself in its truly characteristic form, that there is some danger of yet another, and a no less important, element in this complex character escaping the notice which it deserves—the element of humour. That Dostoievsky was a humorist—and a humorist of a remarkable and original type—has not been sufficiently emphasised by

[1] *The Novels of Fyodor Dostoevsky*. Translated from the Russian by Constance Garnett. Vol. II., *The Idiot*. Vol. III., *The Possessed*. London: William Heinemann.

critics. Perhaps this may be partly explained by the fact that his most famous and widely read work, *Crime and Punishment*, happens to contain less of this particular quality than any of his other books. But to conclude from a perusal of *Crime and Punishment* that Dostoievsky had no humour would be as fallacious as to suppose that Shakespeare had none because he had written *Othello*. Indeed, just as a perspicacious reader, unacquainted with the rest of Shakespeare, might infer from the massive breadth and the penetrating vision of *Othello* the possibility of the early comedies, so the amazing psychological sympathy of *Crime and Punishment* almost suggests a similar phase of work in Dostoievsky. And, as a matter of fact, such work exists. The group of novels (not at present translated into English) of which *Uncle's Dream*, *The Eternal Husband*, and *Another's* are typical examples show Dostoievsky in a mood of wild gaiety, sometimes plunging into sheer farce, but more often reminiscent of the Molière of *Le Médecin Malgré Lui* and *Georges Dandin*, in the elaborate concentration of his absurdities, the brilliance of his satire, and his odd combination of buffoonery and common sense. This mood of pure comedy disappears in *The Double*—a singular and highly interesting work, containing a study of the growth of madness in a feeble intellect overcome by extreme self-consciousness—where the ridicule is piled up till it seems to topple over upon itself, and the furious laughter ends in a gnashing of teeth. Then we have *Crime and Punishment*, in which the humorous faculty is almost entirely suspended; and at last, in *The Idiot* and *The Possessed* (the two latest volumes of Mrs. Garnett's complete translation), Dostoievsky's humour appears in its final and most characteristic form, in which it dominates and inspires all his other qualities—his almost fiendish insight into the human heart, his delight in the extraordinary and the unexpected, his passionate love of what is noble in man, his immense creative force—and endows them with a new and wonderful significance.

The truth is that it is precisely in such cases as Dostoievsky's that the presence or the absence of humour is of the highest importance. With some writers it hardly occurs to us to consider whether they are humorous or not. It makes very little difference to us, for instance, that Tolstoy should scarcely show any signs of humour at all. And the reason for this is clear. Tolstoy is one of those writers who present their imaginary world to us with such calmness, with such exactness, with such an appearance at least of judicial impartiality, that we are immediately satisfied and ask for nothing more. But the imaginary world of a Dostoievsky strikes our senses in a very different fashion; it comes to us amid terror and exorbitance—not in the clear light of day, but in the ambiguous glare of tossing torches and meteors streaming through the heavens. Now writing of that kind may have many advantages: it may arouse the curiosity, the excitement, and the enthusiasm of the reader to a high degree; but there is one great risk that it runs—the risk of unreality. The beckoning lights may turn out to be will-o'-the-wisps, the mysterious landscape nothing but pasteboard scenery. And against that risk the only really satisfactory safeguard is a sense of humour. An author with a sense of humour puts, as it were, a stiff stout walking-stick into the hand of his reader, and bids him lean on that, and, when he is in doubt of the way he is going, feel with it the solid earth under his feet. Balzac is a case in point. He had wit, but no humour; his readers are without that invaluable walking-stick, and the consequence is that they are constantly being tripped up by pieces of stage carpentry, or plunging up to their necks in the bogs of melodrama. If Dostoievsky had been simply what Dr. Brandes describes and nothing more—a genius of excessive acuteness and excessive sensibility—we should have been in the same predicament in his pages. But it was not so. He had humour; and so it happens that, by virtue of that magic power, his wildest fancies have something real and human in them, and his moments of greatest intensity are not melodramatic but tragic. In *The Idiot*, for instance, the unchecked passions of Rogozhin and Nastasya, the morbid agonies of such a figure as Ippolit, the unearthly and ecstatic purity of

217

the Prince—all these things are controlled and balanced by the sheer fun of a hundred incidents, by the ludicrousness of Lebedyev and General Ivolgin, and, above all, by the masterly creation of Madame Epanchin—the sharp-witted, impulsive, irascible old lady, who storms and snorts and domineers through the book with all the vigour of a substantial and familiar reality. Madame Epanchin had many worries, and her daughters were the cause of nearly all of them. Adelaïda, it is true, was engaged to be married, but Alexandra!—

'Sometimes she thought the girl was "utterly hopeless." "She is twenty-five, so she will be an old maid; and with her looks!" Lizaveta Prokofievna positively shed tears at night thinking of her, while Alexandra herself lay sleeping tranquilly. "What is one to make of her? Is she a Nihilist or simply a fool?" That she was not a fool even Lizaveta Prokofievna had no doubt; she had the greatest respect for Alexandra's judgment and was fond of asking her advice. But that she was a *poule mouillée* she did not doubt for a moment; "so calm there's no making her out. Though it's true *poules mouillées* are not calm—foo, I am quite muddled over them." '

The irritatingly phlegmatic Alexandra had a habit which particularly annoyed her mother—she *would* dream the most inept dreams. One day the climax was reached when it transpired that Alexandra had dreamt of nine hens the night before—simply nine hens, and that was all. Madame Epanchin was furious. Such pleasant visions of domestic life are certainly not what one would expect from the inspired epileptic of Dr. Brandes's description; but they are in truth typical of Dostoievsky's art. The thought of those nine hens in Alexandra's dream gives one, somehow, a sense of security amid the storm and darkness of that strange history; one feels that one has one's walking-stick.

But Dostoievsky's humour serves another purpose besides that of being a make-weight to those intense and extreme qualities in his composition which would otherwise have carried him into mere extravagance; it is also the key to his sympathetic treatment of character. There are many ways of laughing at one's fellow-creatures. One may do so with the savage fury of Swift, or the barbed mockery of Voltaire, or the caressing mischief of Jane Austen; but Dostoievsky, in his latest works, uses another sort of laughter—the laughter of lovingkindness. Such laughter is very rare in literature; Shakespeare has some for Falstaff (though there it is complicated by feelings of genuine contempt); it inspired Sterne when he created Uncle Toby, and, of course, there is the classic instance of Don Quixote. Dostoievsky's mastery of this strange power of ridicule, which, instead of debasing, actually ennobles and endears the object upon which it falls, is probably the most remarkable of all his characteristics. *The Idiot* is full of it. It falls in gay cataracts over Madame Epanchin; it lends a humanity to the absurd old General, fallen on evil times, whose romancings drift into imbecility, and who remembers at last quite distinctly that he was one of Napoleon's pages in 1814. But the most elaborate use of it occurs in *The Possessed*, where the figure of Stepan Trofimoyitch, the old idealistic Liberal who comes to his ruin among the hideous realities of modern Nihilism, is presented to us through an iridescent veil of shimmering laughter and tears. The final passage describing his death inevitably recalls the famous pages of Cervantes; and, while it would be rash to say that the Russian writer surpasses his Spanish predecessor in native force, it cannot be doubted that he is the superior in subtlety. Stepan Trofimovitch is a nineteenth-century Quixote—a complex creature of modern civilisation, in whom the noblest aspirations are intertwined with the pettiest personal vanities, in whom cowardice and heroism, folly and wisdom, are inextricably mixed. So consummate is the portraiture that one seems to see the whole nature of the man spread out before one like a piece of shot silk, shifting every moment from silliness to saintliness, from meanness to dignity, from egoism to abnegation. This marvellous synthesis is the work of humour, but of humour which has almost transcended itself— a smile felt so profoundly that it is only shown in the eyes.

1914.

MR. HARDY'S NEW POEMS

MR. HARDY's new volume of poems[1] is a very interesting, and in some ways a baffling book, which may be recommended particularly to æsthetic theorists and to those dogmatic persons who, ever since the days of Confucius, have laid down definitions upon the function and nature of poetry. The dictum of Confucius is less well known than it ought to be. 'Read poetry, oh my children!' he said, 'for it will teach you the divine truths of filial affection, patriotism, and natural history.' Here the Chinese sage expressed, with the engaging frankness of his nation, a view of poetry implicitly held by that long succession of earnest critics for whom the real justification of any work of art lies in the edifying nature of the lessons which it instils. Such generalisations upon poetry would be more satisfactory if it were not for the poets. One can never make sure of that inconvenient and unreliable race. The remark of Confucius, for instance, which, one feels, must have been written with a prophetic eye upon the works of Wordsworth, seems absurdly inapplicable to the works of Keats. Then there is Milton's famous 'simple, sensuous, and passionate' test—a test which serves admirably for Keats, but which seems in an odd way to exclude the complicated style, the severe temper, and the remote imaginations of Milton himself. Yet another school insists upon the necessity of a certain technical accomplishment; beauty is for them, as it was—in a somewhat different connection—for Herbert Spencer, a '*sine quâ non.*' Harmony of sound, mastery of rhythm, the exact and exquisite employment of words—in these things, they declare, lies the very soul of poetry, and without them the noblest thoughts and the finest feelings will never rise above the level of tolerable verse. This is the theory which

[1] *Satires of Circumstance, Lyrics and Reveries, with Miscellaneous Pieces.* By Thomas Hardy. Macmillan. 1914.

Mr. Hardy's volume seems especially designed to disprove. It is full of poetry; and yet it is also full of ugly and cumbrous expressions, clumsy metres, and flat, prosaic turns of speech. To take a few random examples, in the second of the following lines cacophony is incarnate:

> Dear ghost, in the past did you ever find
> Me one whom consequence influenced much?

A curious mixture of the contorted and the jog-trot appears in such a line as:

> And adumbrates too therewith our unexpected troublous
> case;

while a line like:

> And the daytime talk of the Roman investigations

trails along in the manner of an undistinguished phrase in prose. Even Mr. Hardy's grammar is not impeccable. He speaks of one,

> whom, anon,
> My great deeds done,
> Will be mine alway.

And his vocabulary, though in general it is rich and apt, has occasional significant lapses, as, for instance, in the elegy on Swinburne, where, in the middle of a passage deliberately tuned to a pitch of lyrical resonance not to be found elsewhere in the volume, there occurs the horrid hybrid 'naïvely'— a neologism exactly calculated, one would suppose, to make the classic author of *Atalanta* turn in his grave.

It is important to observe such characteristics, because, in Mr. Hardy's case, they are not merely superficial and occasional blemishes; they are in reality an essential ingredient in the very essence of his work. The originality of his poetry lies in the fact that it bears everywhere upon it the impress of a master of prose fiction. Just as the great seventeenth-century writers of prose, such as Sir Thomas Browne and Jeremy Taylor, managed to fill their sentences with the splendour and passion of poetry, while still preserving the texture of an essentially prose style, so Mr. Hardy, by a contrary process, has brought the realism and sobriety of prose into the service of his poetry. The result is a product of a kind very difficult to parallel in our literature. Browning, no doubt, in his intimate and reflective moods—in *By the Fireside* or *Any Wife to Any Husband*—sometimes comes near it; but the full-blooded and romantic optimism of Browning's temper offers a singular contrast to the repressed melancholy of Mr. Hardy's. Browning was too adventurous to be content for long with the plain facts of ordinary existence; he was far more at home with the curiosities and the excitements of life; but what gives Mr. Hardy's poems their unique flavour is precisely their utter lack of romanticism, their common, undecorated presentments of things. They are, in fact, modern as no other poems are. The author of *Jude the Obscure* speaks in them, but with the concentration, the intensity, the subtle disturbing force of poetry. And he speaks; he does not sing. Or rather, he talks—in the quiet voice of a modern man or woman, who finds it difficult, as modern men and women do, to put into words exactly what is in the mind. He is incorrect; but then how unreal and artificial a thing is correctness! He fumbles; but it is that very fumbling that brings him so near to ourselves. In that 'me one whom consequence influenced much,' does not one seem to catch the very accent of hesitating and half-ironical affection? And in the drab rhythm of that 'daytime talk of the Roman investigations,' does not all the dreariness of long hours of boredom lie compressed? And who does not feel the perplexity, the discomfort, and the dim agitation in that clumsy collection of vocables—'And adumbrates too therewith our unexpected troublous case'? What a relief such uncertainties and inexpressivenesses are after the delicate exactitudes of our more polished poets! And how mysterious and potent are the forces of inspiration and sincerity! All the taste, all the scholarship, all the art of the Poet Laureate seem only to end in something that is admirable, perhaps, something that is wonderful, but something that is irremediably remote and cold; while the flat, undistinguished poetry of Mr. Hardy has found out the secret of touching our marrow-bones.

It is not only in its style and feeling that this poetry reveals the novelist; it is also in its subject-matter. Many of the poems—and in particular the remarkable group of 'fifteen glimpses' which gives its title to the volume—consist of compressed dramatic narratives, of central episodes of passion and circumstance, depicted with extraordinary vividness. A flashlight is turned for a moment upon some scene or upon some character, and in that moment the tragedies of whole lives and the long fatalities of human relationships seem to stand revealed:

> My stick! he says, and turns in the lane
> To the house just left, whence a vixen voice
> Comes out with the firelight through the pane,
> And he sees within that the girl of his choice
> Stands rating her mother with eyes aglare
> For something said while he was there.
>
> ' At last I behold her soul undraped!'
> Thinks the man who had loved her more than himself. . . .

It is easy to imagine the scene as the turning-point in a realistic psychological novel; and, indeed, a novelist in want of plots or incidents might well be tempted to appropriate some of the marvellously pregnant suggestions with which this book is crowded. Among these sketches the longest and most elaborate is the *Conversation at Dawn*, which contains in its few pages the matter of an entire novel—a remorseless and terrible novel of modern life. Perhaps the most gruesome is *At the Draper's*, in which a dying man tells his wife how he saw her in a shop, unperceived:

> You were viewing some lovely things. '*Soon required*
> *For a widow, of latest fashion*';
> And I knew 'twould upset you to meet the man
> Who had to be cold and ashen

And screwed in a box before they could dress you
  '*In the last new note of mourning,*'
As they defined it. So, not to distress you,
  I left you to your adorning.

As these extracts indicate, the prevailing mood in this
volume—as in Mr. Hardy's later novels—is not a cheerful
one. And, in the more reflective and personal pieces, the
melancholy is if anything yet more intense. It is the melancholy of regretful recollection, of bitter speculation, of immortal longings unsatisfied; it is the melancholy of one who
has suffered, in Gibbon's poignant phrase, 'the abridgment
of hope.' Mortality, and the cruelties of time, and the ironic
irrevocability of things—these are the themes upon which
Mr. Hardy has chosen to weave his grave and moving variations. If there is joy in these pages, it is joy that is long since
dead; and if there are smiles, they are sardonical. The sentimentalist will find very little comfort among them. Sometimes, perhaps, his hope will rise a little—for the sentimentalist is a hopeful creature; but they will soon be dashed.
'Who is digging on my grave?' asks the dead woman, who has
been forgotten by her lover and her kinsfold and even her
enemy; since it is none of these, who can it be?

> O it is I, my mistress dear,
> Your little dog, who still lives near,
> And much I hope my movements here
>   Have not disturbed your rest.

'Ah, yes!' murmurs the ghost:

> *You* dig upon my grave . . .
> Why flashed it not on me
> That one true heart was left behind?
> What feeling do we ever find
> To equal among human kind
>   A dog's fidelity?

And so, with this comforting conclusion the poem might have
ended. But that is not Mr. Hardy's way.

'Mistress,' comes the reply:

> I dug upon your grave
> To bury a bone, in case
> I should be hungry near this spot
> When passing on my daily trot,
> I am sorry, but I quite forgot
> It was your resting-place.

That is all; the desolation is complete. And the gloom is not even relieved by a little elegance of diction.

1914.

AN ANTHOLOGY

THE book, if you can get it, is worth reading, not only for its curiosity, but for its beauty and its charm. It was published ten years since, and one would be tempted to say that the poetry in it is the best that this generation has known, save that the greater part of it has been written for the last ten centuries. Yet, though it contains so much that is excellent and old, one might travel far without meeting a single reader who had ever heard of the poets of this anthology. Have they, then, been lately rediscovered, dug up, perhaps, from a buried city, and so, after the lapse of ages, restored to the admiration that is their due? By no means! These poems have been printed in innumerable editions, and the names of their writers are familiar words in the mouths of millions. Here are contradictions enough to perplex the most expert of Hegelians, but they are contradictions which, like those of Hegel, may be synthesised quite comfortably, if only you know the trick. The book is a collection of verse translations by Professor Giles, of Cambridge; and the translations are from the Chinese.

It is a faint and curious tone which reaches us, re-echoed so sympathetically by Professor Giles's gracious art, from those far-off, unfamiliar voices of singers long since dead. The strange vibrations are fitful as summer breezes, and fragmentary as the music of birds. We hear them, and we are ravished; we hear them not, and we are ravished still. But, as in the most fluctuating sounds of birds or breezes, we can perceive a unity in their enchantment, and, listening to them, we should guess these songs to be the work of a single mind, pursuing through a hundred subtle modulations the perfection which this earth has never known. We should err; for through the long centuries of Chinese civilisation, poet after poet has been content to follow closely in the footsteps of his prede-

cessors, to handle the very themes which they had handled, to
fit the old music to the old imaginations, to gather none but
beloved and familiar flowers. In their sight a thousand years
seem indeed to have been a moment; the song of the eighteenth
century takes up the burden of the eighth; so that, in this
peculiar literature, antiquity itself has become endowed with
everlasting youth. The lyrics in our anthology, so similar, so
faultless, so compact of art, remind one of some collection of
Greek statues, where the masters of many generations have
multiplied in their eternal marbles the unaltering loveliness of
the athlete. The spirit is the classical spirit—that in which the
beauties of originality and daring and surprise are made an
easy sacrifice upon the altar of perfection; but the classicism
of China affords, in more than one respect, a curious contrast
to that of Greece. The most obvious difference, no doubt, is
the difference in definition. Greek art is, in every sense of the
word, the most finished in the world; it is for ever seeking to
express what it has to express completely and finally; and,
when it has accomplished that, it is content. Thus the most
exquisite of the lyrics in the Greek Anthology are, fundamentally, epigrams—though they are, of course, epigrams
transfigured by passion and the highest splendours of art. One
reads them, and one is filled, in a glorified and ethereal manner, with the same kind of satisfaction as that produced by a
delicious mouthful of wine. One has had a draught of hippo-
crene, a taste of the consummation of beauty, and then one
turns over the page, and pours out another glass. Different,
indeed, is the effect of the Chinese lyric. It is the very converse
of the epigram; it aims at producing an impression which, so
far from being final, must be merely the prelude to a long
series of visions and of feelings. It hints at wonders; and the
revelation which at last it gives us is never a complete one—
it is clothed in the indefinability of our subtlest thoughts.

> A fair girl draws the blind aside
>   And sadly sits with drooping head;
> I see the burning tear-drops glide,
>   But know not why those tears are shed.

'The words stop,' say the Chinese, 'but the sense goes on.'
The blind is drawn aside for a moment, and we catch a
glimpse of a vision which starts us off on a mysterious voyage
down the widening river of imagination. Many of these
poems partake of the nature of the *chose vue*; but they are not
photographic records of isolated facts, they are delicate pastel
drawings of some intimately seized experience. Whatever
sights they show us—a girl gathering flowers while a dragon-
fly perches on her comb—a lonely poet singing to his lute in
the moonlight—pink cheeks among pink peach blossoms;
whatever sounds they make us hear—the nightjar crying
through the darkness—the flute and the swish of the swing
among summer trees—all these things are presented to us
charged with beautiful suggestions and that kind of ulterior
significance which, in our moments of imaginative fervour,
the most ordinary occurrences possess. Here, for instance, is
a description of a sleepless night—a description made up of
nothing but a short list of simple facts, and yet so full of the
very mystery of one of those half-vague, half-vivid watchings
that we feel ourselves the friends of the eleventh-century poet
who wrote the lines:

> The incense-stick is burnt to ash, the water-clock is stilled,
> The midnight breeze blows sharply by and all around is chilled.
> Yet I am kept from slumber by the beauty of the spring:
> Sweet shapes of flowers across the blind the quivering moon-
>   beams fling!

Sometimes the impression is more particular, as in this charming verse:

> Shadows of pairing swallows cross his book,
>   Of poplar catkins, dropping overhead . . .
> The weary student from his window-nook
>   Looks up to see that spring is long since dead.

And sometimes it is more general:

> The evening sun slants o'er the village street;
>   My griefs, alas! in solitude are borne;
> Along the road no wayfarers I meet,—
>   Naught but the autumn breeze across the corn

Here is the essence of loneliness distilled into four simple lines; they were written, in our eighth century, by Kêng Wei.

Between these evanescent poems and the lyrics of Europe there is the same kind of relation as that between a scent and a taste. Our slightest songs are solid flesh-and-blood things compared with the hinting verses of the Chinese poets, which yet possess, like odours, for all their intangibility, the strange compelling powers of suggested reminiscence and romance. Whatever their subject, they remain ethereal. There is much drunkenness in them, much praise of the winecup and the 'liquid amber' of the 'Lan-ling wine'; but what a contrast between their tipsiest lyrics and the debauched exaltation of Anacreon, or the boisterous jovialities of our Western drinking-songs! The Chinese poet is drunk with the drunkenness of a bee that has sipped too much nectar, and goes skimming vaguely among the flowers. His mind floats off at once through a world of delicate and airy dreams:

> Oh, the joy of youth spent in a gold-fretted hall,
> In the Crape-flower Pavilion, the fairest of all,
> My tresses for head-dress with gay garlands girt,
> Carnations arranged o'er my jacket and shirt!
> Then to wander away in the soft-scented air,
> And return by the side of his Majesty's chair. . . .

So wrote the drunken Li Po one summer evening in the imperial garden eleven hundred years ago, on a pink silk screen held up before him by two ladies of the court. This great poet died as he had lived—in a trance of exquisite inebriation. Alone in a pleasure-boat after a night of revelry, he passed the time, as he glided down the river, in writing a poem on himself, his shadow, and the moon:

> The moon sheds her rays on my goblet and me,
> And my shadow betrays we're a party of three . . .
> See the moon—how she glances response to my song;
> See my shadow—it dances so lightly along!
> While sober I feel, you are both my good friends;
> When drunken I reel, our companionship ends.
> But we'll soon have a greeting without a good-bye,
> At our next merry meeting away in the sky.

He had written so far, when he caught sight of the reflection of the moon in the water, and leant over the side of the boat to embrace it. He was drowned; but the poem came safely to shore in the empty boat; it was his epitaph.

Besides their lightness of touch and their magic of suggestion, these lyrics possess another quality which is no less obvious—a recurrent and pervading melancholy. Even their praise of wine is apt to be touched with sadness; it is praise of the power that brings release and forgetfulness, the subtle power which, in one small goblet, can drown a thousand cares. Their melancholy, so delicate and yet so profound, seems almost to be an essential condition of an art which is nothing if not fragmentary, allusive, and dreamy. The gaiety which bubbles over into sudden song finds no place in this anthology. Its poets are the poets of reflection, preoccupied with patient beauties and the subtle relationships of simple things. Thus, from one point of view, they are singularly modern, and perhaps the Western writer whose manner they suggest most constantly is Verlaine. Like him, they know the art of being quiet in verse. Like him, they understand how the fluctuations of temperament may be reflected and accentuated by such outward circumstances as the weather or the time of year. In particular, like him, they are never tired of the rain. They have realised the curious intimacy of its presence, and its pleasures no less than its desolations.

> You ask when I'm coming: alas, not just yet . . .
> How the rain filled the pools on that night when we met!
> Ah, when shall we ever snuff candles again,
> And recall the glad hours of that evening of rain?

But this kind influence which unites can also be a cruel destiny which separates, adding a final bitterness to solitude:

> 'Tis the festival of Yellow Plums! the rain unceasing pours,
> And croaking bull-frogs hoarsely wake the echoes out of doors.
> I sit and wait for him in vain, while midnight hours go by,
> And push about the chessmen till the lamp-wick sinks to die.

That is the melancholy of absence—a strain which is re-echoed again and again among these pages, so that, as we read, we begin to feel that here, in this sad sense of the fragility of human intercourse, lies the deepest inspiration of the book. Poet after poet writes of the burden of solitary love, of the long days of loneliness, of the long nights of recollection—

> Is it thy will, thy image should keep open
> My heavy eyelids to the weary night?

—the lines might have been written in Chinese. Sometimes the theme is varied; thoughts of the beloved lend a sweetness even to absence:

> In absence lovers grieve that nights should be,
> But all the livelong night I think of thee.
> I blow my lamp out to enjoy this rest,
> And shake the gathering dew-drop from my vest. . . .

Or the poet remembers that, after all, sleep has its consolations. 'Drive the young orioles away!' he exclaims—

> Their chirping breaks my slumber through,
> And keeps me from my dreams of you.

And then, often enough, it is the thought of home that haunts these tender singers:

> I wake, and moonbeams play around my bed,
>   Glittering like hoar-frost to my wondering eyes;
> Up towards the glorious moon I raise my head,
>   Then lay me down—and thoughts of home arise.

The exile can never forget the beauties of his birthplace—

> Sir, from my dear old home you come,
>   And all its glories you can name;
> Oh, tell me,—has the winter-plum
>   Yet blossomed o'er the window-frame?

And, when at length he is returning, he trembles and dares not ask the news.

Our finest lyrics are for the most part the memorials of passion, or the swift and exquisite expressions of 'the tender eye-dawn of aurorean love.' In these lyrics of China the stress and the fury of desire are things unknown, and, in their topsy-turvy Oriental fashion, they are concerned far more with memories of love than expectations of it. They look back upon love through a long vista of years which have smoothed away the agitations of romance and have brought with them the calm familiarity of happiness, or the quiet desolation of regret. Thus, while one cannot be certain that this love is not sometimes another name for a sublimated friendship, one can be sure enough that these lovers are always friends. Affection, no doubt, is the word that best describes such feelings; and it is through its mastery of the tones and depths of affection that our anthology holds a unique place in the literature of the world. For this cause, too, its pages, for all their strange antiquity, are fresh to us; their humanity keeps them immortal. The poets who wrote them seem to have come to the end of experience, to have passed long ago through the wonders and the tumults of existence, to have arrived at last in some mysterious haven where they could find repose among memories that were for ever living, and among discoveries that were for ever old. Their poetry is the voice of a civilisation which has returned upon itself, which has achieved, after the revolution of ages, simplicity. It has learnt to say some things so finely that we forget, as we listen to it, that these are not the only things that can be said.

> We parted at the gorge and cried 'Good cheer!'
> The sun was setting as I closed my door;
> Methought, the spring will come again next year,
> But he may come no more.

The words carry with them so much significance, they produce so profound a sense of finality, that they seem to contain within themselves a summary of all that is most important in life. There is something almost cruel in such art as this; one longs, somehow or other, to shake it; and one feels that, if one did, one would shake it into ice. Yet, as it is, it is far from frigid; but it is dry—dry as the heaped rose-leaves in a porcelain vase, rich with the perfume of how many summers! The scent transports us to old gardens, to old palaces; we wander incuriously among forsaken groves; we half expect some wonder, and we know too well that nothing now will ever come again. Reading this book, we might be in the alleys of Versailles; and our sensations are those of a writer whose works, perhaps, are too modern to be included in Professor Giles's anthology:

> Here in the ancient park, I wait alone.
> The dried-up fountains sleep in beds of stone;
> The paths are still; and up the sweeping sward
> No lovely lady passes, no gay lord.
>
> Why do I linger? Ah! perchance I'll find
> Some solace for the desolated mind
> In yon green grotto, down the towering glade,
> Where the bronze Cupid glimmers in the shade.

1908.

ENGLISH LETTER WRITERS

I

THE ELIZABETHANS

THE most lasting utterances of a man are his studied writings; the least are his conversations. His letters hover midway between these two extremes; and the fate which is reserved for them is capable of infinite gradations, from instant annihilation up to immortality. But 'oblivion blindly scattereth her poppy.' The washing-bills of the Pharaohs are preserved to us, but not their love-letters; and the vain chit-chat of Pliny's correspondence has outlived all the gravity of the letters of Tacitus. The end of Time is more favourable to epistolary immortality than its beginnings and its maturity: the barbarism of an early age and the unrest of a vigorous one are alike unpropitious to the preservation of letters. Yet who knows what the present day may not be losing? or what priceless treasures it has not consigned to abolition? Masterpieces lie at the mercy of postmen; preserved correspondences degenerate into culinary employments; and the same flames which devoured a circular may devour a letter from Charles Lamb.

But imagined losses deserve our lamentation less than known ones; and, when we consider the vanished riches of the past, we may indeed lament with good cause. What has become of the letters of Chaucer, and of Marlowe, and of Shakespeare? These, and a hundred other traces of the renowned minds of former ages, have been obliterated for ever from the world. The crowd of geniuses who adorned the most splendid epoch in our literature live for us merely in a few scattered remnants preserved by chance from out the precious mass which has been taken from us.

> Injurious time now with a robber's haste
> Crams his rich thievery up, he knows not how:

and scants us with some meagre relics, when he might have rejoiced us with the entire bodies of the saints.

What remains to us of the correspondence of the Elizabethan era hardly reconciles us to the loss of the rest; but there is enough to give us a clear view of the main characteristics of the letter-writing of those days. These characteristics are particularly interesting because they offer so many points of contrast with the whole current of what was to be the epistolary style of the future. The most distinctively Elizabethan letters which we possess have no descendants in English literature; they do not form a step in the development of the art of letter-writing; they stand by themselves. It will be well to point out their principal peculiarities, with the aid of illustrations.

The Elizabethan age was pre-eminently an age of action, and some of the finest of its letters were written with the object of forwarding some practical end. What would now be a business letter or a political manifesto became endowed in those days with all the attributes of faultless style. Essex begins a letter to Elizabeth with the following sentence: 'From a mind delighting in sorrow, from spirits wasted in passion, from a heart torn in pieces with care, grief, and travail, from a man that hateth himself and all things that keep him alive, what service can your Majesty expect?' And such magnificence of diction was the everyday raiment of an Elizabethan letter. Magnificence, however, could be replaced on occasion by unadorned vigour; with those great spirits the pen was sometimes almost as violent as the sword. Sir Philip Sidney's letter to his father's secretary is a fine example of Elizabethan force.

MR. MOLINEUX,—Few words are best. My letters to my father have come to the eyes of some. Neither can I condemn any but you for it. If it be so, you have played the very knave with me; and so I will make you know, if I have good proof of it. But that for so much as is past. For that is to come, I assure you before God, that if ever I know you do so much as read any letter I write to my father without his commandment, or my consent, I will thrust my dagger into you. And trust to it, for I speak it in earnest. In the meantime, farewell.

Apparently, even for that age, this letter was more than usually forcible; for we find Mr. Molineux declaring in his reply that 'the same is the sharpest I have ever received from any.'

But this combination of practical affairs with literary skill is not the only distinguishing feature of Elizabethan letters. They are even more remarkable for the abundance of their reflexions upon the conduct of life. The crisis of the Reformation had shaken the whole fabric of established thought. Everywhere questions were rising up which had long lain entranced beneath the spell of mother Church; and of these questions none were more important and pressing than the moral ones. The letters of the time show how eagerly men were feeling their way towards the reconstitution of an ethical code. Some of them—such as the letters of Sir Henry Sidney and Lord Strafford to their sons—resemble lay sermons rather than familiar communications. They are filled with maxims, and Latin saws, and careful trains of reasoning; and often, even when their object is not mainly hortatory, their tone is quite distinctly the tone of a moral philosopher. Thus the Lord Chancellor Egerton, writing to Essex to dissuade him from rebellion, says: 'I have begun plainly, be not offended if I proceed so. Bene cedit qui cedit tempori, and Seneca saith, Cedendum est fortunae. The medicine and remedy is not to contend and strive, but humbly to yield and submit. Have you given cause, and ye take a scandal unto you? Then all you can do is too little to make satisfaction. Is cause of scandal given unto you? Yet policy, duty, and religion enforce you to sue, yield, and submit to our sovereign. . . . There can be no dishonour to yield; but, in denying, dishonour and impiety. The difficulty, my good lord, is to conquer yourself, which is the height of true valour and fortitude, whereunto all your honourable actions have tended.'

It was not only in matters of private morals that this power of gnomic exhortation found vent; the morals of politics came equally within its sphere. 'Your father,' wrote Sir Walter Raleigh to the young Prince Henry, 'is called the viceregent of Heaven; while he is good he is the viceregent of Heaven. Shall man have authority from the fountain of good to do evil? No, my prince; let mean and degenerate spirits, which want benevolence, suppose your power impaired by a disability of doing injuries. If want of power to do ill be an incapacity in a prince, with reverence be it spoken, it is an incapacity he has in common with the Deity. . . . Exert yourself, O generous prince, against such sycophants, in the glorious cause of liberty; and assume such an ambition worthy of you, to secure your fellow creatures from slavery; from a condition as much below that of brutes as to act without reason is less miserable than to act against it. Preserve to your future subjects the divine right of free agents; and to your own royal house the divine right of being their benefactors. Believe me, my prince, there is no other right can flow from God.'

Well would it have been for that 'royal house' had it been swayed by such noble counsels! But the right which it preferred to maintain certainly flowed not from God: 'The right divine of kings to govern wrong.'

The elaborate formality of the Elizabethan letter must also be noticed. This effect was doubtless partly produced by the somewhat cumbrous nature of the ordinary prose style, which lent itself much more easily to wealth of ornament than to directness of expression; but it also depended on the fact that the letter was always regarded as a literary exercise. The correspondence of those days was not thrown off in a hurry; letters were given time to mature and grow, and were not despatched till every sentence had blossomed into flower. Those of Dr. Donne provide perhaps the best example of these typically renascent products. They are rich with elaborate discussions upon abstruse questions; they are packed with complicated imagery; they are interweaved with even more complicated compliments. 'Sir,' Donne begins a letter to Sir Henry Goodyer, 'it should be no interruption to your pleasures to hear me often say that I love you, and that you are as much my meditations as myself. I often compare not you and me, but the sphere in which your revolutions are and my wheel, both I hope concentric to God; for methinks the new astronomy is thus appliable well, that we which are a little earth should rather move towards God, than that He which is fulfilling, and can come no whither, should move towards us.' Donne's letters exercise the attention of the reader more than most; but the trouble is well rewarded. The more one broods over them the more one realises the originality of his thought, the beauty of his language, and the subtle splendour of his emotion. Such sentences as these repay much labour: 'I would not that death should take me asleep. I would not have him merely seize me, and only declare me to be dead, but win me and overcome me.'

One further passage even more beautiful and characteristic, perhaps, may be quoted from a letter to Sir T. Lucy: 'I make account that the writing of letters, when it is with any seriousness, is a kind of ecstasy, and a departure and secession and suspension of the soul, which doth then communicate itself to two bodies: and as I would every day provide for my soul's last convoy, though I know not when I shall die, and perchance I shall never die; so for these ecstasies in letters, I oftentimes deliver myself over in writing when I know not when those letters shall be sent to you, and many times they never are, for I have a little satisfaction in seeing a letter written to you upon my table, though I meet no opportunity of sending it.' After which introduction, Donne embarks upon a discussion of the question of Grace, the Primitive Church, St. Augustine, and the doctrine of the Infusion from God.

The preceding quotations will have sufficiently shown the gulf which separates the letters of the Elizabethan era from those of later generations—those of Horace Walpole, for instance, or Gray, or Byron. Since the seventeenth century, the art of letter-writing has turned aside altogether from the affairs of practical life, from the business of ethical exhortation, and from the elaboration of literary beauties. Since that time action has become merely a theme for comment and

description; Latin tags have turned out to be useful as point-
ing, not morals, but epigrams; and the chief end of stylistic
art has come to be the appearance of a colloquial easiness.
The change has not been without its drawbacks; there has
been a loss of profundity, of seriousness, of grandeur. But there
have been corresponding gains—in lightness of touch, in
clarity, and in play of personal feeling. The old style of letter
is the more instructive; the new is the more entertaining.

The letters of James Howell form the point of transition
between the two schools. In them there appears for the first
time a conscious endeavour to be perpetually amusing.
Howell cared for nothing else; and he attained his object. He
had not a spark of the spiritual fire of Donne; he would have
quailed before Sir Philip Sidney; he would not have been able
to follow Raleigh's argument; but he possessed one accomplishment which those great men conspicuously lacked—
he could prattle. It is true that his endless stream of talk is
ornamented after the Elizabethan manner; it meanders
through a grove of the usual conceits and the usual classical
allusions. But it is a stream, and not a piece of artificial water.
He touches upon every subject—love, and Venice, and
Socrates, and letter-writing—always with the same light,
affable, engaging touch. He tells a story admirably; he
can vividly describe places and things; he can talk for pages
about nothing at all. One extract will suffice to show his
quality:

'I was, according to your desire, to visit the late new-
married couple more than once; and to tell you true I never
saw such a disparity between two that were made one flesh
in all my life: he handsome outwardly, but of odd conditions;
she excellently qualified, but hard-favoured; so that the one
may be compared to a cloth of tissue doubled, cut upon coarse
canvas; the other to a buckram petticoat, lined with satin. I
think Clotho had her fingers smutted in snuffing the candle,
when she began to spin the thread of her life, and Lachesis
frowned in twisting it up; but Aglaia, with the rest of the
Graces, were in a good humour when they formed her inner

parts. A blind man is fittest to hear her sing; one would take delight to see her dance if masked; and it would please you to discourse with her in the dark, for there she is best company, if your imagination can forbear to run upon her face. When you marry, I wish you such an inside of a wife; but from such an outward phisnomy the Lord deliver you, and your faithful friend to serve you.'

In spite of its lack of refinement, this is in the true epistolary style. Howell is the direct progenitor of the great eighteenth-century letter-writers.

II

POPE, ADDISON, STEELE, AND SWIFT

In the troubled sea of History two epochs seem to stand out like enchanted islands of delight and of repose—the Age of the Antonines and the eighteenth century. Gibbon's splendid eulogy of 'that period in the history of the world which elapsed from the death of Domitian to the accession of Commodus' suggests at once to our minds the rival glories of his own epoch. Who does not feel that the polished pomp of Gibbon's sentences is the true offspring of the age of Handel and of Reynolds, and yet that it might have been composed as fittingly amid the elaborate colonnades and the Corinthian grandeur of the villa of Adrianus? It is true, indeed, that the comparison might be pushed too far. It would be easy to point out that the eighteenth century was essentially a stage in a great upward movement of mankind, while the golden evening of Marcus Aurelius was succeeded by a night of storm and utter darkness. The eighteenth century was an era of promise, of expansion, of vigorous and increasing life; the Age of the Antonines was one of intellectual decadence, of moral shrinkage, of gradual but inevitable decline. Nevertheless, when all these underlying differences have been taken into account, there yet remains a residuum of resemblance between the two epochs which is obvious enough. The nature of the resemblance is—if we may use a cant phrase—'atmospheric.' The 'atmosphere,' the 'setting'—that complex medium of intimate relations through which every object is presented to our minds—seems to be one and the same when we are considering the younger Pliny and when we are considering the elder Pitt. Both seem most fittingly to live and move and have their being in some well-ordered garden, where the afternoons are long, and the peaches are plump and soft, and the library and the wine and the servants are within comfortable distance. The fact that the brains of the great Commoner turned the scale in the balance of Empires, while those of his Roman predecessor turned nothing of much greater moment than an epigram—that is an irrelevant consideration. Did they not both feel their nectarines ripening in the sun in precisely the same leisurely aristocratic manner? For, if the eighteenth century was profoundly an age of activity, it was also, no less profoundly, an age of leisure. The conflict and torment of the religious struggles, into which the whole energies of the Renaissance had been plunged, were over; the infinite agitations ushered in by the French Revolution had not yet begun. The interval was one of toleration and of repose: of toleration which would have seemed incredible to the age which preceded it; of repose which seems no less incredible to ours. We, from the midst of our obsession of business, of our express trains, our quick lunches, all our hasty, concentrated, conscientious acts, can only look back in wonder upon the days of coaches and of chairs, of pluralities and of sinecures, of jewelled snuff-boxes and powdered hair. What would we say, in our utilitarian fervour, to a statesman who frittered away his mornings in the composition of ribald French verse—in fact, to Frederick the Great? What would we think, in our scientific solemnity, of a man of letters who set about destroying Christianity with no more elaborate an outfit than the Bible and a jest—in fact, of Voltaire? We should surely gasp and stare at such portents almost as much as Horace Walpole would have gasped and stared if he had received, one morning at breakfast, a five-lined whip. The precept 'Il faut cultiver notre jardin' has come down to the degenerate descendants of Candide in the form of 'Have an eye to the main chance'—a very different exhortation. The twentieth century has learned to cultivate its garden so well that it makes a profit of ten per cent. The eighteenth century cared less for the profit and more for the garden. It spent its leisure in the true process of cultivation. It ripened, and it matured; it did not advance. In art, in thought, in the whole conduct of life, what it aimed at was the just, the truly proportioned, the approved and absolute best. Its ideals were stationary because they were so high; and the strict conformity which they enjoined was merely the expression of a hatred and scorn of everything short of perfection. Whether such ideals were ever realised, whether their realisation was even possible, may indeed be doubted: what cannot be doubted is that they formed the framework of the eighteenth-century mind. Thus, when that period is dubbed the age of 'artificiality,' there is one sense in which the imputation is true enough. The age was certainly 'artificial' in so far as it was the very contrary of being spontaneous; it was a highly elaborate, conventional, concocted age. But that it was 'artificial' in another sense, that it was frigid and mechanical and devoid of passion—to suppose this would be to fall into grave error. Doubtless the supposition is often entertained; and it is the more easily held owing to the fact that the great mass of eighteenth-century literature is unemotional. It so happened that the emotions of those days did not seize naturally upon their commonest and most widespread vehicle—the art of writing; they turned instead towards the more recondite arts of painting and music. The wealth of emotion which the eighteenth century brought forth is not to be measured in its poetry; it is to be searched for in the visions of Watteau, of Fragonard, of Gainsborough, in the profound inspirations of Bach, in the triumphant melodies of Gluck, and in the divine symphonies of Mozart.

The least emotional body of literature, however, might be expected to offer an exception to its general character in one of its branches, if in no other—that of familiar letter writing. A letter is only less private than a diary; here, therefore, if anywhere, the public conventions of writing are easily overturned, here, where all the particular accidents of circumstance and character, all the moving actualities of life, press forward, in spite of forms and observances, to make themselves articulate. The eighteenth century is no exception to this rule; and he would be blind indeed who failed to perceive emotion in the *Journal to Stella* or the letters of

Mademoiselle de Lespinasse. Yet upon the whole the letters of that age partake of the qualities of the rest of its literature to an unusual extent. It was not as a vehicle for personal feeling that the letter attracted the majority of the great eighteenth-century letter writers; it was rather as a means for expressing the delicacies and refinements of personal intercourse. The vast vogue which the letter enjoyed was due to the fact that it formed a natural channel through which the elaborate and leisured civilisation of the time might flow. An eighteenth-century letter is the true epitome of the eighteenth century; and the pair of lovers described by Walpole, who sat all day in one room with a screen between them, over which they threw to one another their correspondence, provide the clearest image of that amazing period.

The group of writers who ushered in the new century possessed the characteristics of the dawning age in a striking degree. The letters which passed about between Pope and Bolingbroke and Arbuthnot and Gay might almost be taken for translations of some of Pliny's epistles. Never was a set of letters less spontaneous and more elegant. They are, indeed, essays rather than letters; the subjects with which they are concerned are the commonplaces, and not the occurrences, of life; one does not think of them as having gone through the post; their dates and their signatures are mere rudimentary excrescences; they are the kind of letters which do not require an answer. 'Those indeed who can be useful to all states,' writes Pope to Steele, 'should be like gentle streams, that not only glide through lonely valleys and forests amid the flocks and the shepherds, but visit populous towns in their course, and are at once of ornament and service to them. But there are another sort of people who seem designed for solitude; such, I mean, as have more to hide than to show. As for my own part, I am one of those of whom Seneca says: "Jam umbratiles sunt, ut putent in turbido esse quicquid in luce est." Some men, like some pictures, are fitter for a corner than a full light; and, I believe, such as have a natural bent to solitude (to carry on the former similitude) are like waters, which may be forced into fountains, and, exalted into a great height, may make a noble figure and a louder noise, but after all they would run more smoothly, quietly, and plentifully, in their own natural course upon the ground. The consideration of this would make me very well contented with the possession only of that quiet which Cowley calls the companion of obscurity. But whoever has the Muses too for his companions, can never be idle enough to be uneasy. Thus, Sir, you see, I flatter myself into a good opinion of my own way of living. Plutarch just now told me, that it is in human life . . .' etc. Here we have Seneca, Cowley, Plutarch, and the Muses, and such is the company one becomes best acquainted with in the letters of Pope and his circle. The easy flow of the similes, the pastoral melancholy of the reflexions, the quiet cultivation of the style—these things make pleasant reading for anyone who is content to do without originality and excitement. Sometimes, especially in the hands of the less skilful performers —of Bolingbroke, for instance—this delicate instrument becomes too obviously an echo; the classical note becomes unduly forced. Some of Bolingbroke's letters are stuffed so full with Latin tags that there is no cake for the plums; and as one reads them, one is inevitably reminded of those frigid images which still repose upon the tombs of eighteenth-century magnates, in all their panoply of toga and perruque.

Pope himself avoided these extremes; yet there can be little doubt that it is his poetry rather than his correspondence which reveals the true nature of the man. His extreme sensitiveness, which expressed itself to the full in his verse Epistles, hardly made itself felt in his prose ones. The poignancy of his note to the Miss Blounts on the death of his father—'My poor Father died last night.—Believe, since I did not forget you this moment, I never shall'—finds few parallels in the rest of his correspondence. There was a trait in Pope's character which goes some way to account for this: his feelings were far more easily roused into expression by dislike than by affection. Scorn, hatred, malice, rage—these were the emotions which, with Pope, boiled over almost naturally into fervent language; it is through its mastery of all the shades of these emotions that his verse has gained its immortality. Unfortunately it is part of the nature of things that one does not write familiar letters to one's enemies. Though Addison figures among Pope's correspondents, Atticus does not. Our loss is great. In the undiscovered limbo of dreams and chimæras, Pope's letters to Attossa and to Sporus are among the finest examples of the epistolary art.

The greatest of Pope's enemies has not suffered in the same way. We may be sure that we have got the best of Addison. His letters perfectly reflect that charming, polished, empty personality which the *Spectator* has made familiar to the whole world. 'My dearest Lord,' he writes to the young Earl of Warwick, 'I cannot forbear being troublesome to your lordship whilst I am in your neighbourhood. The business of this is to invite you to a concert of music, which I have found out in a neighbouring wood. It begins precisely at six in the evening, and consists of a blackbird, a thrush, a robin-redbreast and a bull-finch. There is a lark that, by way of overture, sings and mounts till she is almost out of hearing, and afterwards, falling down leisurely, drops to the ground as soon as she has ended her song. The whole is concluded by a nightingale, that has a much better voice than Mrs. Tofts, and something of the Italian manner in her divisions.' That is an exquisite piece of writing about nothing at all; and it snows Addison in his happiest capacity—as the master of the flute in prose. But his character had other, and less agreeable, qualities—qualities which Pope seized upon and emphasised with such bitter virulence in his famous lines on Atticus. Pope's picture is of course painted with a malignant hand; but it is a caricature, not a fancy portrait; it represents at least a portion of the truth. In the *Letter to a Lady* Addison's calm consciousness of superiority, his almost priggish self-sufficiency, his complete mastery of the frigidly polite, become only too glaringly obvious. 'You have passions, you say, Madam; but give me leave to answer, that you have understanding also; you have a heart susceptible of the tenderest impressions, but a soul, if you would choose to wake it, above an unwarranted indulgence of them; and let me entreat you, for your own sake, that no giddy impulse of an ill-placed inclination may induce you to entertain a thought prejudicial to your honour and repugnant to your virtue.' Never was cold water thrown in more refined a manner upon the advances of a lady; the action can hardly be distinguished from a magnificent bow. It is not necessary to remark that Addison was educated at Oxford.

The letters of Steele are as simple as his friend's are elaborate; and indeed their happy *naïveté* is often reminiscent of the preceding age. His notes to Mary Scurlock form a series of exquisite love-letters which might almost have been written by a virtuous and transmogrified Pepys. 'Madam,' he wrote a few days before his marriage, 'It is the hardest thing in the world to be in love and yet attend to business. . . . A gentleman ask'd me this morning what news from Lisbon, and I answer'd she's exquisitely handsome. Another desired to know when I had been last at Hampton Court. I reply'd 'twill be on Tuesday come sennight. Prithee allow me at least to kiss your hand before that day, that my mind may be in some composure. O love! . . .'

The same tone is kept up throughout the correspondence. Many of the letters are nothing but notices of little presents sent to Mrs. Steele by her husband. 'I enclose you a guinea for your pockett.' 'I send you some tea which I doubt not but you will find very good.' 'I send you seven-pen'orth of wall nutts at five a penny, which is the greatest proof I can give you at present of my being with my whole heart yours, Richd. Steele. P.S. There are but 29 wallnutts.' Such are the staple topics of these domestic letters. 'For thee I dye, for thee I languish,' Steele ends a note to his wife after six years of marriage; and four years later is still addressing Mary Steele as 'Ten thousand times my dear, dear, Pretty Prue.'

Steele's nature was one of those fortunate ones which are able to transmute the basest accidents of life into occasions for innocent rejoicing. He could not be otherwise than cheerful. The exact reverse is true of Swift. It is not our purpose, however, to discuss the colossal mind of the great Dean of St. Patrick's. Such an undertaking would be no unworthy task for a Shakespeare; less powerful spirits can only prostrate themselves in dumb worship, like Egyptian priests before the enormous effigies of their gods. It would, besides, be beyond the scope of this essay to attempt an estimation of one whose place in literature depends hardly at all upon his achievements in the domain of letter-writing. Swift's letters are all marked with the indelible stamp of his genius; his *Journal to Stella* reveals to us a whole region of his character which would otherwise have remained unknown; and yet, if all this mass of writing were swept away and utterly abolished, Swift's literary stature would be unchanged. It will be sufficient, perhaps, to notice one particular in which that great man's letters (no less than the rest of his writings) differ in a remarkable degree from those of his contemporaries. In every sense of the term, he is the least artificial of writers. His prose style has been aptly compared to a sheet of plate-glass through which every object appears in the form and colour of absolute reality. It is devoid of any ornament which might impede or deflect the underlying thought; it has no sounding cadences, no splendid figures, no elegant antitheses, no verbal wit. Compared with the sober daylight of Swift's style, that of a writer like Voltaire seems to resemble the brilliancy of drawing-room candles, and that of a writer like Sir Thomas Browne the flare of a midnight torch. Unlike all other prose writers in the world, except Pascal, Swift obtains the whole of his effect by his matter, and by his matter alone.

Sometimes Swift's directness of expression is such that it can hardly be distinguished from brutality. His letter to Miss Waring, for instance, forms a curious contrast to the letter already quoted, which Addison wrote in similar circumstances 'to a Lady.' 'Are you in a condition to manage domestic affairs, with an income of less (perhaps) than £300 a year? Have you such an inclination to my person and humour as to comply with my desires and way of living, and endeavour to make us both as happy as you can? Will you be ready to engage in those methods which I direct for the improvement of your mind, so as to make us entertaining company for each other, without being miserable when we are neither visiting nor visited? Can you bend your love and esteem and indifference to others the same way as I do mine? Shall I have so much power in your heart, or you so much government of your passions, as to grow in good humour upon my approach, though provoked by a ——? Have you so much good-nature as to endeavour by soft words to smooth any rugged humour occasioned by the cross accidents of life? Shall the place wherever your husband is thrown be more welcome than courts or cities without him? . . . These are the questions I have always resolved to propose to her with whom I meant to pass my life; and whenever you can heartily answer them in the affirmative, I shall be blessed to have you in my arms, without regarding whether your person be beautiful or your fortune large. Cleanliness in the first, and competency in the other, is all I look for.'

Addison's method of refusing a lady was to bow her out of the room; Swift's method was to knock her down. Yet no one could doubt for a moment which of the two men was capable of the deeper affections. No letters are more charged with poignant emotion than those which Swift wrote from London to his friends in Ireland, when Stella was dying. 'I have just received yours of August 24,' he wrote to Dr. Sheridan in the last of these; 'I kept it an hour in my pocket with all the suspense of a man who expected to hear the worst news that fortune could give him; and at the same time was not able to hold up my head. These are the perquisites of living long; the last act of life is always a tragedy at best; but it is a bitter aggravation to have one's best friend go before one. . . . I know not whether it be an addition to my grief or not that I am now extremely ill; for it would have been a reproach to me to be in perfect health when such a friend was desperate. I do profess, upon my salvation, that the distressed and desperate condition of my friend makes life so indifferent to me, who by course of nature have so little left, that I do not think it worth the time to struggle; yet I should think, according to what hath been formerly, that I may happen to overcome this present disorder; and to what advantage? Why, to see the loss of that person for whose sake only life was worth preserving. . . . What have I to do in the world? I never was in such agonies as when I received your letter, and had it in my pocket. I am able to hold up my sorry head no longer.'

III

LADY MARY WORTLEY MONTAGU AND LORD CHESTERFIELD

It is curious that the two ladies who have won the greatest reputation as letter writers should present so complete a contrast. Lady Mary Wortley Montagu certainly bears out Professor Raleigh's dictum that in the eighteenth century man lived up to his definition and was a rational animal; and 'a rational animal' is precisely the last designation which anyone would dream of applying to Madame de Sévigné. 'How many readers and admirers,' exclaims Lady Mary, 'has Madame de Sévigné, who only gives us, in a lively manner and fashionable phrases, mean sentiments, vulgar prejudices, and endless repetitions! Sometimes the tittle-tattle of a fine lady, sometimes that of an old nurse, always tittle-tattle.' Nothing could be more unjust; and the injustice obviously springs from an utter lack of sympathy. Lady Mary was the least feminine of women, and Madame de Sévigné was the most. The delicacy, the charm, the tenderness, of the French lady's letters were lost upon the virile mind of the English one. Lady Mary's flashing wit tossed aside the elegance of Madame de Sévigné's with the disdain of a steel rapier tossing aside a piece of silver filigree-work. What could be the value of such a bauble? It was only meant for show!

'Few women would have spoken so plainly as I have done,' Lady Mary wrote in the first of her letters to Edward Wortley; 'but to dissemble is among the things I never do.' And a certain outspoken clarity is perhaps the most conspicuous characteristic of all her letters. She is always absolutely frank and absolutely sensible; yet she manages never to be heavy. Her wit has that quality which is the best of all preservatives against dullness—it goes straight to the point. If she had been a little less sensible, she would have been an eccentric; if she had been a little less witty she would have been a prig. 'To say truth,' she wrote, at the age of sixty-six, 'I think myself an uncommon kind of creature, being an old woman without superstition, peevishness, or censoriousness.' The account was true of all the periods of her life.

Her freedom from prejudice, which was so strikingly demonstrated by her introduction into England of the practice of inoculation, adds a peculiar interest to her letters. Her views on the education of women were especially in advance of her age. 'To say truth, there is no part of the world where our sex is treated with so much contempt as in England. I do not complain of men for having engrossed the government: in excluding us from all degrees of power, they preserve us from many fatigues, many dangers, and perhaps many crimes. . . . But I think it the highest injustice to be debarred the entertainment of my closet, and that the same studies which raise the character of a man should hurt that of a woman. We are educated in the grossest ignorance, and no art omitted to stifle our natural reason; if some few get above their nurses' instructions, our knowledge must rest concealed, and be as useless to the world as gold in a mine.' She returns to the subject again and again in her letters to her daughter, Lady Bute. 'Learning, if she (Lady Bute's daughter) have a real taste for it, will not only make her contented, but happy. No entertainment is so cheap as reading, nor any pleasure so lasting. She will not want new fashions, nor regret the loss of expensive diversions, or variety of company, if she be amused with an author in her closet.' And again: 'The use of learning in our sex, beside the amusement of solitude, is to moderate the passions, and learn to be contented with a small expense, which are the certain effects of a studious life; and it may be preferable even to that fame which men have engrossed themselves, and will not suffer us to share.' 'Most people confound the ideas of sense and cunning,' she again writes, 'though there are really no two things in nature more opposite. It is, in part, from this false reasoning, the unjust custom prevails of debarring our sex from the advantages of learning, the men fancying improvement of our understandings would only furnish us with more art to deceive them; which is directly contrary to the truth. Fools are always enterprising, not seeing the difficulties of deceit or the ill consequences of detection.'

These are admirable reflexions, but Lady Mary is not always so serious. Her letters abound in pointed remarks and spicy anecdotes; and her comments on the persons of her acquaintance are usually most amusing when they are most vitriolic. She is at her best when she is telling her correspondent of the history of some 'beauteous virgin of forty,' and how 'after having refused all the peers in England, because the nicety of her conscience would not permit her to give her hand when her heart was untouched, she remained without a husband till the charms of that fine gentleman, Mr. Smith, who is only eighty-two, determined her to change her condition.' Or in such a character-sketch as this: 'That good creature (as the country saying is) has not a bit of pride in him. I dare swear he purchased his title for the same reason he used to buy pictures in Italy; not because he wanted to buy, but because somebody or other wanted to sell. He hardly ever opened his mouth but to say "What you please, sir"; "At your service"; "Your humble servant," or some gentle expression to the same effect. It is scarce credible that with this unlimited complaisance he should draw a blow upon himself; yet it so happened that one of his countrymen was brute enough to strike him. As it was done before many witnesses, Lord Mansel heard of it; and thinking that if poor Sir John took no notice of it, he would suffer more insults of the same kind, out of pure good nature resolved to spirit him up, at least to some show of resentment, intending to make up their matter afterwards in as honourable a manner as he could for the poor patient. He represented to him very warmly that no gentleman could take a box on the ear. Sir John answered with great calmness, "I know that, but this was not a box on the ear; it was only a slap on the face." '

Every reader of Lady Mary must observe, without subscribing to Pope's scurrilities about 'Sappho,' that a sense of propriety seems rarely to stand in the way of her sense of humour. She was the last person to beat about the bush, when there was a point to be made by plain speaking; and such were precisely the points which presented themselves most frequently to her mind. Thus, when she is coarse, she is always coarse directly; she does not wrap up her meaning in a veil of innuendoes; so that her indecencies have at least this merit: they are nothing if not healthy. Nor can they be denied the saving grace of wit. The following is a typical passage: 'To speak plainly, I am very sorry for the forlorn state of matrimony, which is as much ridiculed by our young ladies as it used to be by young fellows: in short, both sexes have found the inconveniences of it, and the appellation of rake is as genteel in a woman as in a man of quality; it is no scandal to say Miss ——, the maid of honour, looks very well now she is up again, and poor Biddy Noel has never been quite well since her last confinement. You may imagine we married women look very silly; we have nothing to excuse ourselves, but that it was done a great while ago, and we were very young when we did it.' Who would not be amused by that conclusion? And would it not be a somewhat hypocritical severity to laugh and to condemn at the same time?

Lady Mary's straightforwardness was not without its drawbacks. It is only by striking very hard that one can hit the nail on the head; and Lady Mary, solely occupied with that operation, wasted none of her energies in delicate touches. Her letters are all in one key—the C major of this life. They express no subtleties, no discriminations, no changes of mood. They flash; but with a metallic light. Their writer, one feels, was far too sensible either to sink or to soar; and it is an open question whether she was ever much excited. Describing her discussions with the Jesuits, she wrote: 'I have always the advantage of being quite calm on a subject which they cannot talk of without heat.' And that was her attitude in every relation of life. Her very love-letters were made up of arguments upon the ethics of marriage. Her philosophy of life, though it was too witty to be dull, was too dispassionate to be true. The real nature of things was hidden from her, because she could never throw herself into its midst. 'Why are our views so extensive and our power so miserably limited?' she writes. 'This is among the mysteries which (as you justly say) will remain ever unfolded to our shallow capacities. I am much inclined to think we are no more free agents than the queen of clubs when she victoriously takes prisoner the knave of hearts; and all our efforts (when we rebel against destiny) as weak as a card that sticks to a glove when the gamester is determined to throw it on the table. Let us then (which is the only true philosophy) be contented with our chance, and make the best of that very bad bargain of being born in this vile planet; where we may find, however (God be thanked), much to laugh at, though little to approve.' It is hardly an exaggeration to say that, to Lady Mary, life was simply—as she describes it—a game of whist. And the rigour of it was what she most enjoyed.

Lord Chesterfield's letters to his son form a fitting counterpart to Lady Mary Wortley's letters to her daughter. They deal with the same subject—education; though the Earl treats it at infinitely greater length and with infinitely greater wealth of detail. His famous letters are, in fact, hardly familiar letters at all. They are a series of elaborate essays upon manners. The theme is always the same; and the endless repetition of it becomes all the more wearisome from the fact that the variations are conspicuously wanting in variety. It is difficult to conceive a fate more terrible than that which condemned the young Stanhope to the weekly bombardment of his father's packet. Even to us, who can read the four hundred letters with the detachment of creatures of another world, they make gloomy and irritating reading. To Philip, who knew that every sentence in them applied in the most personal manner possible to him, who could look back on an endless vista of identical admonitions, and knew that he must look forward to another vista equally infinite, the horror of their perusal must have been unimaginable. 'Good God!' he used to read at breakfast, 'how I should be shocked, if you came into my room, for the first time, with two left legs, presenting yourself with all the graces and dignity of a tailor, and your clothes hanging upon you, like those in Monmouth Street, upon tenter-hooks!' Could anything be more depressing? But then he had already been informed that 'when we meet, if you are absent in mind, I will soon be absent in body; for it will be impossible for me to stay in the room; and if at table you throw down your knife, plate, bread, etc., and hack the wing of a chicken for half an hour, without being able to cut it off, and your sleeve all the time in another dish, I must rise from table to escape the fever you must certainly give me.' And in a few weeks he was to learn that 'I fear but one thing for you, and that is what one has generally the least reason to fear from one of your age; I mean your laziness: which, if you indulge, will make you stagnate in a contemptible obscurity all your life.' The grave was the one refuge from such a persecution; but who could tell that the grave itself would be safe? Might not a letter from Lord Chesterfield follow one even there, with instructions as to how one should deport oneself in that situation?

The main doctrine which lies at the back of Chesterfield's letters has been expressed by La Bruyère in three sentences: 'Avec de la vertu, de la capacité, et une bonne conduite, on peut être insupportable. Les manières, que l'on néglige comme de petites choses, sont souvent ce qui fait que les hommes décident de vous en bien ou en mal: une légère attention à les avoir douces et polies prévient leurs mauvais jugements. Il ne faut presque rien pour être cru fier, incivil, méprisant, désobligeant: il faut encore moins pour être estimé tout le contraire.' Admitting the truth of the doctrine, were Chesterfield's methods of putting it into practice likely to meet with success? His system of minute instruction falls between two stools—it is either absurdly platitudinous, or uselessly vague. Nobody wants to be told to cut his finger-nails so as to make them form segments of circles; and to tell someone to 'take the tone of his conversation from his company' is the merest mockery. All the important things in manners are either so easy that it is not worth while teaching them, or so difficult that they can never be taught. Chesterfield never seems to have recognised this. On the one hand, he drummed away on carving and blowing one's nose; and on the other, he perpetually attempted to inculcate wit and grace and refinement by the simple process of affirming them to be important and admirable qualities. In any case, such a system of instruction would have been absurd; in the case of Stanhope, an additional fact rendered it peculiarly preposterous. Chesterfield completely failed to see that character was a question of the slightest importance in education. He firmly believed, and constantly reiterated, that a man could learn to be anything—except a poet. If this theory needed refutation, it received it once and for all at the hands of Philip Stanhope. No young man, before or since, was ever more carefully trained in the way that he should go; that he should shine in politics and diplomacy was the one object of his father's life, and of his own endeavours. Alas! he shone in nothing. That was not his nature; and all the pitchforks of Lord Chesterfield were impotent to change it.

Nor can we be sorry that this was the case. Chesterfield's scheme of conduct was odious, not because it was immoral, but because it was blindly conventional. It faithfully crept after all the unthinking prejudices of the age; it definitely aimed at the stupid vulgar ideals of stupid vulgar people; it brushed on one side what was most valuable as trifling and absurd. Place and power were the ends which Stanhope was to pursue with all his might; for their sake he was to flirt with fine ladies, and flatter great ministers; for their sake he was to learn to dance and to wear clean linen every day. He was never to be idle a moment; he was never to reflect, nor brood, nor dream. 'No piping nor fiddling, I beseech you,' exclaims his father; 'no days lost in poring upon almost imperceptible *Intaglios*, and *Cameos*: and do not become a Virtuoso of small wares. Form a taste of Painting, Sculpture, and Architecture, if you please, by a careful examination of the works of the best ancient and modern artists; those are liberal arts, and real taste and knowledge of them become a man of fashion very well. But beyond certain bounds, the man of taste ends, and the frivolous Virtuoso begins.'

It is pleasant to know that this twaddle produced no effect whatever. Philip Stanhope collected, during his travels, a large library of rare old books. It was among these that the happiest hours of his life were spent; and it must have been with no ordinary sense of relief that he turned, after the perusal of one of his father's epistles, to some quiet quarto or some charming Aldus, to some black-letter Luther, some duodecimo Erasmus, or some vast and venerable Bede.

IV

HORACE WALPOLE

THE letter-writing of the eighteenth century reaches its climax in the correspondence of Horace Walpole. The vast period of time which they cover, the immense variety of topics with which they deal, the sustained brilliancy of their execution, give these famous letters a position of pre-eminence unrivalled in English literature, and only paralleled by the letters of Voltaire in the literature of the world. Voltaire, however, threw off his letters in the intervals of a multifarious literary activity —they were little more than incidents in the great work of his life. It would almost be true to say the exact contrary of Walpole. His correspondence was his serious occupation; he did not snatch moments from life to write letters in: he snatched moments from letter-writing in which to live. That he lived so fully, that he was able to indulge in such a variety of occupations and to amass such a wealth of experience, is perhaps almost as wonderful as that Voltaire found the time and the energy wherewith to compile his fourteen volumes of correspondence. In his old age, indeed, Walpole began to degenerate: he wrote letters more and more; he lived less and less. There were occasions towards the end of his life when he deliberately refrained from visiting Lady Ossory, because he knew that then he would have to tell her by word of mouth the anecdotes which he wished to tell her only in a letter. But such conduct was not characteristic of Walpole at his best. He did not spin out his letters, like a silkworm, from his inner consciousness; he nourished them upon the substantial facts of life. His pages are packed with matter. As one turns them over, an enormous panorama unrolls itself before one's eyes. Eminent and brilliant persons, momentous events, epoch-making books, political intrigues, follow one another in endless succession. Now one looks in at a masquerade at

Sir William Hanbury's, now one is at Stowe with the Princess Amelia, now one is superintending the printing of Gray's *Elegy* at Strawberry Hill, now one is sitting down to whist with the 'Archbishopess of Canterbury and Mr. Gibbon,' now one is chatting with Madame du Deffand in Paris, now one is listening to Charles Townshend in the House of Commons. The vigorous and dazzling world of Walpole's London lives again before our eyes. We begin to be intimate with the latter half of the eighteenth century. We have been led in through the back door to the very central chamber of that great period in English History; and we see things, not as outside observers, but as familiar friends.

Walpole's activities were so numerous and so various that readers of the letters are a little apt to emphasise one side of his personality at the expense of the rest, in accordance with their own predilections. This was doubtless also the case with his correspondents. He was probably regarded by Mann as a politician, by Mason as a man of letters, by Cole as an anti-quary, and by Lady Ossory as a gossip. It will be well, there-fore, to consider his letters from these different points of view.

I. Walpole's connection with politics was the natural con-sequence of his parentage. He entered the House of Commons while his father was still in power, and remained a member for twenty-five years; but it was not so much his place in the House, as his place among the great political families, which gave him that inner knowledge of parliamentary workings which is so conspicuous in his letters to Sir Horace Mann. He was thoroughly at home within the narrow circle of the aristocratic society which then controlled the destinies of England. The Lytteltons, the Pitts, the Foxes, the Pelhams, the Bedfords—these were the persons among whom he habitually moved. Besides this, his intimacy with his cousin, General Conway, gave him at one time an almost first-hand acquaintance with affairs. Whether he himself might not have made his mark in politics is perhaps a futile speculation, but it is one which naturally suggests itself to a reader of the letters. It is certain at least that Macaulay's estimate of Walpole's ability was grossly unfair. Walpole cannot be dismissed as an affected and malignant jackanapes. The series of letters to the Earl of Hertford, written while the latter was Ambassador at Paris (1763–5), are sufficient in themselves to show that Walpole was at any rate an acute and sagacious observer, if he was nothing more. But there is some reason to believe that his practice would not have fallen short of his theory. His influence on Conway's party at the time of the Regency Bill (1765) was certainly great, though it was not great enough; and his foresight was proved by the disaster which followed when his advice was neglected. His conflict with George Grenville in the preceding year shows even more clearly how capable he was of taking a practical part in life. Nothing could have been more shrewd and firm than his conduct on that occasion. The qualities which a man must have to be able to baffle and humiliate a Chancellor of the Exchequer were precisely the qualities which would have been most useful to a politician in the time of Walpole.

It is doubtless true that personal motives played a large part in Walpole's politics. But it must be remembered that he never was in any position where the intrusion of personal feelings could lead to any harm; and there is not the slightest reason to suppose that, if he had been in office, he would have allowed his private affections and animosities to interfere with the conduct of affairs. Nor were feelings such as these the only ones which coloured his political views. His hatred of tyranny was certainly genuine; and so was his hatred of corruption. He was not a profound or an original political philosopher, but what principles he had were truly liberal ones; in most disputed questions he was in advance of the majority of his contemporaries. He held the slave trade in detestation. He was bitterly opposed to the American policy of Grenville and North. There was indeed one important topic with regard to which his usual acumen deserted him: he entirely failed to recognise the true significance of the exploits of the East India Company. Clive and Hastings were to him merely types of the successful plunderer who only differs from the common highwayman in that he practises his calling with impunity. But if, in this particular, Walpole erred, he erred in excellent company. It would be too much to expect of a politician that he should be wiser than Burke.

A further instance of Walpole's sagacity is to be seen in the references in his letters from Paris to the condition of France. His jeremiads were never as precise as Lord Chesterfield's, but they display an astonishingly clear appreciation of the trend of events. As early as 1771 Walpole wrote as follows: 'For the misery of his people, and for the dangers of his successors (if he escapes himself) the King, I think, will triumph over his country: a victory most kings prefer, not only to peace, but to foreign laurels. The Princes of the blood are firm, without spirit or sense: the nobility have as little of either; the vigour of Parliamentary remonstrances are hushed by the English remedy—bribery: and the people curse the King, the Chancellor, the mistress; and starve.' It is interesting to find Diderot writing to Wilkes just a month later in the following strain: 'Imaginez un palais immense dont l'aspect majestueux et solide vous en imposoit, promettoit à votre imagination une durée éternelle; imaginez ensuite que les fondements s'ébranlent et que vous voyez tout à coup ses murs énormes se séparer et se disjoindre. Voilà précisément le spectacle que nous offririons à votre spéculation.'[1]

It is not difficult to explain why, in spite of his position and his attainments, Walpole never took an active part in public life. In the first place, the whole cast of his mind was eminently unsuited to the rough-and-tumble of the parliamentary arena. He could not speak with ease; and in the heat of battle he would certainly have cut a sorry figure. His extreme sensitiveness to ridicule, doubtless the main cause of his abstention from debate, shut off from him for ever all hope of a political career. Secondly, Walpole's interests were far from being exclusively political; and it is open to question whether,

[1] From an unpublished letter in the British Museum. The date is October 19, 1771.

even if the highest places had been offered to him, he would have accepted them. Doubtless he had ambitions; but he also had Strawberry Hill. His books, his china, his ladies, his leisure—why should he sacrifice all these things for the sake of a little uncomfortable power? Was the game worth the candle, after all?

II. The literary side of Walpole is to be studied chiefly in the series of letters to Mason, which are little more than a running criticism of the books and plays of the time. Walpole's taste was certainly not in advance of his age; perhaps it was on the whole behind it. His admiration of Gibbon was unstinted; but so was his admiration of Dr. Robertson. The poetry of Gray he declared to be immortal; but then he paid the same compliment to the poetry of Mason. These were all conventional eighteenth-century judgments, which were certainly made by Walpole's bookseller no less than by Walpole himself. But his lack of literary discrimination went further than this. 'At present nothing is talked of, nothing admired,' he wrote in 1760, 'but what I cannot help calling a very insipid and tedious performance; it is a kind of novel, called "The Life and Opinions of Tristram Shandy," the great humour of which consists in the whole narration always going backwards. . . . The characters are tolerably kept up, but the humour is for ever attempted and missed.' Nothing could be more superficial. It does not seem to have entered Walpole's head that Sterne was a master of English prose, or that one might as well praise the characters of Iago and Macbeth for being 'tolerably kept up' as those of Uncle Toby and Mr. Shandy.

The truth is that Walpole's interest in literature as an art was very small. It is only necessary to compare him with Gray, for instance, to see at once how merely skin-deep his literary feelings were. Literature amused him, it interested him; but it never moved him. Reading was for him an elegant recreation, and nothing more. It has been constantly pointed out that his dealings with Chatterton throw no discredit upon him whatever; it is not the business of every rich gentleman to assist unfortunate poets. This defence is complete, but it is irrelevant, unless one fact is clearly recognised—that Walpole belonged to a class which cannot be expected to have a real appreciation of art. Walpole found that he had been deceived by a beggarly young poet; he would have no more to say to him. Nothing could be more natural or require less excuse; for Walpole did not know what a poet was.

Even more marked than his lack of true artistic feeling was Walpole's antipathy to abstract speculation. It was this characteristic which put him altogether out of touch with the most important literary movement of his time—that great revolt against the superstition and prejudice of the Past, which was set on foot by Voltaire, and carried to its height by the Encyclopædists. Diderot, d'Alembert, Condorcet, Hume—these great names only served to raise the contempt of Walpole. 'The *savants*—I beg their pardons, the *philosophes*—are insupportable, superficial, overbearing, and fanatic.' 'The French,' he wrote from Paris, 'affect philosophy, literature, and freethinking; the first never did, and never will, possess me; of the two others I have long been tired. Freethinking is for one's self, surely not for society; besides, one has settled one's way of thinking, or knows it cannot be settled, and for others I do not see why there is not as much bigotry in attempting conversions from any religion as to it. . . . For literature, it is very amusing when one has nothing else to do. I think it rather pedantic in society; tiresome when displayed professedly; and besides, in this country one is sure it is only the fashion of the day. Their taste in it is worst of all: could one believe that when they read our authors, Richardson and Mr. Hume should be their favourites? The latter is treated here with perfect veneration.'

It is fortunately possible to be a good letter writer without being even a tolerable critic or philosopher. Though Walpole's thought was never deep, it was always vivacious; and excellence of style was meted out to him, though not the faculty of perceiving it in others. The distinguishing mark of his writing is a curious mixture of the careless and the elaborate. He is able to spin the most fanciful similes, to heap image upon image and embroidery upon embroidery, and yet to preserve an almost colloquial tone. 'Poor human nature,' he wrote to Lady Ossory at the age of sixty-four, 'what a contradiction it is! To-day it is all rheumatism and morality, and sits with a death's head before it: to-morrow it is dancing! Oh! my Lady, my Lady, what will you say, when the next thing you hear of me after my last letter is that I have danced three country dances with a whole set, forty years younger than myself! Shall not you think I have been chopped to shreds and boiled in Medea's kettle? Shall not you expect to see a print of Vestris teaching me?—and Lord Brudenell dying with envy? You may stare with all your expressive eyes, yet the fact is true. Danced—I do not absolutely say *danced*—but I swam down three dances very gracefully, with the air that was so much in fashion after the battle of Oudenard, and that was still taught when I was fifteen, and that I remember General Churchill practising before a glass in a gouty shoe.'

Such is a specimen of Walpole's style at its best; and to say that he nowhere, in the whole of his fifty years of correspondence, falls very far short of this level of excellence is no mean compliment. On every page there is the same ease, the same ingenuity, the same constant succession of surprises, the same exquisite balance of rhythm. It is reported of Walpole that he often wrote his letters in a room full of company; and the story is not only interesting as an illustration of the facility with which he wrote. For the precise impression produced upon us by the best of his letters is that they were written by some one who had the sound of a refined conversation still in his ears.

III. No description of Walpole would be complete without an allusion to him as antiquary and connoisseur. The letters are full of references to the various curiosities and objects of vertu which he took so much pride in collecting around him—the Roman Eagle, the medals, the spurs of King Charles, the Domenichinos, the manuscripts, the rare prints —all the multitude of treasures contained in the 'Tribune' at

Strawberry Hill. There can be no doubt that it was a characteristic of Walpole's mind to be pleased by oddities more easily than by things of more solid worth. He liked Gothic architecture, not because he thought it beautiful, but because he found it queer; and accordingly the Gothic castles (whether of Otranto or of Strawberry) which he himself constructed, were more remarkable for their queerness than for their beauty. His love of peculiarity, however, never outweighed his hatred of the ridiculous; he always remained within the boundaries of common sense. Macaulay's strictures on this head are as exaggerated as the rest of his brilliant diatribe; and indeed, even if Walpole had been carried by his mania for collecting into excesses of folly undreamt of by Macaulay himself, how could we help forgiving them in the face of a passage such as this?—'You are to know, Madam, that I have in my custody the individual ebony cabinet in which Madame de Sévigné kept her pens and paper for writing her matchless letters. It was preserved near Grignan by an old man who mended her pens, and whose descendant gave it last year to Mr. Selwyn, as truly worthy of such a sacred relic. It wears, indeed, all the outward and visible signs of such venerable preciousness, for it is clumsy, cumbersome, and shattered, and inspires no more idea of her spirit and *légèreté* than the mouldy thigh-bone of a saint does of the unction of his sermons.'

IV. It is as a commentary on the everyday doings and sayings of the brilliant society of his age that Walpole's letters exercise their firmest hold over the hearts of his readers. At least one-half of the correspondence is taken up with this fleeting unessential side of life, which finds a perfect reflection in the delicate polish of Walpole's periods. His letters to Lady Ailesbury and Lady Ossory, and later to the Miss Berrys, are made up of a stream of anecdotes, of small-talk, of descriptions of fine houses, of accounts of balls and theatricals, of *vers de société*, of gossiping reminiscences of ancient days. After every social event Walpole hurried to send off a comment on it to whichever of his favourite Countesses might happen to be out of town; and when great occasions were lacking, the ordinary occurrences of the day furnish abundance of matter for his pen. 'My resolutions of growing old and staid,' he wrote to Lady Hervey, 'are admirable; I wake with a sober plan, and intend to pass the day with my friends—then comes the Duke of Richmond, and hurries me down to Whitehall to dinner—then the Duchess of Grafton sends for me to loo in Upper Grosvenor Street—before I can get thither, I am begged to step to Kensington, to give Mrs. Anne Pitt my opinion about a bow-window—after the loo, I am to march back to Whitehall to supper—and after that, am to walk with Miss Pelham on the terrace till two in the morning, because it is moonlight and her chair is not come. All this does not help my morning laziness; and, by the time I have break-fasted, fed my birds and my squirrels, and dressed, there is an auction ready. In short, Madam, this was my life last week, and is I think every week, with the addition of forty episodes.'

Such was the round of trivial gaieties and dissipations in which most of Walpole's time was spent. But it would be an error to suppose that his intercourse with the men and women about him was always of this ephemeral nature; he was cap-able both of sincere attachments and of strong dislikes. Every-thing that we know of him leads us to the conclusion that he was sensitive to an extraordinary degree; and the defects—for defects they certainly were—which he showed in social intercourse, were caused by an excess of this quality of sensitiveness rather than by a lack of genuine feeling. His angry, cutting sentences, his constant mockery of his enemies, his constant quarrels with his friends, all these things were certainly not the result of a coldness of heart. And there was another element in his character which must never be for-gotten in any estimate of Walpole's relations with other people—his pride. At heart he was a complete aristocrat; it was almost impossible for him to be unreserved. The masks he wore were imposed upon him by his caste, by his breeding, by his own intimate sense of the decencies and proprieties of life; so that his hatreds and his loves, so easily aroused and so intensely cherished, were forced to express themselves in spiteful little taunts and in artificial compliments. Sometimes for a moment or two the veil is withdrawn. In his account of his quarrel with Gray, for instance, in his letter to Mason, after the former's death, when he says 'I treated him insolently. He loved me, and I did not think he did,' one must be very blind indeed to see in such words as those nothing more than a frigid indifference. But perhaps the most interesting of his confidences is in his letter to Conway, written on his sixtieth birthday. It is one of the rare passages in the letters which was obviously not intended for publication. 'Though I am threescore to-day, I should not think that an age for giving everything up; but it is, for whatever one has not strength to perform . . . my spirits are never low; but they seldom will last out the whole day; and though I dare to say I appear to many capricious, and different from the rest of the world, there is more reason in my behaviour than there seems. . . . It would be ridiculous to talk so much of myself, and to enter into such trifling details, but *you* are the person in the world that I wish to convince that I do not act merely from humour or ill-humour; though I confess at the same time that I want your *bonhomie*, and have a disposition not to care at all for people that I do not absolutely like. I could say a great deal more on this head, but it is not proper; though, when one has pretty much done with the world, I think with Lady Blandford, that one may indulge oneself in one's own whims and partialities in one's own house. . . . I will never say any more on these subjects, because there may be as much affectation in being over old, as folly in being over young. My idea of age is, that one has nothing really to do but what one ought, and what is reasonable. All affectations are pretentions; and pretending to be anything one is not, cannot deceive when one is known, as everybody must be that has lived long. . . . Family love and pride make me interest myself about the young people of my own family—for the whole rest of the young world, they are as indifferent to me as puppets or black children. This is my creed, and a key to my whole conduct, and the more likely to remain my creed, as

I think it *raisonné*. If I could paint my opinions instead of writing them—and I don't know whether it would not make a new sort of alphabet—I should use different colours for different affections at different ages. When I speak of love, affection, friendship, taste, liking, I should draw them rose colour, carmine, blue, green, yellow, for my contemporaries; for new comers, the first would be no colour; the others, purple, brown, crimson, and changeable. Remember, one tells one's creed only to one's confessor, that is *sub sigillo*. I write to you as I think; to others as I must. Adieu!'

There is something almost austere in the resignation and the disillusionment of these lines. One feels that there are depths beneath. One may not pity; one may perhaps admire.

V

GRAY AND COWPER

THE main interest of the correspondence of Walpole is that it reflects for us to the full the bustle and glamour of the age in which he lived. The fascination of Gray's letters is of a very different nature; it is almost entirely personal. The subjects with which they deal are not the living momentary actions of every day which we find recorded with such zest in the pages of Walpole; they are the quiet reflected topics which might naturally present themselves to a recluse of any epoch—poetry, and botany, and the beauties of nature, and the almost stationary incidents of University life. But whatever it is that Gray is writing of, we are certain to find the mark of his personality indelibly stamped upon it; everything he lays hands on becomes part of himself; his essence lingers about all his pages, like a subtle and mysterious and pervading scent. As we read on, the attraction which this mind exercises over us becomes stronger and stronger; we cannot tear ourselves away; we begin to be as much absorbed in a catalogue of Latin books and the dates of birds singing as we were in Lady Mary's raciest anecdote or Horace Walpole's most elaborate compliment; we find ourselves becoming endeared to the Cambridge gossip of five generations back; we do not know why this should be, and that very fact intensifies the enchantment. Is Gray's refinement the thing about him which captivates us most? It would, indeed, be difficult to imagine a person more perfectly refined; as Bonstetten said, many years after his friend was dead, 'Gray was the ideal of a gentleman.' The busy ornament of Walpole's style seems almost vulgar after Gray's easy grace. Gray's prose, though far less studied than his verse, is just as faultless. It is the prose of one who is a complete master of the art of writing; it is natural, yet never weak; expressive, yet never out of taste. It could not have been written by anyone who was not a scholar, nor by anyone who was not a man of the world.

Or is it the breadth of Gray's sympathies which lies at the root of our admiration? This quality of his mind was the natural consequence of his good taste. His literary judgments are always excellent; his enjoyment of Shakespeare did not blind his eyes to the merits of Gresset; he admired Froissart no less than Voltaire. He was passionately fond of flowers and of birds. In his love of nature he was one of the earliest precursors of the school of Wordsworth; and some of the finest passages in his letters are his descriptions of scenery among the Lakes. 'As I advanced,' he writes to Wharton, describing a mountain walk, 'the crags seemed to close in, but discovered a narrow entrance turning to the left between them. I followed my guide a few paces, and lo, the hills opened again into no large space, and then all further way is barred by a stream, that at the height of above fifty feet gushes from a hole in the rock, and spreading in large sheets over its broken front, dashes from steep to steep, and then rattles away in a torrent down the valley. The rock on the left rises perpendicular with stubbed yew-trees and shrubs starting from its side to the height of at least three hundred feet; but those are not the things; it is that to the right under which you stand to see the fall that forms the principal horror of the place. From its very base it begins to slope forward over you in a black and solid mass, without any crevice in its surface, and overshadows half the area below with its dreadful canopy. When I stood at (I believe) full four yards distance from its foot, the drops which perpetually distill from its brow, fell on my head, and in one part of the top more exposed to the weather, there are loose stones that hang in the air, and threaten visibly some idle spectator with instant destruction. It is safer to shelter yourself close to its bottom, and trust the shelter of that enormous mass which nothing but an earthquake can stir. The gloomy uncomfortable day well suited the savage aspect of the place, and made it still more formidable.'

'I stayed there (not without shuddering),' Gray adds, 'a

quarter of an hour, and thought my trouble richly paid, for the impression will last for life.'

Or is what most delights us in Gray his sense of humour? A subtle smile seems to play over his letters—a smile which often eludes our vision, and meets us when we least expect to find it. His humour is quiet; but it is singularly free from restraint. There is no subject upon which it may not suddenly perch, with a touch as light as a bird's. The death of Mr. Walpole's cat, and the death of a head of a college from a surfeit of mackerel, equally afford matter for his delicate laughter, just as his own death does. 'The spirit of laziness,' he writes from Cambridge, '(the spirit of the place) begins to possess even me, that have so long declaimed against it. Yet has it not so prevailed, but that I feel that discontent with myself, that ennui, that ever accompanies it in its beginnings. Time will settle my conscience, time will reconcile my languid companion; we shall smoke, we shall tipple, we shall doze together, we shall have our little jokes, like other people, and our long stories. Brandy will finish what port begun; and a month after the time you will see in some corner of a London Evening Post "Yesterday died the Rev. Mr. John Grey, Senior-Fellow of Clare Hall, a facetious companion, and well respected by all that knew him. His death is supposed to have been occasioned by a fit of an apoplexy, being found fallen out of bed with his head in a chamber-pot." ' Such was Gray's humour—the humour of the gently ironical suggestion, not the humour of the loud guffaw. The wild hilarity of a Lamb, and the sombre sarcasm of a Swift were alike alien to his spirit. Nor did he know the Shandean giddiness; he never (to quote his own criticism of Sterne) 'threw his periwig in the face of his audience'; his was the least ostentatious of wits; it was born to blush unseen.

When we have mentioned Gray's exquisite taste, his wide culture, and his peculiar humour, we have not exhausted the list of qualities which go to make up that charm which we have noticed as distinctively his. There is another quality of even greater importance than these—his melancholy. Gray was never in high spirits; there was always a little sediment of depression lurking at the bottom of his happiest moods. His melancholy was indeed the quintessential part of him—the true substance of his being; and, in his letters, one perceives it, mixing with his other qualities, and giving them a strange significance, like a French horn among a company of strings. Perhaps it is in his letters to Bonstetten that this underlying characteristic of Gray's finds its clearest expression. Gray was nearing the end of his life when the arrival of that vivacious young foreigner in Cambridge seemed to open up to him a vista of delightful hopes. 'I never saw such a boy,' he wrote to Nicholls; 'our breed is not made on this model. He is busy from morning to night, has no other amusement than that of changing one study for another; likes nobody that he sees here; and yet wishes to stay longer, though he has passed a whole fortnight with us already.' In the weeks which followed, Gray's affection for Bonstetten steadily deepened; and when at last the latter was obliged to return to Switzerland, his departure left an aching void in Gray's life. 'Alas!' Gray wrote to him, 'How do I every moment feel the truth of what I have somewhere read,—"Ce n'est pas le voir, que de s'en souvenir";—and yet that remembrance is the only satisfaction I have left. My life now is but a conversation with your shadow—the known sound of your voice still rings in my ears—there, on the corner of the fender you are standing, or tinkling on the pianoforte, or stretched at length on the sofa. . . . I cannot bear this place where I have spent many tedious years in less than a month since you left me.' Three weeks later he writes again, after a journey to Suffolk: 'The thought that you might have been with me there has embittered all my hours: your letter has made me happy, as happy as so gloomy, so solitary a being as I am, is capable of being made. I know and have too often felt the disadvantages I lay myself under, how much I hurt the little interest I have in you, by this air of sadness so contrary to your nature and present enjoyments; but sure you will forgive though you cannot sympathize with me. . . . All that you say to me, especially on the subject of Switzerland, is infinitely acceptable. It feels too pleasing ever to be fulfilled, and as often as I read over your truly kind letter, written long since from London, I stop at these words: "La mort qui peut glacer nos bras avant qu'ils soient entre-lacés." '

The same distinction pervades Gray's melancholy as all his other feelings. His grief has in it 'no weakness, no contempt, dispraise or blame,' there is no high-pitched exclamation in it —there is only a tender regret. The same note is to be heard in the *Elegy* and in the *Sonnet to West*. One is reminded, as one listens to it, of the exquisite emotion of a sonata by Mozart.

It is difficult to believe that Gray could have lived among more appropriate surroundings than those which were actually his. His spirit seems still to hover about Cambridge. Those retired gardens, those cloistered courts, are as fitted now for his footstep and his smile as they were a hundred years ago. It seems hardly rash, when the midnight fire has been piled up, when sleep has descended upon the profane, when a deeper silence has fallen upon the night, when the unsported oak still stands invitingly ajar, to expect—in spite of the impediments of time and of mortality—a visit from Gray.

The letters of Cowper, though they rank high in English literature, do not require much comment. As far as they go, they are perfect, but they hardly go anywhere at all. Their gold is absolutely pure; but it is beaten out into the thinnest leaf conceivable. They are like soap-bubbles—exquisite films surrounding emptiness, and almost too wonderful to be touched.

Cowper had nothing to say, and he said it beautifully; yet it is difficult not to wish that he had had something more to say, even at the expense of expressing it a little less well. His letters are stricken with sterility; they are dried up; they lack the juices of life. In them, the vast and palpitating eighteenth century seems suddenly to dwindle into a quiet and well-appointed grave. The wheel had come full circle: the flute of Addison was echoed at last by the flute of Cowper; perfection had returned upon itself.

The following extract shows the highest point which Cowper's mastery of art of making bricks without straw ever reached. 'My dear Friend, you like to hear from me. This is a very good reason why I should write—but I have nothing to say. This seems equally a good reason why I should not. Yet if you had alighted from your horse at our door this morning, and at this present writing, being five o'clock in the afternoon, had found occasion to say to me—"Mr. Cowper, you have not spoken since I came in, have you resolved never to speak again?" it would be but a poor reply, if in answer I should plead inability as my best and only excuse. And this, by the way, suggests a seasonable piece of instruction, and reminds me of what I am apt to forget, when I have any epistolary business in hand; that a letter may be written on anything or nothing, just as that anything or nothing happens to occur. A man that has a journey before him twenty miles in length, which he is to perform on foot, will not hesitate, and doubt, whether he shall set out or not, because he does not readily conceive how he shall ever reach the end of it; for he knows, that by the simple operation of moving one foot forward first, and then the other, he shall be sure to accomplish it. So it is in the present case, and so it is in every similar case. A letter is written as a conversation is maintained, or a journey performed, not by preconcerted or premeditated means, a new contrivance, or an invention never heard before; but merely by maintaining a progress, and resolving, as a postillion does, having once set out, never to stop, till we reach the appointed end. If a man may talk without thinking, why may not he write upon the same terms? A grave gentleman of the last century, a tie-wig, square-toe, Steinkirk figure, would say— "My good sir, a man has no right to do either." But it is to be hoped that the present century . . .' After all, it was only to be expected that, when Cowper set out to write a letter about nothing at all, it would be too long to quote.

VI

BYRON, SHELLEY, KEATS, AND LAMB

THE reader who passes suddenly from the letters of Walpole, Gray, and Cowper to those of Byron, Shelley, and Keats experiences a strange and violent shock. His sensations resemble those of a rower who has been meandering for many days down a broad and quiet river, among fields and gardens and spacious villas, and who, in a moment, finds himself upon the sea. He has left behind him the elegance, the seclusion, the leisure of the eighteenth century; he has embarked upon the untrammelled ocean of a new age, where he will be refreshed, astonished, and delighted, but where he will find no rest. The contrast is so complete that one is tempted to believe that an intelligent reader from another planet might almost, by the aid of these letters alone, infer the French Revolution. Everything has changed; not only the 'atmosphere,' the general point of view; but the very form and manner of the expressions, the very clothing of the meanest thoughts, have undergone a mysterious transmutation. The old city has been ploughed up, the old landmarks have been thrown down, new streets and buildings obliterate the buried remnants of the past. The inhabitants have new faces, and speak a language which was never heard before.

The letters of Byron are completely typical of the new spirit. In three respects they differ profoundly from all the letters which preceded them. In the first place their extreme vitality makes the most vivacious passages of Walpole and Lady Mary Wortley Montagu seem bloodless in comparison. It is only possible to appreciate their energy to the full when a great number of them have been read. The cumulative effect of Byron's vigour acts upon the reader like a tonic or a seabreeze; he himself begins to wish to throw his ink-bottle through the window, to practise pistol-shooting in bed, to scatter his conversation with resounding oaths. The true essence of Byron cannot be distilled into two or three quotations; but the following extract may serve as an instance of the peculiar masculinity of his style. As an example of this particular quality in Byron it is especially applicable for two reasons: it is one of the rare pieces of description in his letters, and is thus comparatively free from other characteristics which will be considered later; and its subject suggests an interesting comparison with a similar passage by Walpole. It will be best to quote Walpole first: 'The scaffold was immediately new-strewed with saw-dust, the block new-covered, the executioner new dressed, and a new axe brought. Then came old Balmerino, treading with the air of a general. As soon as he mounted the scaffold, he read the inscription on his coffin, as he did again afterwards: he then surveyed the spectators, who were in amazing numbers, even upon masts of ships in the river; and pulling out his spectacles, read a reasonable speech. . . . He took the axe and felt it, and asked the headsman how many blows he had given Lord Kilmarnock; and gave him three guineas. Two clergymen, who attended him, coming up, he said, "No, gentlemen, I believe you have already done me all the service you can." Then he went to the corner of the scaffold, and called very loud for the warder, to give him his periwig, which he took off, and put on a night-cap of Scotch plaid, and then pulled off his coat and waistcoat and lay down; but being told he was on the wrong side, vaulted round, and immediately gave the sign by tossing up his arm, as if he were giving the signal for battle. He received three blows, but the first certainly took away all sensation. . . . Balmerino certainly died with the intrepidity of a hero, but with the insensibility of one too. As he walked from his prison to execution, seeing every window and top of house filled with spectators, he cried out "Look, look, how they are all piled up like rotten oranges!" '

Byron, writing sixty years later, gives the following account of a similar incident: 'The day before I left Rome I saw three robbers guillotined. The ceremony—including the *masked* priests; the half-naked executioners; the bandaged criminals; the black Christ and his banner; the scaffold; the soldiery; the slow procession, and the quick rattle and heavy fall of the axe; the splash of blood, and the ghastliness of the exposed heads— is altogether more impressive than the vulgar and ungentle- manly dirty "new drop" and dog-like agony of infliction upon the sufferers of the English sentence. Two of these men behaved calmly enough, but the first of the three died with great terror and reluctance, which was very horrible. He would not lie down; then his neck was too large for the aperture, and the priest was obliged to drown his exclamations by still louder exhortations. The head was off before the eye could trace the blow; but from an attempt to draw back the head, notwithstanding it was held forward by the hair, the first head was cut off close to the ears; the other two were taken off more cleanly. It is better than the oriental way, and (I should think) than the axe of our ancestors. The pain seems little; and yet the effect to the spectator, and the preparation to the criminal, are very striking and chilling. The first turned me quite hot and thirsty, and made me shake so that I could hardly hold the opera-glass (I was close, but determined to see, as one should see everything, once, with attention); the second and third (which shows how dreadfully soon things grow indifferent), I am ashamed to say, had no effect on me as a horror, though I would have saved them if I could.'

There are few passages in Byron's letters so elaborate as this; yet it is clear enough that even this was dashed off at white heat. The careful elegance of the eighteenth century was utterly alien to Byron's manner of writing. He is never ingenious, or polished, or ornamental. His nearest approach to an epigram is a bad pun. He rushes on helter-skelter, as the fancy takes him, into postscripts longer than his letters, and post-postscripts longer than all. His vocabulary is often coarse; his constructions are liable to lose themselves in the current of his thoughts; he is always amusing, but he is very rarely polite. 'You are to print in what form you please,' he writes to Murray on the subject of the publication of *Manfred*—

'that is your concern; as far as your connection with myself has gone, you are the best judge how far you have lost or gained—probably sometimes one and sometimes the other, but when you come to me with your *"can"* and talk to me about the copy of Manfred as if the "force of purchase would no further go—to *make* a book he separates the two," I say unto you, verily it is not so; or, as the Foreigner said to the Waiter, after asking him to bring a glass of water, to which the man answered "I will, sir,"—"You *will*!—God damn,—I say, you *mush*!"'

The Byron of the letters is the Byron of *Don Juan* and *The Vision of Judgment*, not the Byron of *Childe Harold* and *The Corsair*. Hardly a trace is to be found in them of the sentimentalising and philosophising 'Pilgrim'; it is the actual living man of the world whom they display. The picture is not only astonishingly vivid, it is astonishingly different from any other picture in the world. Byron's letters bear the impress of a far more distinct and individual personality than any of the letters of his predecessors. It was not that he was greater than they; it was simply that he was differentiated from his contemporaries to a greater degree; he was the first of those dominating and isolated figures which were to be produced in such profusion in the first half of the nineteenth century.

Unfortunately Byron's character was marred by a defect only too common to men of this particular type: he was a complete egoist. And round this fault a multitude of others naturally clustered—narrowness of interests, lack of real enthusiasms, vulgarity, affectation. His letters are concerned with one subject, and one alone—himself. His own actions, his own thoughts, his own books, his own hopes, his own disappointments and regrets—these were the staple topics of his correspondence. Nor was he content with this direct sort of self-appreciation. He was perpetually trying to rake in a little more admiration than even he was willing to admit to be his due. He was an inveterate *poseur*; and his poetry was merely the result of one out of a large number of his poses. He wished to be thought a philosopher, and a man of feeling, and a republican, and a gay dog; he also wished to be thought a poet. That he convinced the world that he was, is doubtless the most striking proof of his genius. Few save Byron could ever have carried the lack of ear, of taste, and of common sense so far, as would have enabled them to commit to paper the hideous balderdash, for instance, which goes by the name of *Cain*; none save Byron could have hypnotised Europe into believing that that work was worthy of the combined efforts of Milton and Æschylus. It is difficult to decide which was the more amazing achievement. But perhaps after all it is not in his poetry that we find Byron at his worst. It is only necessary to cast one's eye over the blasphemies and obscenities which he poured forth in his letters to Moore upon the author of *Hyperion* to reach the true measure of the depths of degradation to which Byron's taste could sink. It is satisfactory to know that Keats at any rate was under no delusion as to the value of Byron's poetry. Some recently discovered lines have brought his opinion of it to light.[1]

Byron as a reckless and amused adventurer is an object pleasanter to contemplate than Byron as a poet. In the former capacity, his Venetian letters give a view of him which is undoubtedly all the more entertaining owing to the fact that it distinctly oversteps the bounds of propriety. Many of Byron's most human, vigorous, and entertaining qualities seem to have been called out in his dealings with a certain class of women. The story of the 'Fornarina' (Letter to Murray, August 1, 1819) is a piece of racy narrative worthy of Fielding at his best. It is too long to quote, but the powers of description which it displays make it clear that the world would have been the gainer if Byron had written novels instead of poetry.

Trelawney says, in his *Reminiscences*, that Byron, since his

---

[1] "Apollo! faded! O far-flown Apollo!
    Where is thy misty pestilence to creep
    Into the dwellings, through the door-crannies
    Of all mock-lyrists, large self-worshippers,
    And careless Hectorers in proud bad verse?"
                         (The Fall of Hyperion.)

'school hallucinations,' had never had a friend. It is certainly true that Byron's letters bear out this statement. Indeed, he was probably incapable of friendship. There was no give and take about his nature; and his vanity was such that he preferred to be flattered by an insignificant mind, like Moore's, to being treated as an equal by a noble one, like Shelley's. The exception, however, which Trelawney makes as to his 'school hallucinations' suggests that there may have been a time when it was otherwise with Byron. His affection for Lord Clare may have been, after all, no 'hallucination'; it may have been the one real friendship of his life. 'I never hear the word "Clare," ' he wrote in his *Detached Thoughts*, in 1821, 'without a beating of the heart even now, and I write it with the feelings of 1803–4–5– ad infinitum.' A few weeks later it happened that the friends met on the road between Imola and Bologna. 'This meeting,' Byron wrote, 'annihilated for a moment all the years between the present time and the days of Harrow. It was a new and inexplicable feeling, like rising from the grave, to me. . . . We were but five minutes together, and in the public road; but I hardly recollect an hour of my existence which could be weighed against them. . . . Of all I have ever known, he has always been the least altered in every thing from the excellent qualities and kind affections which attached me to him so strongly at school.'

One seems to discern, in these few sentences, a warm and genuine feeling struggling out through the cold wrappings with which years and the world and his own self-conceit had involved the soul of Byron. For a moment or two he had been innocent once more.

The few existing letters of Shelley are chiefly remarkable for their exquisite descriptions of Italian scenery, and their criticisms of Italian literature and art. They do not add materially to our knowledge of the man—that 'one thing,' as a living poet has said, 'sweeter than his own songs were'— though they must increase our admiration of the artist. Shelley's prose is, like his poetry, romantic, coloured, and luxuriant, to the highest degree. Two sentences will give a fair example of the fertile imagination of his style: 'The hand-writing of Ariosto is a small, firm and pointed character, expressing, as I should say, a strong and keen, but circumscribed energy of mind; that of Tasso is large, free, and flowing, except that there is a checked expression in the midst of its flow, which brings the letters into a smaller compass than one expected from the beginning of the word. It is the symbol of an intense and earnest mind, exceeding at times its own depth, and admonished to return by the chillness of the waters of oblivion striking upon its adventurous feet.'

Both Byron and Shelley, no less than Keats, were pagans; but Byron's paganism was that of a Roman Emperor, while the two latter poets were pagans of the Athenian mould. Nothing could be in more complete contrast with the vulgar blasphemies of Byron than this passage, written by Shelley after a visit to Pompeii: 'I now understand why the Greeks were such great poets; and, above all, I can account, it seems to me, for the harmony, the unity, the perfection, the uniform excellence, of all their works of art. They lived in a perpetual commerce with external nature, and nourished themselves upon the spirit of its forms. Their theatres were all open to the mountains and the sky. Their columns, the ideal types of a sacred forest, with its roof of interwoven tracery, admitted the light and wind; the odour and the freshness of the country penetrated the cities. The temples were mostly upaithric; and the flying clouds, the stars, or the deep sky, were seen above. O, but for that series of wretched wars which terminated in the Roman conquest of the world; but for the Christian religion, which put the finishing stroke on the ancient system; but for those changes that conducted Athens to its ruin,—to what an eminence might not humanity have arrived!'

Before leaving Shelley, it is impossible not to quote one more passage—the pathetic and beautiful description of the Protestant cemetery at Rome: 'The English burying-place is a green slope near the walls, under the pyramidal tomb of Cestius, and is, I think, the most beautiful and solemn cemetery I ever beheld. To see the sun shining on its grass, fresh, when we first visited it, with the autumnal dews, and hear the whispering of the wind among the leaves of the trees which have overgrown the tomb of Cestius; and the soil which is stirring in the sun-warm earth, and to mark the tombs, mostly of women and young people who were buried there, one might, if one were to die, desire the sleep they seem to sleep. Such is the human mind, and so it peoples with its wishes vacancy and oblivion.' It is fortunately as needless as it is impossible to make any comment upon writing such as this.

The letters of Keats throw far more fresh light upon their writer than those of Shelley. Without them, we should hardly be aware of even the outlines of the character of that most impersonal of poets. It is sometimes asserted that Keats was effeminate and anæmic, that he was a weak voluptuary, whose interests were bounded by the physical forms of things; and such a view of his nature might, indeed, be supported with some show of truth by quotations from his poems. His letters, however, provide a striking illustration of how erroneous judgments of this kind are liable to be. Passage after passage in them reveals to us the fact that Keats's mind was in reality no less remarkable for its intellectual activity and strength than for its love of beauty. His thought ranged easily from criticism to psychology, from reflexions upon political history to reflexions upon the conduct of life; and his thought was never commonplace, never superficial, never slipshod, and never at rest. 'From the "Paradise Lost" and other works of Milton,' he wrote to Reynolds in 1818, 'I hope it is not too presuming, even between ourselves, to say, that his Philosophy, human and divine, may be tolerably understood by one not much advanced in years. In his time, Englishmen were just emancipated from a great superstition, and men had got hold of certain points and resting-places in reasoning which were too newly born to be doubted, and too much opposed by the mass of Europe not to be thought ethereal and authentically divine. Who could gainsay his ideas on virtue, vice, and chastity, in "Comus," just at the time of the dismissal of codpieces and a hundred other disgraces? Who would not rest satisfied with his hintings at good and evil in the "Paradise Lost," when just free from the Inquisition and burnings in Smithfield? The Reformation produced such immediate and great benefits, that Protestantism was considered under the immediate eye of heaven, and its own remaining dogmas and superstitions, then, as it were, regenerated, constituted those resting-places and seeming sure points of Reasoning from that I have mentioned. Milton, whatever he may have thought in the sequel, appears to have been content with these by his writings. He did not think into the human heart as Wordsworth has done. Yet Milton as a philosopher had sure as great powers as Wordsworth. What is then to be inferred? O, many things. It proves there is really a grand march of intellect, it proves that a mighty Providence subdues the mightiest minds to the service of the time being, whether it be in human knowledge or Religion.' With trains of thought such as this the letters are crowded; nothing could be less remote from lasciviousness and morbidity, nor bear more obviously the impress of a bold, original, and ripening, though not yet mature, intelligence. When it is remembered that this passage was written when Keats was twenty-two, that he had enjoyed the most meagre of educations, that the apex of his intellectual surroundings was Leigh Hunt, one cannot doubt that if he had lived his mind would have scaled to heights which none of his contemporaries ever reached. 'I will essay to reach to as high a summit in poetry,' he wrote, 'as the nerve bestowed upon me will suffer. The faint conceptions I have of poems to come bring the blood frequently into my forehead.' Keats, at any rate, was by no means unaware of his own powers. Indeed, his extreme consciousness, his acute sensitiveness to every perception, to every feeling, to every stimulus,—this was what lay at the basis of his character. 'I carry all matters to an extreme,' he says, 'so that when I have any little vexation, it grows in five minutes into a theme for Sophocles.'

A vexation, a train of ideas, a beautiful vision—whatever the stimulus, the same activity of thought and feeling was sure to follow. His love of beauty was intense: 'I feel assured I should write from the mere yearning and fondness I have for the beautiful, even if my night's labours should be burnt every morning, and no eye ever shine upon them.' But his mind responded no less vividly to very different impressions. 'On our return from Belfast, we met a sedan—the Duchess of Dunghill. It is no laughing matter though. Imagine the worst dog-kennel you ever saw, placed upon two poles from a mouldy fencing. In such a wretched thing sat a squalid old woman, squat like an ape half-starved from a scarcity of biscuit in its passage from Madagascar to the Cape, with a pipe in her mouth, and looking out with a round-eyed skinny-lidded inanity; with a sort of horizontal idiotic movement of her head, while two ragged, tattered girls carried her along. What a thing would be a history of her life and sensations!' In Keats's own history it was the violence of his sensations which was the culminating tragedy of his life. His last letters to Fanny Brawne and to Brown, in the intensity of the emotions which they display, are unsurpassed in the whole of literature. The same sacred horror of passion speaks in them as speaks in the lyrics of Catullus and of Heine, and in some of the sonnets of Shakespeare. But it is something of a desecration even to refer to such agonies and such splendours; to cut pieces out of them for notice and for admiration would be almost to commit the unforgivable sin.

It is difficult to believe that the letters of Lamb ever went through the same post as those of Byron and Keats. Indeed, it is difficult to believe that they ever went through the post at all. They are letters which a voyaging angel might write to the City of Heaven; they bear no marks of time or space or such sublunary accidents; one doubts whether it was ever true that they were not. Nothing shows more clearly Lamb's detachment from his age than his attitude towards Nature. 'I must confess,' he says, 'that I am not romance-hit about *Nature*.

The earth, and sea, and sky (when all is said) is but as a house to dwell in. . . . Just as important to me (in a sense) is all the furniture of my world; eye-pampering, but satisfies no heart. Streets, streets, streets, streets, markets, theatres, churches, Covent Gardens, shops sparkling with pretty faces of industrious milliners, neat sempstresses, ladies cheapening, gentlemen behind counters lying, authors in the street with spectacles, George Dyers (you may know them by their gait), lamps lit at night, pastry-cooks' and silversmiths' shops, beautiful Quakers of Pentonville, noise of coaches, drowsy cry of mechanic watchmen at night, with rakes reeling home drunk; if you happen to wake at midnight, cries of "Fire!" and "Stop thief!", inns of court, with their learned air, and halls and butteries, just like Cambridge colleges; old book-stalls, "Jeremy Taylors," "Burtons on Melancholy," and "Religio Medicis" on every stall. These are thy pleasures, O London! with thy many sins. O City, abounding in w——s, for these may Keswick and her giant brood go hang!'

Though the friend of Wordsworth and Coleridge can hardly be counted as of their generation, his very power of overstepping the limits of time made him a keener admirer of their poetry. 'I had rather be a doorkeeper in your margin,' he bursts out to Wordsworth, who had been maltreated by the reviewers, 'than have their proudest text swelling with my eulogies.' Yet his failure to appreciate either Keats or Shelley shows that even Lamb's critical eye might be dazzled by too much radiance. The quality of his imagination was so wholly different from theirs that their speech fell upon his ears like a strange language. The images which moved him were neither materially beautiful nor spiritually exalted; they were too human to lose themselves in the tropical luxuriances of *Endymion* or upon the mountain snows of the *Prometheus Unbound*. They remained beside the fire, in the candle-light, among midnight folios and innocent jests. And, in its own way, Lamb's fancy was no less exuberant than that of his great contemporaries. 'Why do cats grin in Cheshire?' he exclaims in a sudden parenthesis. 'Because it was once a County Palatine, and the cats cannot help laughing whenever they think of it, though I see no great joke in it.' But it is in its longer flights that his imagination displays itself in its most fantastic forms. The *Essays of Elia* are, of course, rich in such passages; but the letters occasionally soar off into even more wonderful regions of unrestrained fooling—regions where the absurd and the serious, the jovial and the pathetic, the true and the false, seem to be inextricably fused together to form one enchanting whole. Perhaps the example which exhibits the peculiar quality of Lamb's imagination more admirably than any other is the letter to Manning, written on the eve of the latter's return from China. 'Down with the pagodas!' Lamb bursts out. 'Down with the idols—Ching-chong-fo—and his foolish priesthood! Come out of Babylon, O my friend! for her time is come. . . . And in sober sense what makes you so long from amongst us, Manning? You must not expect to see the same England again which you left.' This is the text of the letter; the rest is commentary. 'Empires have been overturned,' it goes on, 'crowns trodden into dust, the face of the Western world quite changed.' (Lamb was writing in Waterloo year, and so far he has truth with him.) 'Your friends have all got old,' he proceeds—'those you left blooming; myself (who am one of the few that remember you) those golden hairs which you recollect my taking a pride in, turned to silvery and grey.' This forms the transition stage from reality to fantasia; with his 'golden hairs' Lamb takes a final spring from the earth into the Empyrean: 'Mary has been dead and buried many years; she desired to be buried in the silk gown you sent her. Rickman that you remember active and strong, now walks out supported by a servant maid and a stick. Martin Burney is a very old man. The other day an aged woman knocked at my door, and pretended to my acquaintance. It was long before I had the most distant cognition of her; but at last, together we made her out to be Louisa, the daughter of Mrs. Topham, formerly Mrs. Morton, who had been Mrs. Reynolds, formerly Mrs. Kenney, whose first husband was Holcroft, the dramatic writer of the last century. St. Paul's

Church is a heap of ruins; the Monument isn't half so high as you knew it, divers parts being successively taken down which the ravages of time had rendered dangerous; the horse at Charing Cross is gone, no one knows whither; and all this has taken place while you have been settling whether Ho-hing-tong should be spelt with a — or a —.'

'Poor Godwin!' the letter continues, piling vision upon vision. 'I was passing his tomb the other day in Cripplegate Churchyard. There are some verses upon it written by Miss ——, which if I thought good enough I would send you. He was one of those who would have hailed your return, not with boisterous shouts and clamours, but with the complacent gratulations of a philosopher anxious to promote knowledge as leading to happiness; but his theories are ten feet deep in Cripplegate mould. Coleridge is just dead, having lived just long enough to close the eyes of Wordsworth, who paid the debt to Nature but a week or two before. Poor Col., but two days before he died he wrote to a bookseller proposing an epic poem on the "Wanderings of Cain" in twenty-four books. It is said he said he has left behind him more than forty thousand treatises in criticism, metaphysics, and divinity, but few of them in a state of completion. They are now destined, perhaps, to wrap up spices. You see what mutations the busy hand of Time has produced.'

This is Lamb in his lightest and happiest vein. It is only occasionally that the other side of him—the tragic side— makes its appearance in his letters. When it does, the beauty of the expression is as perfect as ever. 'All my strength is gone,' he wrote to Miss Wordsworth, during one of his sister's temporary confinements, 'and I am like a fool, bereft of her co-operation. I dare not think, lest I should think wrong; so used am I to look up to her in the least and the biggest perplexity. To say all that I know of her would be more than I think any body could believe, or even understand; and when I hope to have her well again with me, it would be sinning against her feelings to go about to praise her; for I can conceal nothing that I do from her. She is older and wiser and better than I, and all my wretched imperfections I cover to myself by resolutely thinking on her goodness.' In the light of such words as these, the words which Coleridge addressed to his friend seem no longer strange to us: 'I look upon you as a man called by sorrow and anguish and a strange desolation of hopes into quietness, and a soul set apart and made peculiar to God.'

1905.

INDEX

[Figures in italics indicate the more important references]

INDEX

Printed in England
SPOTTISWOODE, BALLANTYNE & CO. LTD.
London & Colchester